NEW DIMENSIONS IN LITERATURE

INTRODUCTION

TO NONFICTION

John R. Arscott
Coordinator, Senior Division
West Essex High School
North Caldwell, New Jersey

Editorial Board   Don M. Wolfe
John R. Arscott
Hardy R. Finch

McCORMICK-MATHERS PUBLISHING COMPANY, INC.
Wichita, Kansas 67201

Grateful acknowledgment is made for permission to reprint the following selections:

"Mickey" from *The Open Heart* by Edward Weeks, by permission of Little, Brown and Co.—Atlantic Monthly Press. Copyright, ©, 1947 by Edward Weeks.

From *Black Boy* by Richard Wright. Copyright 1945 by Richard Wright. Reprinted with the permission of Harper & Row, Publishers, Incorporated. Copyright © 1937 by Richard Wright. Reprinted by permission of Paul R. Reynolds & Son.

"I Get a Colt to Break In" from *The Autobiography of Lincoln Steffens,* copyright, 1931, by Harcourt, Brace & World, Inc.; renewed, 1959, by Peter Steffens. Reprinted by permission of the publishers.

"Much Pomp and Several Circumstances" reprinted by permission of the publisher from *The Court of Boyville* by William Allen White. Copyright 1899 by William Allen White, copyright 1910 by The Macmillan Company.

"Ring Out, Wild Bells" reprinted by permission of Dodd, Mead & Company from *Bed of Neuroses* by Wolcott Gibbs. Copyright, 1936, by Wolcott Gibbs.

From *Act One,* by Moss Hart. © Copyright 1959 by Catharine Carlisle Hart and Joseph M. Hyman, Trustees. Reprinted by permission of Random House, Inc. Also reprinted by permission of Martin Secker & Warburg Limited.

"The Champawat Man-Eater" from *Man-Eaters of India* by Jim Corbett. Copyright © 1957 by Oxford University Press, Inc. Reprinted by permission. Also from *Man-Eaters of Kumaon* by Jim Corbett reprinted by permission of Oxford University Press.

"The Fifty-first Dragon" from *Seeing Things at Night* by Heywood Broun. Copyright © 1921, 1949 by Heywood Hale Broun. Reprinted by permission of Heywood Hale Broun and Constance M. Broun by arrangement with Marie Rodell.

From *Adventures in Two Worlds* by A. J. Cronin by permission of Little, Brown and Co. Copyright, 1935, 1937, 1938, 1939, 1943, 1946, 1948, 1949, 1950, 1951, 1952 by A. J. Cronin. Also reprinted by permission of Dr. A. J. Cronin by arrangement with A. M. Heath & Company Limited.

CONTENTS

INTRODUCTION

The purpose of this anthology is to provide the reader with a collection of interest-catching and thought-provoking nonfiction selections.

The breadth of nonfiction is truly overwhelming, including autobiography, biography, essays, and entire volumes on adventure, travel, science, history, and literary criticism. The editor in choosing selections for this volume has kept in mind two indispensable yardsticks: timelessness and variety.

There is an abundance of contemporary material in this anthology, but there has been no worshiping at the shrine of modernity. That which is contemporary may all too quickly pass away. Today's raging inferno may be tomorrow's tempest in a teapot. The emphasis has rather been on timelessness, for that which is timeless is assuredly timely. Man's place in time and space may change, but human nature seems to possess enduring and unchanging qualities.

The selections, a careful blend of light and heavy, bitter and sweet, should appeal to a wide variety of tastes and interests. The reader may move from the irrepressible mirth of Robert Benchley and Wolcott Gibbs to such tragic, yet inspiring, accounts of human courage as are told by John Gunther in *Death Be Not Proud* and by Anne Frank in her *Diary of a Young Girl.* His reading whisks him aloft in a flimsy mail plane high above the Andes as it struggles to survive a raging storm, or transports him to the rugged Himalayan hills of India for a tiger-shoot in which the prize is a dangerously lethal man-eater. History comes alive for him as he reads the words of Pericles, Woodrow Wilson, and John F. Kennedy. There is material to stimulate the appetite of the reluctant reader and yet sufficient scope to satisfy the appetite of the more demanding.

The study aids—introductions, questions and comments, word studies, and composition exercises—have all been designed to facilitate and enrich the reader's understanding and enjoyment of these selections.

Finally, it is the hope of the editor that this volume will serve as a springboard to further meaningful and enjoyable reading experiences.

Mickey is an old dog. He is slowing down; his senses aren't what they used to be; he's not enjoying the same status he used to have with the other dogs in the neighborhood. He feels absolutely dependent upon the family from whom he has received affection, recognition, and a sense of belonging.

Anyone who has ever loved a dog and watched with helplessness and sorrow as it started to grow old will find it easy to share the feelings of Edward Weeks in this tender portrait of Mickey.

MICKEY

Edward Weeks

OVERHEAD the oak leaves stir against the cloudless blue, and the shadow in which I am reading ripples like running water. At my feet on the borderline between the sunny and the cool grass lies Mickey dozing, gray muzzle pointed toward the driveway up which the family will return from their expedition. Periodically he rouses himself, shakes the catkins from his black curls, and moves closer to the sun. His movement renews the scolding of the mother robin in the bittersweet and interrupts my intake of print. I watch him, and through the forming impressions of the book in my lap, memory thrusts its feeling.

This is probably our last summer together. Mickey is sixteen and that is a great age for a cocker spaniel given to eating any old thing; indeed a great age for any dog. Implicit in every friendship is the trust that it will never break. Mick has no reason to doubt us, but we who note his fading hearing and his inability to spot us at any distance on the beach live with the warning to make these months good.

I remember William Morton Wheeler's remarking on the silent communication between dogs, and how, when he had taken one of his for a walk through the Arboretum, the others would gather about the traveler instantly on his return and by scent and emanation have all the news in a matter of seconds. On the Common with other dogs Mick is eager, quivering, and gregarious when I am along, and hair-on-end belligerent when accompanying his mistress. In canine years he is now well past the century mark, so it is small wonder that dogs in their prime have only a passing curiosity in what he has to say. They pause, there is the usual tail-wagging introduction. Then, while he is still standing on his dignity, they suddenly lope off. Mick will start after and then resign himself to his own grass, which he scratches up with a "What the hell." For ladies he has, I gather, the charm of an aging colonel. There is a honey-colored spaniel who, after the nosing, will describe mad circles about him as he stands immovable on the moonlit Common. But if she pushes him too roughly he loses his balance and shows his lip, and so they part.

At home his expressions are stressed for our benefit. His humor, as when with jaws open and tongue half a yard out he stands there grinning; his sneeze of expectation; his mutter—a kind of controlled yip—of annoyance; his jumping recognition of those most important words in a city dog's vocabulary, "Going out" and "Down country" (is it the special note that colors our voices as we say them?); his sharp demanding bark when his water dish is empty or when brownies, his passion, are cooking—these are a language no one could miss. So too his boredom when, after a decent interval in our friend's house, he fetches his leash and stands obdurate with it in his jaws.

And in his play, he loves to tease. Mickey came to us when he was three weeks old and in the pecking order[1] he established himself as a contemporary of my daughter Sara and as

[1] *pecking order:* among chickens, the right of the more aggressive to peck at and dominate the weak and more timid of the flock

a senior in every respect to young Ted. In his youth we spent the winters in an apartment on the Fenway, and here Mickey devised a series of games for his own and our amusement. There was one he liked to play with a Malaga grape. A grape would be given him and he would go through the motions of chewing it. Then he would lie down facing us, his head cocked on one side. With a sudden twist he would fling the grape, perfectly intact, over his shoulder and pounce upon it as it rolled along the rug or under the table. Again the mock seriousness of swallowing it, the fixed stare in our direction, and again, the quick projection. The wonder was that he could keep this up for such a long time without puncturing the thin-skinned grape.

He loved to tease Sara about her dollhouse. The open rooms were just right for his inspection, and the inmates—known as Mr. and Mrs. Brewster—were much to his taste. He would stand gazing into the living room until he was sure Sara was watching him; then with a quick dart he would seize one of the little dolls and be off, up the hall, through the kitchen, through the dining room, across the living room, and into the hall again. It was a lovely circle, and Sara could seldom catch him without the help of May, the cook. Sara's revenge was unpremeditated. One evening she set Mr. and Mrs. Brewster at the dinner table and served each of them a chocolate-covered Ex-lax[1] for their supper, and after she had gone to sleep Mickey ate both. On rising the next morning, I found that he used the bathroom in a hurry, and Sara, all unknowing, supplied the perfect caption at breakfast: "Now, Mother, I told you the dolls were alive. They ate their candy."

I remember those times when he seemed to speak my language, once for instance when in his puppyhood he was sick from a distemper injection. He began vomiting at midnight and at four I got the car and drove him to the vet's. He was so weak that he leaned limply against the corner of seat

---

[1] *Ex-lax:* a common laxative

and door, but in answer to my hand his eyes said, "I'm sorry to be such a mess. But I *am* sick." And again, years later, when he had to apologize for his hunting. It was summer and our little cottage adjoined the orchard and vegetable garden of our big neighbor. At sundown rabbits would make free with the tender lettuce and carrots, and their scent—when Mickey got it—drove him wild. One evening from our screened porch I spotted a cottontail in the green. Mick was asleep, but quietly opening the door I pointed him at the quarry and he got the idea. Rabbit and spaniel disappeared over the horizon with yips marking every second bound. Two hours went by, and then in darkness there was Mick scratching at the screen. "No luck," he said, and in his mouth was the half-eaten carrot the rabbit had dropped in his haste. "No luck."

Mickey is by his nature a hunter and a retriever. But now, with his teeth gone, his retrieving is limited to fisherman's corks as they curve ahead of him on the beach, and to apples in the orchard. He fancied himself a hunter, and for years he nourished a grudge against squirrels. I used to tease him about this. Walking close to one of our oaks, I would peer up into the leaves and touch the bark significantly; whereupon Mick would leave the ground jumping and scrabbling as high as my arm.

The squirrels, for their part, enjoyed the feud: they knew he could never catch them. I remember one summer day when Mickey was lying on the open porch soaking up the sun which radiated from the warm boards. Close to the house stood an old apple tree, one of whose branches reached over the porch. Along this bridge, as Mickey slept, stole one of his bushy-tailed enemies. With mathematical precision the squirrel nipped clean a hard green apple, which hit the porch with a thump an inch from Mickey's nose. It was as nice a piece of natural comedy as I have ever witnessed; and the aftermath was noisy.

That dogs remember, we know from their habits and from their twitching dreams when they are so palpably reliving some activity. But how far back does their memory reach, and do those little half-uttered cries indicate that, like man, they are long haunted by old fears? If so, then Mick may still feel the most painful terror of domesticated animals—the fear of desertion. The autumn of his second year, my wife and I had to answer a sudden call to New York. We closed the cottage, packed up the daughter, and to save time left the pup with the maid. She took him to her home in Watertown, and from it he naturally escaped in search of us. That was on Friday afternoon. They saw him for an instant at the garbage pail Saturday morning, and then he was gone for good.

By our return on Monday there wasn't a clue. We drove the unfamiliar streets and we put our appeal in the newspapers and on the air. In twenty-four hours we had heard from seventeen spaniel owners, fifteen of whom had lost their own dogs. But one of them gave us a tip. In their search they had seen a small black dog in the vast reaches of the Watertown Arsenal. So, with the Governor's permission, we drove through the gates—this was long before the war—to explore the cement strips which led between the huge closed buildings. A sergeant's son gave us hope. "Sure," he said, "a little black dog. He's here all right, only you can't get close to him." "Don't scare him," I said. "Find him if you can." Whistling and calling, we went to point after point, and once on the knoll above a huge oil tank I thought I heard the short familiar bark, but nothing moved. Three hours later we came back to the same spot, and there was the boy lying full-length on the cement wall aiming an imaginary gun. "The buffalo is down here," he called. Ten yards farther, and I saw Mick's nest and his unmistakable head. "Mickey," I shouted. Then up the slope he came on the dead run, his ears brown pancakes of burr.

Is it the fear of our leaving him that so troubles him when he can now no longer hear us as we move about the house? The sight of an open suitcase makes him more doleful than does a thunderstorm. When we pack for the country there is no way to tell him that he will surely come too. In his heart of hearts Mick knows that he is dependent upon four people, and no comfort of maid or sitter can distract his vigil when we are gone for the evening. Our woods are his woods. The squirrels who used to scold him he no longer hears. He begins not to hear us. But we shall hear him long after he is gone.

Questions and Comments

1. How old is Mickey? What signs of his failing health warn the author to "make these months good"?

2. What does the author mean by "the silent communication between dogs"? How do the other dogs now treat Mickey?

3. What are some of the gestures and expressions Mickey uses to make his wishes known?

4. The author says that Mickey loved to tease. What examples does he cite to demonstrate this quality in the dog?

5. What interesting question does the author pose about the memory of dogs?

6. What does the author call "the most painful terror of domesticated animals"? What incident involving Mickey does he recount to demonstrate this?

7. What is the meaning of the last line of the selection?

Word Study

1. Mickey shakes the *catkins* from his black curls. What are catkins?

2. In the third paragraph the author uses the words *emanation, gregarious, belligerent,* and *lope.* What do these words mean?

3. An early meaning of the word *aftermath* is "a second-growth crop." Explain the relationship of this early meaning to the meaning of the word in "the aftermath was noisy."

4. Give the meaning of the italicized words, using clues in the context of the selection wherever possible. Check your guesses in a dictionary.

   "*Implicit* in every friendship is the trust that it will never break." (page 3)

   ". . . he fetches his leash and stands *obdurate* with it in his jaws." (page 4)

   "Sara's revenge was *unpremeditated*." (page 5)

   "That dogs remember, we know from their habits and from their twitching dreams when they are so *palpably* reliving some activity." (page 6)

   "The sight of an open suitcase makes him more *doleful* than does a thunderstorm." (page 7)

Composition

1. Is the author's portrayal of Mickey objective? Sympathetic? Sentimental? Cite examples from the selection to prove your point.

2. Perhaps you, too, have a dog, a cat, or some other pet. Discuss (a) the circumstances of his arrival; (b) his good and bad qualities; (c) his special likes and dislikes; (d) anecdotes concerning his quirks of character, adventures, or misadventures.

3. State your opinion of the following idea: "Implicit in every friendship is the trust that it will never break."

Childhood is usually a happy, carefree time when the basic human needs—food, clothing, and shelter—are provided by loving parents. For Richard Wright, however, childhood was a time of deprivation and struggle. In the following selection he encounters a formidable and relentless enemy —hunger.

from BLACK BOY

Richard Wright

HUNGER stole upon me so slowly that at first I was not aware of what hunger really meant. Hunger had always been more or less at my elbow when I played, but now I began to wake up at night to find hunger standing at my bedside, staring at me gauntly. The hunger I had known before this had been no grim, hostile stranger; it had been a normal hunger that had made me beg constantly for bread, and when I ate a crust or two I was satisfied. But this new hunger baffled me, scared me, made me angry and insistent. Whenever I begged for food now my mother would pour me a cup of tea which would still the clamor in my stomach for a moment or two; but a little later I would feel hunger nudging my ribs, twisting my empty guts until they ached. I would grow dizzy and my vision would dim. I became less active in my play, and for the first time in my life I had to pause and think of what was happening to me.

"Mama, I'm hungry," I complained one afternoon.

"Jump up and catch a kungry," she said, trying to make me laugh and forget.

"What's a *kungry?*"

"It's what little boys eat when they get hungry," she said.

"What does it taste like?"

"I don't know."

"Then why do you tell me to catch one?"

"Because you said that you were hungry," she said smiling.

I sensed that she was teasing me and it made me angry.

"But I'm hungry. I want to eat."

"You'll have to wait."

"But I want to eat now."

"But there's nothing to eat," she told me.

"Why?"

"Just because there's none," she explained.

"But I want to eat," I said, beginning to cry.

"You'll just have to wait," she said again.

"But why?"

"For God to send some food."

"When is He going to send it?"

"I don't know."

"But I'm hungry!"

She was ironing and she paused and looked at me with tears in her eyes.

"Where's your father?" she asked me.

I stared in bewilderment. Yes, it was true that my father had not come home to sleep for many days now and I could make as much noise as I wanted. Though I had not known why he was absent, I had been glad that he was not there to shout his restrictions at me. But it had never occurred to me that his absence would mean that there would be no food.

"I don't know," I said.

"Who brings food into the house?" my mother asked me.

"Papa," I said. "He always brought food."

"Well, your father isn't here now," she said.

"Where is he?"

"I don't know," she said.

"But I'm hungry," I whimpered, stomping my feet.

"You'll have to wait until I get a job and buy food," she said.

As the days slid past the image of my father became associated with my pangs of hunger, and whenever I felt hunger I thought of him with a deep biological bitterness.

My mother finally went to work as a cook and left me and my brother alone in the flat each day with a loaf of bread and a pot of tea. When she returned at evening she would be tired and dispirited and would cry a lot. Sometimes, when she was in despair, she would call us to her and talk to us for hours, telling us that we now had no father, that our lives would be different from those of other children, that we must learn as soon as possible to take care of ourselves, to dress ourselves, to prepare our own food; that we must take upon ourselves the responsibility of the flat while she worked. Half frightened, we would promise solemnly. We did not understand what had happened between our father and our mother and the most that these long talks did to us was to make us feel a vague dread. Whenever we asked why father had left, she would tell us that we were too young to know.

One evening my mother told me that thereafter I would have to do the shopping for food. She took me to the corner store to show me the way. I was proud; I felt like a grownup. The next afternoon I looped the basket over my arm and went down the pavement toward the store. When I reached the corner, a gang of boys grabbed me, knocked me down, snatched the basket, took the money, and sent me running home in panic. That evening I told my mother what had happened, but she made no comment; she sat down at once, wrote another note, gave me more money, and sent me out to the grocery again. I crept down the steps and saw the same gang of boys playing down the street. I ran back into the house.

"What's the matter?" my mother asked.

"It's those same boys," I said. "They'll beat me."

"You've got to get over that," she said. "Now, go on."

"I'm scared," I said.

"Go on and don't pay any attention to them," she said.

I went out of the door and walked briskly down the sidewalk, praying that the gang would not molest me. But when I came abreast of them someone shouted.

"There he is!"

They came toward me and I broke into a wild run toward home. They overtook me and flung me to the pavement. I yelled, pleaded, kicked, but they wrenched the money out of my hand. They yanked me to my feet, gave me a few slaps, and sent me home sobbing. My mother met me at the door.

"They b-beat m-me," I gasped. "They t-t-took the m-money."

I started up the steps, seeking the shelter of the house.

"Don't you come in here," my mother warned me.

I froze in my tracks and stared at her.

"But they're coming after me," I said.

"You just stay right where you are," she said in a deadly tone. "I'm going to teach you this night to stand up and fight for yourself."

She went into the house and I waited, terrified, wondering what she was about. Presently she returned with more money and another note; she also had a long heavy stick.

"Take this money, this note, and this stick," she said. "Go to the store and buy those groceries. If those boys bother you, then fight."

I was baffled. My mother was telling me to fight, a thing that she had never done before.

"But I'm scared," I said.

"Don't you come into this house until you've gotten those groceries," she said.

"They'll beat me; they'll beat me," I said.

"Then stay in the streets; don't come back here!"

I ran up the steps and tried to force my way past her into the house. A stinging slap came on my jaw. I stood on the sidewalk, crying.

"Please, let me wait until tomorrow," I begged.

"No," she said. "Go now! If you come back into this house without those groceries, I'll whip you!"

She slammed the door and I heard the key turn in the lock. I shook with fright. I was alone upon the dark, hostile streets and gangs were after me. I had the choice of being beaten at home or away from home. I clutched the stick, crying, trying to reason. If I were beaten at home, there was absolutely nothing that I could do about it; but if I were beaten in the streets, I had a chance to fight and defend myself. I walked slowly down the sidewalk, coming closer to the gang of boys, holding the stick tightly. I was so full of fear that I could scarcely breathe. I was almost upon them now.

"There he is again!" the cry went up.

They surrounded me quickly and began to grab for my hand.

"I'll kill you!" I threatened.

They closed in. In blind fear I let the stick fly, feeling it crack against a boy's skull. I swung again, lamming another skull, then another. Realizing that they would retaliate if I let up for but a second, I fought to lay them low, to knock them cold, to kill them so that they could not strike back at me. I flayed with tears in my eyes, teeth clenched, stark fear making me throw every ounce of my strength behind each blow. I hit again and again, dropping the money and the grocery list. The boys scattered, yelling, nursing their heads, staring at me in utter disbelief. They had never seen such frenzy. I stood panting, egging them on, taunting them to come on and fight. When they refused, I ran after them and they tore out for their homes, screaming. The parents of the boys rushed into the streets and threatened me, and for the first time in my life I shouted at grownups, telling them that I would give them the same if they bothered me. I finally found my grocery list and the money and went to the store. On my way back I kept my stick poised for instant use, but there was not a single boy in sight. That night I won the right to the streets of Memphis.

Questions and Comments

Richard Wright, the author of this selection, was a Negro writer who died in 1960. In his writings—for example, *Uncle Tom's Children, Native Son,* and *Black Boy,* from which the above selection is taken—he maintains the belief that society's primary responsibility is that of providing an environment in which the Negro people can realize their true potential.

1. What is the difference between the hunger the author experiences and that which he had known earlier?

2. Why is the author's family poverty-stricken?

3. What duties does the author's mother say he and his brother must assume while she is working? What is her state of mind at this time? Why?

4. How does Richard react when he is asked to buy groceries for the first time?

5. What happens to him on the way to the grocery store? What does his mother tell him when he returns the second time without having completed his errand?

6. What does the author's mother force him to do? Why?

7. What happens when the author ventures into the street for the third time?

Word Study

1. Try to guess the meaning of the italicized words from their context. Then use a dictionary to check your guesses.

   "When she returned at evening she would be tired and *dispirited* and would cry at lot." (page 12)

   "Realizing that they would *retaliate* if I let up for but a second, I fought to lay them low. . . ." (page 14)

   "I *flayed* with tears in my eyes, teeth clenched, *stark* fear making me throw every ounce of my strength behind each blow." (page 14)

2. The verb *egg* used in this selection has nothing in common with the noun *egg* except spelling. Look up *egg* as in "I stood panting, egging them on" in an unabridged dictionary and give the derivation of the word.

Composition

1. In this selection the central character faces a great conflict within himself which he eventually overcomes. Describe the conflict and tell whether you feel the author did or did not portray it convincingly. Cite evidence from the selection to support your opinion.

2. The author's mother forced her son to do something that he did not want to do. Explain why you think her action was or was not the correct one for this situation. Discuss what might have happened if she had done otherwise.

3. Under what conditions do you feel fighting is justified? Describe a fight that you have witnessed or read about. Try to evaluate the cause of the encounter and tell how it might have been avoided.

Have you ever tried to train a horse, a dog, or some other animal? If so, you will readily appreciate some of the difficulties that Lincoln Steffens encountered in his attempt to break in a colt. The selection that follows is a chapter from *The Autobiography of Lincoln Steffens*. In this chapter Lincoln Steffens exhibits patience, persistence, and determination—qualities which later characterized his career as an astute and severe critic of the American political and economic scene. He became famous for his magazine articles exposing various forms of racketeering that developed in the early years of the twentieth century.

I GET A COLT
TO BREAK IN

Lincoln Steffens

COLONEL CARTER gave me a colt. I had my pony, and my father meanwhile had bought a pair of black carriage horses and a cow, all of which I had to attend to when we had no "man." And servants were hard to get and keep in those days; the women married, and the men soon quit service to seize opportunities always opening. My hands were pretty full, and so was the stable. But Colonel Carter seemed to think that he had promised me a horse. He had not; I would have known it if he had. No matter. He thought he had, and maybe he did promise himself to give me one. That was enough. The kind of man that led immigrant trains across the continent and delivered them safe, sound, and together where he promised would keep his word. One day he drove over from Stockton, leading a two-year-old which

17

he brought to our front door and turned over to me as mine. Such a horse!

She was a cream-colored mare with a black forelock, mane, and tail and a black stripe along the middle of her back. Tall, slender, high-spirited, I thought then—I think now that she was the most beautiful of horses. Colonel Carter had bred and reared her with me and my uses in mind. She was a careful cross of a mustang mare and a thoroughbred stallion, with the stamina of the wild horse and the speed and grace of the racer. And she had a sense of fun. As Colonel Carter got down out of his buggy and went up to her, she snorted, reared, flung her head high in the air, and, coming down beside him, tucked her nose affectionately under his arm.

"I have handled her a lot," he said. "She is kind as a kitten, but she is as sensitive as a lady. You can spoil her by one mistake. If you ever lose your temper, if you ever abuse her, she will be ruined for ever. And she is unbroken. I might have had her broken to ride for you, but I didn't want to. I want you to do it. I have taught her to lead, as you see; had to, to get her over here. But here she is, an unbroken colt; yours. You take and you break her. You're only a boy, but if you break this colt right, you'll be a man—a young man, but a man. And I'll tell you how."

Now, out west, as everybody knows, they break in a horse by riding out to him in his wild state, lassooing, throwing, and saddling him; then they let him up, frightened and shocked, with a yelling broncho-buster astride of him. The wild beast bucks, the cowboy drives his spurs into him, and off they go, jumping, kicking, rearing, falling, till by the weight of the man, the lash, and the rowels, the horse is broken—in body and spirit. This was not the way I was to break my colt.

"You must break her to ride without her ever knowing it," Colonel Carter said. "You feed and you clean her—you; not the stable man. You lead her out to water and to walk. You put her on a long rope and let her play, calling her to you and gently pulling on the rope. Then you turn her loose in the grass lot there and, when she has romped till tired, call her. If she won't come, leave her. When she wants water or food, she will run to your call, and you will pet and feed and care for her." He went on for half an hour, advising me in great detail how to proceed. I wanted to begin right away. He laughed. He let me lead her around to the stable, water her, and put her in the stable and feed her.

There I saw my pony. My father, sisters, and Colonel Carter saw me stop and look at my pony.

"What'll you do with him?" one of my sisters asked. I was bewildered for a moment. What should I do with the little red horse? I decided at once.

"You can have him," I said to my sisters.

"No," said Colonel Carter, "not yet. You can give your sisters the pony by and by, but you'll need him till you have taught the colt to carry you and a saddle—months; and you must not hurry. You must learn patience, and you will if you give the colt time to learn it, too. Patience and control. You can't control a young horse unless you can control yourself. Can you shoot?" he asked suddenly.

I couldn't. I had a gun and I had used it some, but it was a rifle, and I could not bring down with it such game as there was around Sacramento—birds and hares. Colonel Carter looked at my father, and I caught the look. So did my father. I soon had a shotgun. But at the time Colonel Carter turned to me and said:

"Can't shoot straight, eh? Do you know what that means? That means that you can't control a gun, and that means that you can't control yourself, your eye, your hands, your nerves. You are wriggling now. I tell you that a good shot is always a good man. He may be a 'bad man' too, but he is quiet, strong, steady in speech, gait, and mind. No matter, though. If you break in this colt right, if you teach her her paces, she will teach you to shoot and be quiet."

He went off downtown with my father, and I started away with my colt. I fed, I led, I cleaned her, gently, as if she were made of glass; she was playful and willing, a delight. When Colonel Carter came home with my father for supper, he questioned me.

"You should not have worked her today," he said. "She has come all the way from Stockton and must be tired. Yes, yes, she would not show fatigue; too fine for that, and too young to be wise. You have got to think for her, consider her as you would your sisters."

Sisters! I thought; I had never considered my sisters. I did not say that, but Colonel Carter laughed and nodded to my sisters. It was just as if he had read my thought. But he went on to draw on my imagination a centaur;[1] the colt as a horse's body—me, a boy, as the head and brains of one united creature. I liked that. I would be that. I and the colt: a centaur.

After Colonel Carter was gone home I went to work on my new horse. The old one, the pony, I used only for business: to go to fires, to see my friends, run errands, and go hunting with my new shotgun. But the game that had all my attention was the breaking in of the colt, the beautiful cream-colored mare, who soon knew me—and my pockets. I carried sugar to reward her when she did right, and she discovered where I carried it; so did the pony, and when I was busy they would push their noses into my pockets, both of which were torn down a good deal of the time. But the colt learned. I taught her to run around a circle, turn and go the other way at a signal. My sisters helped me. I held the long rope and the whip (for signaling), while one of the girls led the colt; it was hard work for them, but they took it in turns. One would lead the colt round and round till I snapped the whip; then she would turn, turning the colt, till the colt did it all by herself. And she was very quick. She shook hands with each of her four feet. She let us run under her, back and forth. She was slow only to carry me. Following Colonel Carter's instructions, I began by laying

[1] *centaur:* in Greek mythology, one of a race of creatures that were half man, half horse

my arm or a surcingle over her back. If she trembled, I drew it slowly off. When she could abide it, I tried buckling it, tighter and tighter. I laid over her, too, a blanket, folded at first, then open, and, at last, I slipped up on her myself, sat there a second, and as she trembled, slid off. My sisters held her for me, and when I could get up and sit there a moment or two, I tied her at a block, and we, my sisters and I, made a procession of mounting and dismounting. She soon got used to this and would let us slide off over her rump, but it was a long, long time before she would carry me.

That we practiced by leading her along a high curb where I could get on as she walked, ride a few steps, and then, as she felt me and crouched, slip off. She never did learn to carry a girl on her back; my sisters had to lead her while I rode. This was not purposeful. I don't know just how it happened, but I do remember the first time I rode on my colt all the way around the lot and how, when I put one of the girls up she refused to repeat. She shuddered, shook and frightened them off.

While we were breaking in the colt a circus came to town. The ring was across the street from our house. Wonderful! I lived in that circus for a week. I saw the show but once, but I marked the horse-trainers, and in the mornings when they were not too busy I told them about my colt, showed her to them, and asked them how to train her to do circus tricks. With their hints I taught the colt to stand up on her hind legs, kneel, lie down, and balance on a small box. This last was easier than it looked. I put her first on a low big box and taught her to turn on it; then got a little smaller box upon which she repeated what she did on the big one. By and by we had her so that she would step up on a high box so small that her four feet were almost touching, and there also she would turn.

The circus man gave me one hint that was worth all the other tricks put together. "You catch her doing something of herself that looks good," he said, "and then you keep her at it." It was thus that I taught her to bow to people. The first day I rode her out on to the streets was a proud one for me and for the colt, too, apparently. She did not walk, she danced; perhaps she was excited, nervous; anyhow I liked the way she threw up her head, champed at the bit, and went dancing, prancing down the street. Everybody stopped to watch us, and so, when she began to sober down, I picked her up again with heel and rein, saying, "Here's people, Lady," and she would show off to my delight. By constant repetition I had her so trained that she would single-foot, head down, along a country road till we came to a house or a group of people. Then I'd say, "People, Lady," and up would go her head, and her feet would dance.

But the trick that set the town talking was her bowing to any one I spoke to. "Lennie Steffens' horse bows to you," people said, and she did. I never told how it was done; by accident. Dogs used to run out at us, and the colt enjoyed it; she kicked at them sometimes with both hind hoofs. I joined her in the game, and being able to look behind more conveniently than she could, I watched the dogs until they were in range, then gave the colt a signal to kick. "Kick, gal," I'd say, and tap her ribs with my heel. We used to get dogs together that way; the colt would kick them over and over and leave them yelping in the road. Well, one day when I met a girl I knew I lifted my hat, probably muttered a "Good day," and I must have touched the colt with my heel. Anyway, she dropped her head and kicked—not much; there was no dog near, so she had responded to my unexpected signal by what looked like a bow. I caught the idea and kept her at it. Whenever I wanted to bow to a girl or anybody else, instead of saying "Good day," I muttered "Kick, gal," spurred her lightly, and—the whole centaur bowed and was covered with glory and conceit.

Yes, conceit. I was full of it, and the colt was quite as bad. One day my chum Hjalmar came into town on his Black Bess, blanketed. She had had a great fistule cut out of her shoulder and had to be kept warm. I expected to see her weak and dull, but no, the good old mare was champing and dancing, like my colt.

"What is it makes her so?" I asked, and Hjalmar said he didn't know, but he thought she was proud of the blanket. A great idea. I had a gaudy horse blanket. I put it on the colt and I could hardly hold her. We rode down the main street together, both horses and both boys, so full of vanity that everybody stopped to smile. We thought they admired, and maybe they did. But some boys on the street gave us another angle. They, too, stopped and looked, and as we passed, one of them said, "Think you're hell, don't you?"

Spoilsport!

We did, as a matter of fact; we thought we were hell. The recognition of it dashed us for a moment; not for long, and the horses paid no heed. We pranced, the black and the yellow, all the way down J Street, up K Street, and agreed that we'd do it again, often. Only, I said, we wouldn't use blankets. If the horses were proud of a blanket, they'd be proud of anything unusually conspicuous. We tried a flower next time. I fixed a big rose on my colt's bridle just under her ear and it was great—she pranced downtown with her head turned, literally, to show off her flower. We had to change the decoration from time to time, put on a ribbon, or a bell, or a feather, but, really, it was not necessary for my horse. Old Black Bess needed an incentive to act up, but all I had to do to my horse was to pick up the reins, touch her with my heel, and say, "People"; she would dance from one side of the street to the other, asking to be admired. As she was. As we were.

I would ride down to my father's store, jump off my prancing colt in the middle of the street, and run up into the shop. The colt, free would stop short, turn, and follow me right up on the sidewalk, unless I bade her wait. If any one approached her while I was gone, she would snort, rear, and strike. No stranger could get near her. She became a frightened, frightening animal, and yet when I came into sight

she would run to me, put her head down, and as I straddled her neck, she would throw up her head and pitch me
into my seat, facing backward, of course. I whirled around
right, and off we'd go, the vainest boy and the proudest
horse in the State.

"Hey, give me a ride, will you?" some boy would ask.

"Sure," I'd say, and jump down and watch that boy try
to catch and mount my colt. He couldn't. Once a cowboy
wanted to try her, and he caught her; he dodged her fore-
feet, grabbed the reins, and in one spring was on her back.
I never did that again. My colt reared, then bucked, and, as
the cowboy kept his seat, she shuddered, sank to the ground,
and rolled over. He slipped aside and would have risen with
her, but I was alarmed and begged him not to. She got up
at my touch and followed me so close that she stepped on
my heel and hurt me. The cowboy saw the point.

"If I were you kid," he said, "I'd never let anybody mount
that colt. She's too good."

That, I think, was the only mistake I made in the rearing of Colonel Carter's gift-horse. My father differed from
me. He discovered another error or sin, and thrashed me
for it. My practice was to work hard on a trick, privately,
and when it was perfect, let him see it. I would have the
horse out in our vacant lot doing it as he came home to supper. One evening, as he approached the house, I was standing, whip in hand, while the colt, quite free, was stepping
carefully over the bodies of a lot of girls, all my sisters and
all their girl friends. (Grace Gallatin, later Mrs. Thompson-
Seton, was among them.) My father did not express the
admiration I expected; he was frightened and furious. "Stop
that," he called, and he came running around into the lot,
took the whip, and lashed me with it. I tried to explain;
the girls tried to help me explain.

I had seen in the circus a horse that stepped thus over a
row of prostrate clowns. It looked dangerous for the clowns,
but the trainer had told me how to do it. You begin with
logs, laid out a certain distance apart; the horse walks over

them under your lead, and whenever he touches one you rebuke him. By and by he will learn to step with such care that he never trips. Then you substitute clowns. I had no clowns, but I did get logs, and with the girls helping, we taught the colt to step over the obstacles even at a trot. Walking, she touched nothing. All ready thus with the logs, I had my sisters lie down in the grass, and again and again the colt stepped over and among them. None was ever touched. My father would not listen to any of this; he just walloped me, and when he was tired or satisfied and I was in tears, I blubbered a short excuse: "They were only girls." And he whipped me some more.

My father was not given to whipping; he did it very seldom, but he did it hard when he did it at all. My mother was just the opposite. She did not whip me, but she often smacked me, and she had a most annoying habit of thumping me on the head with her thimbled finger. This I resented more than my father's thorough-going thrashings, and I can tell why now. I would be playing Napoleon and as I was reviewing my Old Guard, she would crack my skull with that thimble. No doubt I was in the way; it took a lot of furniture and sisters to represent properly a victorious army; and you might think as my mother did that a thimble is a small weapon. But imagine Napoleon at the height of his power, the ruler of the world on parade, getting a sharp rap on his crown from a woman's thimble. No. My father's way was more appropriate. It was hard. "I'll attend to you in the morning," he would say, and I lay awake wondering which of my crimes he had discovered. I know what it is to be sentenced to be shot at sunrise. And it hurt, in the morning, when he was not angry but very fresh and strong. But you see, he walloped me in my own person; he never humiliated Napoleon or my knighthood, as my mother did. And I learned something from his discipline, something useful.

I learned what tyranny is and the pain of being misunderstood and wronged, or, if you please, understood and set right; they are pretty much the same. He and most parents and teachers do not break in their boys as carefully as I broke in my colt. They haven't the time that I had, and they have not some other incentives I had. I saw this that day when I rubbed my sore legs. He had to explain to my indignant mother what had happened. When he had told it his way, I gave my version: how long and cautiously I had been teaching my horse to walk over logs and girls. And having shown how sure I was of myself and the colt, while my mother was boring into his silence with one of her reproachful looks, I said something that hit my father hard.

"I taught the colt that trick, I have taught her all that you see she knows, without whipping her. I have never struck her; not once. Colonel Carter said I mustn't, and I haven't."

And my mother, backing me up, gave him a rap: "There," she said, "I told you so." He walked off, looking like a thimble-rapped Napoleon.

Questions and Comments

1. What does the author say is the usual way of breaking a horse out west? How was the author to break in his own colt?

2. Colonel Carter says, "You must learn patience, and you will if you give the colt time to learn it, too. Patience and control." Does the author learn patience and control? Give evidence from the selection.

3. What does Colonel Carter mean by saying that a good shot is always a good man even though he may be a bad one?

4. What is the greatest hint given to the author by the horse trainers of the circus? What use does the author make of it?

5. What one mistake does the author think he made in the rearing of his horse? What other mistake does his father think he made?

6. How does the punishment administered by the author's mother differ from that administered by his father? Which does the author resent more? Why?

7. What is the significance of the last paragraph?

Word Study

1. Tell the meaning of the italicized words, all of which are connected with horses:

   "She was a careful cross of a *mustang mare* and a *thorough-bred stallion.* . . ." (page 18)

   ". . . by the weight of the man, the lash, and the *rowels,* the horse is broken—in body and spirit." (page 18)

   "I began by laying my arm or a *surcingle* over her back." (page 21)

   "I had her trained so that she would *single-foot,* head down, along a country road. . . ." (page 22)

   "She had had a great *fistule* cut out of her shoulder. . . ." (page 22)

2. The colt champed at the bit; that is, she gnashed the bar in her mouth. What does *champ at the bit* mean when applied to a person?

Composition

1. Explain the significance of Colonel Carter's statement "You're only a boy, but if you break this colt right, you'll be a man—a young man, but a man."

2. Write of your own experiences in caring for and training a pet animal, telling what you learned from the animal as well as what you taught the animal.

3. Give your own opinion on the need for discipline and the most effective manner of administering it.

William Allen White is known for his warm, nostalgic accounts of Middle Western, small-town American life. As editor of the *Emporia Gazette* he bequeathed to the world a rich legacy of human-interest stories, essays, and penetrating editorials. Many find *The Court of Boyville,* from which the following account is taken, one of his most delightful and enduring works. The period in which the action takes place is late in the nineteenth century.

MUCH POMP AND SEVERAL CIRCUMSTANCES

William Allen White

BACK of Pennington's barn, which was the royal castle of the Court of Boyville, ran a hollow. In the hollow grew a gnarly box-elder tree. This tree was the courtiers' hunting-lodge. In the crotches of the rugged branches Piggy Pennington, Abe Carpenter, Jimmy Sears, Bud Perkins, and Mealy Jones were wont to rest of a summer afternoon, recounting the morning's adventures in the royal tourney of the marble-ring, planning for the morrow's chase, meditating upon the evil approach of the fall school term, and following such sedentary pursuits as to any member of the court seemed right and proper. One afternoon late in August the tree was alive with its arboreal aristocracy. Abe Carpenter sat on the lowest branch, plaiting a four-strand, square-braided "quirt";[1] Jimmy Sears was holding the ends. Piggy was casually skinning cats, hanging by his legs, or chinning on an almost horizontal limb, as he took his part

[1] *quirt:* a short-handled riding whip

in the lagging talk. Hidden by the foliage in the thick of the tree, in a three-pronged seat, Bud Perkins reclined, his features drawn into a painful grimace, as his right hand passed to and fro before his mouth, rhythmically twanging the tongue of a jew's-harp,[1] upon which he was playing "To My Sweet Sunny South Take Me Home." He breathed heavily and irregularly. His eyes were on the big white clouds in the blue sky, and his heart was filled with the poetry of lonesomeness that sometimes comes to boys in pensive moods. For the days when he had lived with his father, a nomad of the creeks that flowed by half a score of waterways into the Mississippi, were upon the far horizon of his consciousness, and the memory of those days made him as sad as any memory ever can make a healthy, carefree boy. He played "Dixie," partly because it was his dead father's favorite tune, and partly because, being sprightly, it kept down his melancholy. Later he took out a new mouth-organ, which his foster-mother had given to him, and to satisfy his boyish idea of justice played "We Shall Meet, but We Shall Miss Him," because it was Miss Morgan's favorite. While he played the jew's-harp his tree friends flung ribald remarks at him. But when Bud began to waver his hand for a tremulo[2] upon the mouth-organ as he played "Marsa's in de Col', Col' Groun'," a peace fell upon the company, and they sat quietly and heard his repertoire,—"Ol'Shadey," "May, Dearest May," "Lilly Dale," "Dey Stole My Chile Away," "Ol' Nicodemus," "Sleeping, I Dream, Love," and "Her Bright Smile." He was a Southern boy—a bird of passage caught in the North—and his music had that sweet, soothing note that cheered the men who fought under the Stars and Bars.[3]

Into this scene rushed Mealy Jones, pell mell, hat in hand, breathless, bringing war's alarms. "Fellers, fellers,"

[1] *jew's-harp:* a small lyre-shaped musical instrument
[2] *tremulo:* the rapid repetition of a musical tone so as to produce a fluttering effect
[3] *Stars and Bars:* Confederate flag

screamed Mealy, half a block away, "it's a-comin' here! It's goin' to be here in two weeks. The man's puttin' up the boards now, and you can get a job passin' bills."

An instant later the tree was deserted, and five boys were running as fast as their legs would carry them toward the thick of the town. They stopped at the new pine billboard, and did not leave the man with the paste bucket until they had seen "Zazell" flying out of the cannon's mouth, the iron-jawed woman performing her marvels, the red-mouthed rhinoceros with the bleeding native impaled upon its horn and the fleeing hunters near by, "the largest elephant in captivity," carrying the ten-thousand dollar beauty, the acrobats whirling through space, James Robinson turning handsprings on his dapple-gray steed, and, last and most ravishing of all, little Willie Sells in pink tights on his three charging Shetland ponies, whose breakneck course in the picture followed one whichever way he turned. When these glories had been pasted upon the wall and had been discussed to the point of cynicism, the Court of Boyville reluctantly adjourned to get in the night wood and dream of a wilderness of monkeys.

During the two weeks after the appearance of the glad tidings on the billboards, the boys of Willow Creek spent many hours in strange habiliments, making grotesque imitations of the spectacles upon the boards. Piggy Pennington rolled his trousers far above his knees for tights, and galloped his father's fat delivery horse up and down the alley, riding sideways, standing, and backwards, with much vainglory. To simulate the motley[1] of the tightrope-walking clown, Jimmy Sears wore the calico lining of his clothes outside, when he was in the royal castle beyond his mother's ken. Mealy donned carpet slippers in Pennington's barn, and wore long pink-and-white striped stockings of a suspiciously feminine appearance, fastened to his abbreviated shirt waist with stocking-suspenders, hated of all boys. Abe

---

[1] *motley:* a cloth or garment of many colors

Carpenter, in a bathing-trunk, did shudder-breeding trapeze tricks, and Bud Perkins, who nightly rubbed himself limber in oil made by hanging a bottle of angleworms in the sun to fry, wore his red calico baseball clothes, and went through keg-hoops in a dozen different ways. In the streets of the town the youngsters appeared disguised as ordinary boys. They revelled in the pictured visions of the circus, but were sceptical about the literal fulfilment of some of the promises made on the bills. Certain things advertised were eliminated from reasonable expectation: for instance, the boys all knew that the giraffe would not be discovered eating off the top of a cocoanut-tree; nor would the monkeys play a brass band; and they knew that they would not see the "Human Fly" walk on the ceiling at the "concert." For no boy has ever saved enough money to buy a ticket to the "concert." Nevertheless, they gloated over the pictures of the herd of giraffes and the monkey-band and the graceful "Human Fly" walking upside down "defying the laws of gravitation"; and they considered no future, however pleasant, after the day and date on the bills. Thus the golden day approached, looming larger and larger upon the horizon as it came. In the interim, how many a druggist bought his own bottles the third and fourth time, how many a junk-dealer paid for his own iron, how many bags of carpet rags went to the ragman, the world will never know.

Now, among children of a larger growth, in festive times hostile demonstrations cease; animosities are buried; but in Boyville a North-ender is a North-ender, a South-ender is a South-ender, and a meeting of the two is a fight. Boyville knows no times of truce. It asks nor offers quarter. When warring clans come together, be it workday, holiday, or even circus day, there is a clatter of clods, a patter of feet, and retreating hoots of defiance. And because the circus billboards were frequented by boys of all kiths[1] and clans, clashes occurred frequently, and Bud Perkins, who was the fighter of

---

[1] *kiths:* neighborhoods

the South End, had many a call to arms. Indeed, the approaching circus unloosed the dogs of war rather than nestled the dove of peace. For Bud Perkins, in a moment of pride, issued an ukase[1] which forbade all North End boys to look at a certain billboard near his home. This ukase and his strict enforcement of it made him the target of North End wrath. Little Miss Morgan, his foster-mother, who had adopted him at the death of his father the summer before the circus bills were posted, could not understand how the lad managed to lose so many buttons, nor how he kept tearing his clothes. She ascribed these things to his antecedents and to his deficient training. She did not know that Bud, whom she called Henry, and whose music on the mouth-organ seemed to come from a shy and gentle soul, was the Terror of the South End. Her guileless mind held no place for the important fact that North End boys generally travelled by her door in pairs for safety. Such is the blindness of women. Cupid probably got his defective vision from his mother's side of the house.

The last half of the last week before circus day seemed a century to Bud and his friends. Friday and Saturday crept by, and Mealy Jones was the only boy at Sunday-school who knew the Golden Text, for an inflammatory rumor that the circus was unloading from the side-track at the depot swept over the boys' side of the Sunday-school room, and consumed all knowledge of the fifth chapter of Acts, the day's lesson. After Sunday-school the boys broke for the circus grounds. There they feasted their gluttonous eyes upon the canvas-covered chariots, and the elephants, and the camels, and the spotted ponies, passing from the cars to the tents. The unfamiliar noises, the sight of the rising "sea of canvas," the touch of mysterious wagons containing so many wonders, and the intoxicating smell that comes only with much canvas, many animals, and the unpacking of Pandora's box,[2] stuffed the boys' senses until they viewed with utter

[1] *ukase:* in Russia, an imperial order having the force of law; any official decree

[2] *Pandora's box:* in Greek mythology, a box containing all human ills

stoicism the passing dinner hour and the prospect of finding only cold mashed potatoes and the necks and backs of chickens in the cupboards. They even affected indifference to parental scoldings, and lingered about the enchanting spot until the shadows fell eastward and the day was old.

When a boy gets on his good behavior he tempts Providence. And the Providence of boys is frail and prone to yield. So when Bud Perkins, who was burning with a desire to please Miss Morgan the day before the circus, went to church that Sunday night, any one can see that he was provoking Providence in an unusual and cruel manner. Bud did not sit with Miss Morgan, but lounged into the church, and took a back seat. Three North End boys came in and sat on the same bench. Then Jimmy Sears shuffled past the North Enders, and sat beside Bud. After which the inevitable happened. It kept happening. They "passed it on," and passed it back again; first a pinch, then a chug, then a cuff, then a kick under the bench. Heads craned toward the boys occasionally, and there came an awful moment when Bud Perkins found himself looking brazenly into the eyes of the preacher, who had paused to glare at the boys in the midst of his sermon. The faces of the entire congregation seemed to turn upon Bud automatically. A cherub-like expression of conscious innocence and impenetrable unconcern beamed through Bud Perkins's features. The same expression rested upon the countenances of the four other malefactors. At the end of the third second Jimmy Sears put his hand to his mouth and snorted between his fingers. And four young men looked down their noses. In the hush, Brother Baker—a tiptoeing Nemesis[1]—stalked the full length of the church toward the culprits. When he took his seat beside the boys the preacher continued his discourse. Brother Baker's unctuousness angered Bud Perkins. He felt the implication that his conduct was bad, and his sense of guilt spurred his temper. Satan put a pin in Bud's hand. Slowly, almost imperceptibly, Satan moved the boy's arm on the back of the pew,

[1] *Nemesis:* goddess of retribution

around Jimmy Sears. Then an imp pushed Bud's hand as he jabbed a pin into the back of a North Ender. The boy from the North End let out a yowl of pain. Bud was not quick enough. Brother Baker saw the pin; two hundred devout Methodists saw him clamp his fingers on Bud Perkin's ear, and march him down the length of the church and set him beside Miss Morgan. It was a sickening moment. The North End grinned as one boy under its skin, and was exceeding glad. So agonizing was it for Bud that he forgot to imagine what a triumph it was for the North End—and further anguish is impossible for a boy.

Miss Morgan and Bud Perkins left the church with the congregation. Bud dreaded the moment when they would leave the crowd and turn into their side street. When they did turn, Bud was lagging a step or two behind. A boy's troubles are always the fault of the other boy. The North End boy's responsibility in the matter was so clear—to Bud —that, when he went to justify himself to Miss Morgan, he was surprised and hurt at what he considered her feminine blindness to the fact. After she had passed her sentence she asked: "Do you really think you deserve to go, Henry?"

The blow stunned the boy. He saw the visions of two weeks burst like bubbles, and he whimpered: "I dunno." But in his heart he did know that to deny a boy the joy of seeing Willie Sells on his three Shetland ponies, for nothing in the world but showing a North-ender his place, was a piece of injustice of the kind for which men and nations go to war. At breakfast Bud kept his eyes on his plate. His face wore the resigned look of a martyr. Miss Morgan was studiously gracious. He dropped leaden monosyllables into the cheery flow of her conversation, and after breakfast put in his time at the woodshed.

At eight o'clock that morning the town of Willow Creek was in the thrall of the circus. Country wagons were passing on every side street. Delivery carts were rattling about with unusual alacrity. By half-past nine dressed-up children were flitting along the side streets hurrying their seniors. On the main thoroughfare flags were flying, and the streams of strangers that had been flowing into town were eddying at the street corners. The balloon-vender wormed his way through the buzzing crowd, leaving his wares in a red and blue trail behind him. The bark of the fakir[1] rasped the tightening nerves of the town. Everywhere was hubbub; everywhere was the dusty, heated air of the festival; every-where were men and women ready for the marvel that had come out of the great world, bringing pomp and circum-stance in its gilded train; everywhere in Willow Creek the spirit which put the blue sash about the country girl's waist and the flag in her beau's hat ran riot, save at the home of Miss Morgan. There the bees hummed lazily over the old-fashioned flower garden; there the cantankerous jays jabbered in the cottonwoods; there the muffled noises of the town festi-val came as from afar; there Miss Morgan puttered about her morning's work, trying vainly to croon a gospel hymn; and there Bud Perkins, prone upon the sitting-room sofa, made parallelograms and squares and diamonds with the dots and lines on the ceiling paper. When the throb of the drum and the blare of the brass had set the heart of the town to dancing, some wave of the ecstasy seeped through the li-lac bushes and into the quiet house. The boy on the sofa started up suddenly, checked himself ostentatiously, walked to the bird cage, and began to play with the canary. The wave carried the little spinster to the window. The circus had a homestead in human hearts before John Wesley staked his claim, and even so good a Methodist as Miss Morgan could not be deaf to the scream of the calliope nor the tinkle of cymbals.

To emphasize his desolation, Bud left the room, and sat down by a tree in the yard, with his back to the kitchen door and window. There Miss Morgan saw him playing mumble-peg in a desultory fashion. When the courtiers of Boyville

[1] *fakir:* in India, a wonder-worker

came home from the parade they found him; and because
he sat playing a silent, sullen, solitary game, and responded
to their banter only with melancholy grunts, they knew
that the worst had befallen him. Much confab followed, in
which the pronoun "she" and "her" were spoken. Otherwise
Miss Morgan was unidentified. For the conversation ran
thus, over and over:—

"You ask her."

"Naw, I've done ast 'er."

" 'T won't do no good for me to ast 'er. She don't like me."

"I ain't 'fraid to ast 'er."

"Well, then, why don't you?"

"Why don't *you?*"

"Let's all ast 'er."

"S'pose she will, Bud?"

"I dunno."

Then Piggy and Abe and Jimmy and Mealy came trapes-
ing up to Miss Morgan's kitchen door. Bud sat by the tree
twirling his knife at his game. Piggy, being the spokesman,
stood in the doorway. "Miss Morgan," he said, as he slapped
his leg with his hat.

"Well, Winfield?" replied the little woman, divining his
mission, and hardening her heart against his purpose.

"Miss Morgan," he repeated, and then coaxed sheepishly,
"can't Bud go to the show with us, Miss Morgan?"

"I'm afraid not to-day," smiled back Miss Morgan, as she
went about her work. A whisper from the doorstep prompted
Piggy to "ask her why," whereas Piggy echoed: "Why can't
he, Miss Morgan?"

"Henry misbehaved in church last night, and we've agreed
that he shall stay home from the circus."

Piggy advanced a step or two inside the door, laughing
diplomatically: "O—no, Miss Morgan; don't you think he's
agreed. He's just dyin' to go."

Miss Morgan smiled, but did not join in Piggy's hilarity
—a bad sign. Piggy tried again: "They got six elephants,

and one's a trick elephant. You'd die a-laughin' if you saw him." And Piggy went into a spasm of laughter.

But it left Miss Morgan high and dry upon the island of her determination.

Piggy prepared for an heroic measure, and stepped over to the kitchen table, leaning upon it as he pleaded: "This is the last circus this year, Miss Morgan, and it's an awful good one. Can't he go just this once?"

The debate lasted ten minutes, and at the end four boys walked slowly, with much manifestation of feeling, back to the tree where the fifth sat. There was woe and lamentation after the manner of boykind. When the boys left the yard it seemed to Miss Morgan that she could not look from her work without seeing the lonesome figure of Bud. In the afternoon the patter of feet by her house grew slower, and then ceased. Occasionally a belated wayfarer sped by. The music of the circus band outside of the tent came to Miss Morgan's ears on gusts of wind, and died away as the wind ebbed. She dropped the dish-cloth three times in five minutes, and washed her cup and saucer twice. She struggled bravely in the Slough of Despond[1] for awhile, and then turned back with Pliable.[2]

"Henry," she said, as the boy walked past her carrying peppergrass to the bird, "Henry, what made you act so last night?"

The boy dropped his head and answered: "I dunno."

"But, Henry, didn't you know it was wrong?"

"I dunno."

"Why did you stick that little boy with the pin?"

"Well—well—" he gasped, preparing for a defence. "Well —he pinched me first."

"Yes, Henry, but don't you know that it's wrong to do those things in church? Don't you see how bad it was?"

"I was just a-playin', Miss Morgan; I didn't mean to."

[1] *Slough of Despond:* in John Bunyan's *Pilgrim Progress,* a deep bog into which the hero, Christian, falls
[2] *Pliable:* the companion of Christian in *Pilgrim's Progress*

Bud did not dare to trust his instinctive reading of the signs. He went on impulsively: "I wanted him to quit, but he just kept right on, and Brother Baker didn't touch him."

The wind brought the staccato[1] music of the circus band to the foster-mother's ears. The music completed her moral decay, for she was thinking, if Brother Baker would only look after his own children as carefully as he looked after those of other people, the world would be better. Then she said: "Now, Henry, if I let you go, just this once—now just this once, mind you—will you promise never to do anything like that again?"

Blackness dropped from the boy's spirit, and by main strength he strangled a desire to yell. The desire revived when he reached the alley, and he ran whooping to the circus grounds.

There is a law of crystallization among boys which enables molecules of the same gang to meet in whatever agglomeration they may be thrown. So ten minutes after Bud Perkins left home he found Piggy and Jimmy and old Abe and Mealy in the menagerie tent. Whereupon the South End was able to present a bristling front to the North End —a front which even the pleasings of the lute in the circus band could not break. But the boys knew that the band playing in the circus tent meant that the performance in the ring was about to begin. So they cut short an interesting dialogue with a keeper, concerning the elephant that remembered the man who gave her tobacco ten years ago, and tried to kill him the week before the show came to Willow Creek. But when the pageant in the ring unfolded its tinselled splendor in the Grand Entry, Bud Perkins left earth and walked upon clouds of glory. His high-strung nerves quivered with delight as the ring disclosed its treasures—Willie Sells on his spotted ponies, James Robinson on his dapple gray, the "8 funny clowns—count them 8," the Japanese jugglers and tumblers, the bespangled women on the rings, the

---

[1] *staccato:* in music, having a sharp, abrupt, disjointed character

dancing ponies, and the performing dogs. The climax of his joy came when Zazell, "the queen of the air," was shot from her cannon to the trapeze. Bud had decided, days before the circus, that this feature would please him most. Zazell's performance was somewhat tame, but immediately thereafter a really startling thing happened. A clown holding the trick mule called to the boys near Bud, who nudged him into the clown's attention. The clown, drawing from the wide pantaloons a dollar, pantomimed to Bud. He held it up for the boy and all the spectators to see. Alternately he pointed to the trick mule and to the coin, coaxing and questioning by signs, as he did so. It took perhaps a minute for Bud's embarrassment to wear off. Then two motives impelled him to act. He didn't propose to let the North-enders see his embarrassment, and he saw that he might earn the dollar for Miss Morgan's missionary box, thus mitigating the disgrace he had brought upon her in church. This inspiration literally flashed over Bud, and before he knew it, he was standing in the ring, with his head cocked upon one side to indicate his utter indifference to everything in the world. Of course it was a stupendous pretence. For under his pretty starched shirt, which Miss Morgan had forced on him in the hurry of departure, his heart was beating like a little windmill in a gale. As Bud bestrode the donkey the cheers of the throng rose, but above the tumult he could hear the North End jeering him. He could hear the words the North-enders spoke, even their "ho-o-oho-os," and their "nyayh-nyayh-nyayahs," and their "look-at-old-pretty-boy's," and their "watch-him-hit-the-roof's," and their "get-a-basket's," and similar remarks less desirable for publication. As the donkey cantered off, Bud felt sure he could keep his seat. Once the animal bucked. Bud did not fall. The donkey ran, and stopped quickly. Bud held on. Then the donkey's feet twinkled—it seemed to Bud in the very top of the tent—and Bud slid off the animal's neck to the ring. The clown brought the boy his hat, and stood over him as he rose. Bud laughed

stupidly into the chalked face of the clown, who handed
Bud a dollar, remarking in a low voice, "Well, son, you're a
daisy. They generally drop the first kick."

What passed in the ring as Bud left it, bedraggled and
dusty, did not interest him. He brushed himself as he went.
The band was playing madly, and the young woman in the
stiff skirts was standing by her horse ready to mount. The
crowd did not stop laughing; Bud inclined his head to dust
his knickerbockers, and then in a tragic instant he saw
what was convulsing the multitude with laughter. The outer
seam of the right leg of his velveteen breeches was gone,
and a brown leg was winking in and out from the flapping
garment as he walked. Wildly he gathered the parted garment, and it seemed to him that he never would cover the
ground between the ring and the benches. In the course of
several æons—which the other boys measured by fleeting
minutes—the wave of shame that covered Bud subsided.
Pins bound up the wounds in his clothes. He drew a natural
breath, and was able to join the mob which howled down the
man who announced the concert.

After that the inexorable minutes flew by until the performance ended. In the menagerie tent Bud and his
friends looked thirstily upon the cool, pink "schooners" of
lemonade, and finally, when they had spent a few blissful
moments with the monkeys and had enjoyed a last, long,
lingering look at the elephants, they dragged themselves un-
willingly away into the commonplace of sunshine and trees
and blue sky. Only the romantic touch of the side-show ban-
ners and the wonder of the gilded wagons assured them that
their memories of the passing hour were not empty dreams.

The boys were standing enraptured before the picture
of the fat woman upon the swaying canvas. Bud had drifted
away from them to glut his eyes upon the picture of the
snakes writhing around the charmer. The North-enders had
been following Bud at a respectful distance, waiting for the
opportunity which his separation from his clan gave to
them. They were enforced by a country boy of great reputed

prowess in battle. Bud did not know his danger until they pounced upon him. In an instant the fight was raging. Over the guy ropes it went, under the ticket wagon, into the thick of the lemonade stands. And when Piggy and Abe and Jimmy had joined it, they trailed the track of the storm by torn hats, bruised, battle-scarred boys, and the wreckage incident to an enlivening occasion. When his comrades found Bud, the argument had narrowed down to Bud and the boy from the country, the other wranglers having dropped out for heavy repairs. The fight, which had been started to avenge ancient wrongs, particularly the wrongs of the bill-board, only added new wrongs to the list. The country boy was striking wildly, and trying to clinch his antagonist, when the town marshal—the bogie-man of all boys—stopped the fight. But of course no town marshal can come into the thick of a discussion in Boyville and know much of the merits of the question. So when the marshal of Willow Creek saw Bud Perkins putting the finishing touches of a good trouncing on a strange boy, and also saw Bill Pennington's boy, and Henry Sears's boy, and Mrs. Carpenter's boy, and old man Jones's boy dancing around in high glee at the performance, he quietly gathered in the boys he knew, and let the stranger go.

Now no boy likes to be marched down the main street of his town with the callous finger of the marshal under his shirt-band. The spectacle operates distinctly against the peace and dignity of Boyville for months thereafter. For passing youths who forget there is a morrow jibe at the culprits, and thus plant the seeds of dissensions which bloom in fights. It was a sweaty, red-faced crew that the marshal dumped into Pennington's grocery with, "Here, Bill, I found your boy and these young demons fightin' down 't the circus ground, and I took 'em in charge. You 'tend to 'em, will you?"

Mr. Pennington's glance at his son showed that Piggy was unharmed. A swift survey of the others gave each, save Bud, a bill of health. But when Mr. Pennington's eyes fell on Bud, he leaned on a show-case and laughed till he shook all over; for Bud, with a rimless hat upon a towelled head, with a face scratched till it looked like a railroad map, with a torn shirt that exposed a dirty shoulder and a freckled back, with trousers so badly shattered that two hands could hardly hold them together,—as Mr. Pennington expressed it, Bud looked like a second-hand boy. The simile pleased Pennington so that he renewed his laughter, and paid no heed to the chatter of the pack clamoring to tell all in one breath, the history of the incident that had led to Bud's dilapidation. Also they were drawing gloomy pictures of the appearance of his assailants, after the custom of boys in such cases. Because his son was not involved in the calamity, Piggy's father was not moved deeply by the story of the raid of the North-enders and their downfall. So he put the young gentlemen of the Court of Boyville into the back room of his grocery store, where coal-oil and molasses barrels and hams and bacon and black shadows of many mysterious things were gathered. He gave the royal party a cheese knife and a water-melon, and bade them be merry, a bidding which set the hearts of Piggy and Abe and Jimmy and Mealy to dancing, while Bud's heart, which had been sinking lower and lower into a quagmire of dread, beat on numbly and did not join the joy. As the time for going home approached, Bud shiv-ered in his soul at the thought of meeting Miss Morgan. Not even the watermelon revived him, and when a watermelon will not help a boy his extremity is dire. Still he laughed and chatted with apparent merriment, but he knew how hollow was his laughter and what mockery was in his cheer. When the melon was eaten business took its regular order.

"Say, Bud, how you goin' to get home?" asked Abe.

Bud grinned as he looked at his rags.

"Gee," said Mealy, "I'm glad it ain't me."

"Aw, shucks," returned Bud, and he thought of the stricken Ananias[1] in the Sunday-school lesson leaf as he

[1] *Ananias:* in the Bible, a man who fell dead after Peter rebuked him for lying

spoke; "run right through like I always do. What I got to be 'fraid of?"

"Yes, Mr. Bud, you can laugh, but you know you'll catch it when you get home."

This shaft from Jimmy Sears put in words the terror in Bud's heart. But he replied: "I'll bet you I don't."

Bud's instinct piloted him by a circuitous route up the alley to the kitchen door. Miss Morgan sat on the front porch, waiting for the boy to return before serving supper. He stood helplessly in the kitchen for a minute, with a weight of indecision upon him. He feared to go to the front porch, where Miss Morgan was. He feared to stay in the kitchen. But when he saw the empty wood-box a light seemed to dawn. Instinct guided him to the woodpile, and the law of self-preservation filled his arms with wood, and instinct carried him to the kitchen wood-box time and again, and laid the wood in the box as gently as if it had been glass and as softly as if it had been velvet. Not until the pile had grown far above the wainscoting on the kitchen wall, did a stick crashing to the floor tell Miss Morgan that Bud was in the house.

But there is a destiny that shapes our ends, and just as the falling wood attracted Miss Morgan's attention, it was diverted by a belligerent party at her front gate. This belligerent party was composed of two persons, to wit: one mother from the north end of Willow Creek, irate to the spluttering point, and one boy lagging as far behind the mother as his short arm would allow him to lag. The mother held the short arm, and was literally dragging her son to Miss Morgan's gate to offer him in evidence as "Exhibit A" in a possible cause of the State of Kansas *vs.* Henry Perkins. Exhibit A was black and blue as to the eyes, torn as to the shirt, bloody as to the nose, tumbled and dusty as to the hair, and as to the countenance, clearly and unquestionably sheep-faced. The mother opened the bombardment with: "Miss Morgan, I just want you to look at my boy."

Miss Morgan looked in horror, and exclaimed: "Well, for mercy sakes! Where on earth's he been?"

And the leader of the war party returned: "Where's he been? Well, I'll tell you where he's been. And I just want you to know who done this." Here Exhibit A got behind a post. The recital of the details of his catastrophe was humiliating. But the mother continued: "Henry Perkins done this. I don't believe in stirring up neighborhood quarrels and all that, but I've just stood this long enough. My boy can't stick his nose out of the door without that Perkins boy jumpin' on him. If you can't do anything with that Perkins boy, I'll show him there's a law in this land."

Miss Morgan wilted as the speech proceeded. She had voice only to say, "I'm sure there's some mistake"; and then remembering the crash of the wood on the kitchen floor, she called: "Henry, come here!"

As Bud shambled through the house, the spokesman of the belligerents replied: "No, there isn't no mistake either. My boy is a good little boy, and just as peaceable a boy as there is in this town. And because I don't allow him to fight, that Perkins boy picks on him all the time. I've told him to keep out of his way and not to play with Henry Perkins, but he can't be runnin' all over this town to keep———"

And then Exhibit B, with scratched face, tattered raiment, and grimy features, stood in the doorway. The witness for the State looked in dumb amazement at the wreck. Miss Morgan saw Bud, and her temper rose—not at him, but at his adversary. Exhibit A sulkily turned his face from Exhibit B, and Exhibit B seemed to be oblivious of the presence of Exhibit A; for the boys it was a scene too shameful for mutual recognition. Miss Morgan broke the heavy silence with: "Henry, where on earth have you been?"

"Been t' the circus," replied the boy.

"Henry, did you blacken that little boy's eyes, and tear his clothes that way?" inquired Miss Morgan when her wits returned.

"Why—no 'm—I didn't. But he was one of four fellers that picked on me comin' home from the circus, and tried to lick me."

"Willie," demanded the head of the attacking posse, "did you pick a fight with that Perkins boy?"

"Oh, no 'm, no 'm! I was just playin' round the tent, me and another boy, and Bud he come up and jumped on us." And then to add verisimilitude to his narrative, he appended: "Him and four other boys."

"Henry," asked Miss Morgan, as she surveyed the debris of Henry's Sunday clothes, and her womanly wrath for the destroyer of them began to boil, "Henry, now tell me honestly, is this little boy telling the truth? Now, don't you story to me, Henry."

"Honest injun, Miss Morgan, I cross my heart and hope to drop dead this minute if I ain't tellin' you the way it was. Him and them North-enders, why they come along and called me names, and he tried to hit me, and I just shoved him away like this," and Henry executed a polite pantomine. "And I was swingin' my arms out to keep 'em all from hittin' me, and he got in the way, and I couldn't help it. And they was all a pickin' on me, and I told 'em all the time I didn't want to fight."

But Exhibit A kept looking at his mother and shaking his head in violent contradiction of Bud, as the story was told.

Miss Morgan asked: "Who scratched your face so, Henry?"

"Him; he's all the time fightin' me."

"No, ma, I didn't. You know I didn't."

Exhibit A and Exhibit B were still back to back. Then Exhibit B responded: "Miss Morgan, you ast him if he didn't cuss and damn me, and say he was goin' to pound me to death if I ever come north of Sixth."

To which the leader of the raiders returned in great scorn: "The very idea! Just listen at that! Why, Miss Morgan, that Perkins boy is the bully of this town. Come on,

Willie, your pa will see if there is no law to protect you from such boys as him." Whereupon the war party faced about, and walked down the sidewalk and away.

Miss Morgan and Bud watched the North End woman and her son depart. Miss Morgan turned to Bud, and spoke spiritedly: "Now, Henry, don't ever have anything to do with that kind of trash again. Now, you won't forget, will you, Henry?"

Bud examined his toes carefully, and replied, "No 'm."

In the threshold she put her hand on the boy's shoulder, and continued: "Now, don't you mind about it, Henry. They sha'n't touch you. You come and wash, and we'll have supper."

When a boy has a woman for a champion, if he is wise, he trusts her to any length. So Bud went to the kitchen, picked up the water-bucket, and went to the well, partly to keep from displaying a gathering wave of affection for his foster-mother, and partly to let the magnificence of the wood-box burst upon her in his absence. When he returned, he found Miss Morgan pointing toward the wood-box and beaming upon him. Bud grinned, and fished in his pocket for the coin.

"Here's a dollar I got for ridin' the trick mule," he faltered. "I thought it would be nice for the missionary society." That he might check any weak feminine emotions, he turned his attention to the supper-table, and blurted: "Gee, we're goin' to have pie, ain't we? I tell you, I'm mighty pie hungry."

The glow of Miss Morgan's melted heart shone upon her face. Through a seraphic[1] smile she spoke: "It's apple pie, too, Henry—your kind." As she put the supper upon the table, she asked: "Did you have a good time at the circus, Henry?"

The boy nodded vehemently, and said: "You bet!" and then went on, after a pause, "I guess I tore my pants a little gettin' off of that mule; but I thought you'd like the dollar."

[1] *seraphic:* resembling a seraph, or an angel

It was the finest speech he could make. "I guess I can mend them, Henry," she answered; and then she asked, with her face in the cupboard, "Sha'n't we try some of the new strawberry preserves, Henry?"

As she was opening the jar she concluded that Henry Perkins was an angel—a conclusion which, in view of the well-known facts, was manifestly absurd.

Questions and Comments

1. Who is Miss Morgan? How does Bud feel about her? Cite evidence from the selection to support your answer.

2. How do the boys amuse themselves for the two weeks before the circus opens?

3. What kind of reputation does Bud have among the boys of Boyville? What did he do that angered the North End boys?

4. What does the author mean when he says, "When a boy gets on his good behavior he tempts Providence"? Is this true of Bud? Explain your answer.

5. What happens to Bud during church? What action does Miss Morgan take against Bud as a result of the episode in church? Why does she undergo a change of heart?

6. What are Bud's two motives for riding the trick mule? Why does the crowd laugh when Bud leaves the ring?

7. Why does Miss Morgan defend Bud when the mother of the North End boy comes to complain about Bud's treatment of her son?

8. What does the author mean when he says, "A boy's troubles are always the fault of the other boy"? Who do you think is mostly at fault for Bud's troubles? Cite evidence from the selection to support your answer.

9. What is the author's opinion of Bud? Reread the last sentence of the selection and tell what it means.

Word Study

1. William Allen White used big words to create a humorous effect. An example of this is "There is a law of *crystallization* among boys which enables *molecules* of the same gang to meet in whatever *agglomeration* they may be thrown." State the author's idea in simpler terms.

2. Use the clues to give the meaning of the italicized words:

   "There they feasted their *gluttonous* eyes. . . ." (A glutton is a person who eats to great excess.)

   "Brother Baker's *unctuousness* angered Bud Perkins." (Unction is an oil used in certain religious rites.)

   ". . . he had lived with his father, a *nomad* of the creeks. . . ." (Members of wandering tribes were nomads.)

   ". . . Miss Morgan could not be deaf to the scream of the *calliope*. . . ." (Calliope was the muse of heroic poetry.)

3. Tell the meaning of the following words, using a dictionary if clues in the context are not sufficient: *sedentary* (page 28), *habiliments* (page 30), *vainglory* (page 30), *desultory* (page 35), *inexorable* (page 40), *quagmire* (page 42), *wainscoting* (page 43), *verisimilitude* (page 45).

Composition

1. In his description of Boyville, William Allen White vividly portrayed the sights, sounds, and pace of life in a small Middle Western town. Discuss some of the devices and methods he used to help you to see and feel life in Boyville.

2. Perhaps you have recently taken a trip to the circus, to a ball game, or even to the World's Fair. Describe some of the things you saw that especially impressed you. Try to recapture in words some of the excitement you experienced.

3. Compare growing up in small towns with growing up in large cities. Discuss some of the benefits and disadvantages of both and tell which you prefer.

The stage is set; the houselights dim; an expectant hush falls over the theater as the curtain slowly rises. Another amateur dramatic performance has begun at the Riverdale Country School. Doting parents settle back in their seats to watch their offspring cavort through Shakespeare's comedy, *A Midsummer Night's Dream*. An unusual costume, however, initiates a series of comic effects not in the original script—effects for which Shakespeare cannot be held responsible.

RING OUT, WILD BELLS

Wolcott Gibbs

WHEN I finally got around to seeing Max Reinhardt's cinema version of "A Midsummer Night's Dream," and saw a child called Mickey Rooney playing Puck, I remembered suddenly that long ago I had taken the same part.

Our production was given on the open-air stage at the Riverdale Country School, shortly before the war. The scenery was only the natural scenery of that suburban dell, and the cast was exclusively male, ranging in age from eleven to perhaps seventeen. While we had thus preserved the pure, Elizabethan note of the original, it must be admitted that our version had its drawbacks. The costumes were probably the worst things we had to bear, and even Penrod,[1] tragically arrayed as Launcelot in his sister's stockings and his father's drawers, might have been embarrassed for us. Like Penrod, we were costumed by our parents, and like the Schofields, they seemed on the whole a little weak historically. Half

[1] *Penrod:* the twelve-year-old hero of Booth Tarkington's novel *Penrod*, who was noted for constantly getting into scrapes

49

of the ladies were inclined to favor the Elizabethan, and
they had constructed rather bunchy ruffs[1] and farthingales[2]
for their offspring; others, who had read as far as the
stage directions and learned that the action took place
in an Athenian wood, had produced something vaguely
Athenian, usually beginning with a sheet. Only the fairies
had a certain uniformity. For some reason their parents had
all decided on cheesecloth, with here and there a little ill-
advised trimming with tinsel.

My own costume was mysterious, but spectacular. As
nearly as I have ever been able to figure things out, my
mother found her inspiration for it in a Maxfield Parrish[3]
picture of a court jester. Beginning at the top, there was a
cap with three stuffed horns; then, for the main part, a pair
of tights that covered me to my wrists and ankles; and finally
slippers with stuffed toes that curled up at the ends. The
whole thing was made out of silk in alternate green and red
stripes, and (unquestionably my poor mother's most demented stroke) it was covered from head to foot with a
thousand tiny bells. Because all our costumes were obviously
perishable, we never wore them in rehearsal, and naturally
nobody knew that I was invested with these peculiar sound
effects until I made my entrance at the beginning of the second act.

Our director was a man who had strong opinions about
how Shakespeare should be played, and Puck was one of his
favorite characters. It was his theory that Puck, being "the
incarnation of mischief," never ought to be still a minute, so
I had been coached to bound onto the stage, and once there
to dance up and down, cocking my head and waving my arms.

"I want you to be a little whirlwind," this man said.

Even as I prepared to bound onto the stage, I had my own
misgivings about those dangerously abundant gestures, and

---

[1] *ruff:* an elaborate lace collar worn in Elizabethan times
[2] *farthingale:* a hoop worn beneath the skirt
[3] *Maxfield Parrish:* an American artist and illustrator

their probable effect on my bells. It was too late, however, to invent another technique for playing Puck, even if there had been room for anything but horror in my mind. I bounded onto the stage.

The effect, in its way, must have been superb. With every leap I rang like a thousand children's sleighs, my melodies foretelling God knows what worlds of merriment to the enchanted spectators. It was even worse when I came to the middle of the stage and went into my gestures. The other ringing had been loud but sporadic. This was persistent, varying only slightly in volume and pitch with the vehemence of my gestures. To a blind man, it must have sounded as though I had recklessly decided to accompany myself on a xylophone. A maturer actor would probably have made up his mind that an emergency existed, and abandoned his gestures as impracticable under the circumstances. I was thirteen, and incapable of innovations. I had been told by responsible authorities that gestures went with this part, and I continued to make them. I also continued to ring—a silvery music, festive and horrible.

If the bells were hard on my nerves, they were even worse for the rest of the cast, who were totally unprepared for my new interpretation. Puck's first remark is addressed to one of the fairies, and it is mercifully brief.

I said, "How now, spirit! Whither wander you?"

This unhappy child, already embarrassed by a public appearance in cheesecloth and tinsel, was also burdened with an opening speech of sixteen lines in verse. He began bravely:

> "Over hill, over dale,
> Through brush, through brier,
> Over park, over pale,
> Through flood, through fire . . ."

At the word "fire," my instructions were to bring my hands up from the ground in a long, wavery sweep, intended to represent fire. The bells pealed. To my startled ears, it sounded more as if they exploded. The fairy stopped in his lines and looked at me sharply. The jingling, however, had diminished; it was no more than as if a faint wind stirred my bells, and he went on:

> "I do wander everywhere,
>   Swifter than the moone's sphere . . ."

Here again I had another cue, for a sort of swoop and dip indicating the swiftness of the moone's sphere. Again the bells rang out, and again the performance stopped in its tracks. The fairy was clearly troubled by these interruptions. He had, however, a child's strange acceptance of the inscrutable, and was even able to regard my bells as a last-minute adult addition to the program, nerve-racking but not to be questioned. I'm sure it was only this that got him through that first speech.

My turn, when it came, was even worse. By this time the audience had succumbed to a helpless gaiety. Every time my bells rang, laughter swept the spectators, and this mounted and mingled with the bells until everything else was practically inaudible. I began my speech, another long one, and full of incomprehensible references to Titania's changeling.[1]

"Louder!" said somebody in the wings. "You'll have to talk louder."

It was the director, and he seemed to be in a dangerous state.

"And for heaven's sake, stop that jingling!" he said.

I talked louder, and I tried to stop the jingling, but it was no use. By the time I got to the end of my speech, I was shouting and so was the audience. It appeared that I had very lit-

---

[1] *Titania's changeling:* The Indian child in *A Midsummer Night's Dream* whom Puck helps Oberon obtain from Titania by means of trickery

tle control over the bells, which continued to jingle in spite of my passionate efforts to keep them quiet.

All this had a very bad effect on the fairy, who by this time had many symptoms of a complete nervous collapse. However, he began his next speech:

> "Either I mistake your shape and making quite,
> Or else you are that shrewd and knavish sprite
> Called Robin Goodfellow: are you not he
> That..."

At this point I forgot that the rules had been changed and I was supposed to leave out the gestures. There was a furious jingling, and the fairy gulped.

"Are you not he that, that..."

He looked miserably at the wings, and the director supplied the next line, but the tumult was too much for him. The unhappy child simply shook his head.

"Say anything!" shouted the director desperately. "Anything at all!"

The fairy only shut his eyes and shuddered.

"All right!" shouted the director. "All right, Puck. *You* begin *your* next speech."

By some miracle, I actually did remember my next lines, and had opened my mouth to begin on them when suddenly the fairy spoke. His voice was a high, thin monotone, and there seemed to be madness in it, but it was perfectly clear.

"Fourscore and seven years ago," he began, "our fathers brought forth on this continent a new nation, conceived..."

He said it right through to the end, and it was certainly the most successful speech ever made on that stage, and probably one of the most successful speeches ever made on any stage. I don't remember, if I ever knew, how the rest of us ever picked up the dull, normal thread of the play after that extraordinary performance, but we must have, because I know it went on. I only remember that in the next intermission the director cut off my bells with his penknife, and after that things quieted down and got dull.

Questions and Comments

1. What does the author mean when he says that the costumes for the production were "a little weak historically"? Why were some of the costumes "vaguely Athenian"?

2. What feature of his costume does the author call his mother's "most demented stroke"? Why had the costume never been worn during rehearsal?

3. How does the director instruct the author to play the role of Puck? What is the result of the author's following the director's instructions?

4. What effect does the author's costume have on the rest of the cast—particularly the fairy?

5. What unexpected speech does the fairy recite? Why?

6. What does the director do to Puck's costume during intermission? According to the author, what effect does this have on the play?

Word Study

1. From the context give the meaning of the italicized words: "The other ringing had been loud but *sporadic*. This was persistent, varying only slightly in volume and pitch with the *vehemence* of my gestures."

2. Show how the derivation helps to reveal the meaning of the following words:

   demented as in "my poor mother's most demented stroke"
   —The Latin *ment* is a form of *mens* meaning "mind."

incarnation as in "the incarnation of mischief"—The Latin *carn* is a form of *caro* meaning "flesh."

innovations as in "incapable of innovations"—The Latin word *novus* means "new."

inscrutable as in "a child's strange acceptance of the inscrutable"—The Latin verb *scrutare* means "search," and here the prefix *in* means "not."

Composition

1. Tell what you feel to be the most humorous moment in the selection, and explain what steps the author took to achieve this moment.

2. It is not unusual for the most carefully laid plans to backfire. Describe an incident which you have heard about—or perhaps even been involved in—where despite careful planning everything went hopelessly awry.

Reflecting his love for the theater, Moss Hart entitled the autobiography of his early years *Act One*. In this book we read about his poverty-haunted days in a tenement neighborhood of New York early in the century. In the selection that follows we see him trying to win status in the gang. Physically frail and inept at sports, he wins recognition in a rather unusual way.

from ACT ONE

Moss Hart

I WANTED, of course, to be an actor. It never occurred to me that these godlike creatures did not themselves make up the words that flowed so effortlessly and magnificently from their lips. I think I believed they created a play as they went along —a belief, I am convinced, that some portions of a matinée audience still cling to. More than once, sitting in the audience at a play of mine, I have heard the lady behind me exclaim, "The clever things actors say! Aren't they wonderful!" And I have been tempted to say, "Not *that* wonderful, madame!" But I have understood her bewitchment. Not even in my wildest dreams of glory did I ever imagine that I would one day write the words for actors to speak on the stage, and not until long afterward did I come to know that there were more important figures in the theatre than the gods of my idolatry.

Had I had the wit to perceive it, there was already a hint that I was a dramatist; even then I could dramatize a story and hold an audience, and when I inadvertently stumbled on this gift, I used it the way other boys use a good pitching arm or a long reach in basketball. It gave me the only standing I was ever to have in the tough and ruthless world of boys of my own age, and I wielded the tiny sense of power it gave me hungrily and shrewdly. Even in the long-ago days when I was growing up, the cult of "toughness" in American life was beginning to blossom and flower. The non-athletic boy, the youngster who liked to read or listen to music, who could not fight or was afraid to, or the boy who had some special interest that was strange or alien to the rest, like the theatre in my case, was banished from the companionship of the others by rules of the "tough" world that was already beginning to prevail.

It is a mistake to believe that this cult of "toughness" was limited to the poor neighborhood in which we lived. It had begun to pervade other levels of American life, and I suspect that today's bland dismissal of the intellectual and the overwhelming emphasis placed on the necessity of competing and of success are due in part to the strange taboo we have set against that softness in ourselves which brings men closest to the angels. A nation of poets would be no more desirable than a nation of athletes, but I wonder if that toughness and competitiveness, which have become an ingrained part of our character as a people and a symbol of our way of life as a nation, are not a sign of weakness as well as of strength. Is our cultural life not robbed of a necessary dimension and our emotional life of an element of grace? And I wonder if the fear of a lack of toughness in our children does not sometimes rob them of an awakening awareness and sensitivity in the realm of the spirit that are each child's birthright and his weapon of rebellion against the accepted norm of his time. This lack of toughness and the inability to compete were a constant agony of my own childhood, and I lived it through as best I could.

A city child's summer is spent in the street in front of his home, and all through the long summer vacations I sat on the curb and watched the other boys on the block play baseball or prisoner's base or gutter hockey. I was never asked to take part even when one team had a member missing—not out of any special cruelty, but because they took it for granted

I would be no good at it. They were right, of course. Yet much of the bitterness and envy and loneliness I suffered in those years could have been borne better if a single wise teacher or a knowledgeable parent had made me understand that there were compensations for the untough and the non-athletic; that the world would not always be bounded by the curbstone in front of the house.

One of those compensations I blundered into myself, and its effect was electric on both me and the tough world of the boys on the block. I have never forgotten the joy of that wonderful evening when it happened. There was no daylight-saving in those days, and the baseball and other games ended about eight or eight thirty, when it grew dark. Then it was the custom of the boys to retire to a little stoop that jutted out from the candy store on the corner and that somehow had become theirs through tribal right. No grownup ever sat there or attempted to. There the boys would sit, talking aimlessly for hours on end. There were the usual probings of sex and dirty jokes, not too well defined or clearly understood; but mostly the talk was of the games played during the day and of the game to be played tomorrow. Ultimately, long silences would fall and then the boys would wander off one by one. It was just after one of those long silences that my life as an outsider changed, and for one glorious summer I was accepted on my own terms as one of the tribe. I can no longer remember which boy it was that summer evening who broke the silence with a question; but whoever he was, I nod to him in gratitude now. "What's in those books you're always reading?" he asked idly. "Stories," I answered. "What kind?" asked somebody else without much interest.

Nor do I know what impelled me to behave as I did, for usually I just sat there in silence, glad enough to be allowed to remain among them; but instead of answering his question, I launched full tilt into the book I was immersed in at the moment. The book was *Sister Carrie*[1] and I told them

---

[1] *Sister Carrie:* a novel by Thedore Dreiser

the story of Sister Carrie for two full hours. They listened bug-
eyed and breathless. I must have told it well, but I think
there was another and deeper reason that made them so flat-
tering an audience. Listening to a tale being told in the
dark is one of the most ancient of man's entertainments, but
I was offering them as well, without being aware of doing
it, a new and exciting experience.

The books they themselves read were the *Rover Boys*[1] or
Tom Swift[2] or G. A. Henty.[3] I had read them too, but at
thirteen I had long since left them behind. Since I.was much
alone I had become an omnivorous reader and I had gone
through the books-for-boys-series in one vast gulp. In those
days there was no intermediate reading material between
children's and grownups' books, or I could find none, and
since there was no one to say me nay, I had gone right from
Tom Swift and His Flying Machine to Theodore Dreiser and
Sister Carrie. Dreiser had hit my young mind and senses
with the impact of a thunderbolt, and they listened to me
tell the story with some of the wonder that I had had in
reading it.

It was, in part, the excitement of discovery—the discovery
that there could be another kind of story that gave them a
deeper kind of pleasure than the *Rover Boys*—blunder-
ingly, I was giving them a glimpse of the riches contained
outside the world of *Tom Swift*. Not one of them left the
stoop until I had finished, and I went upstairs that wonderful evening not only a member of the tribe but a figure in
my own right among them.

The next night and many nights thereafter, a kind of un-
spoken ritual took place. As it grew dark, I would take my
place in the center of the stoop and, like Scheherazade,[4]

[1] *Rover Boys:* a famous series of books for boys by Edward Stratemeyer
[2] *Tom Swift:* the hero of a popular series of books for boys
[3] *G. A. Henty:* English writer of books for boys. The action of his novels
took place in various historical periods.
[4] *Scheherazade:* in *The Arabian Nights,* the bride of a murderous sultan,
who tricks him into sparing her life by telling him an exciting story each
night

begin the evening's tale. Some nights, in order to savor my triumph more completely, I cheated. I would stop at the most exciting part of a story by Jack London or Frank Norris or Bret Harte, and without warning tell them that that was as far as I had gone in the book and it would have to be continued the following evening. It was not true, of course; but I had to make certain of my new-found power and position, and with a sense of drama that I did not know I possessed, I spun out the long summer evenings until school began again in the fall. Other words of mine have been listened to by larger and more fashionable audiences, but for that tough and grimy one that huddled on the stoop outside the candy store, I have an unreasoning affection that will last forever. It was a memorable summer, and it was the last I was to spend with the boys on the block.

The following summer, since I was now thirteen years old, I would be able to obtain "working papers" and get a job downtown for the summer months. The prospect of getting away from "the block," of nudging closer to that small shimmering area where Broadway lay, made life more endurable. All that winter I concocted grandiose dreams of getting a job as office boy for Klaw & Erlanger,[1] or Florenz Ziegfeld,[2] or Sam Harris,[3] and somehow, some way, working my way down from the office and through the stage door. As the last days of school loomed ahead, I scanned the Sunday advertisements more and more desperately, searching for an ad that would read, "Office or errand boy wanted in theatrical office." There were none, of course. There were errand and office boy ads by the dozen, office and errand boys wanted by every other business under the sun; but no such ad as I looked for ever appeared, and in time to come I learned why none was ever likely to. Nepotism runs through

---

[1] *Klaw & Erlanger:* American theatrical producers

[2] *Florenz Ziegfeld:* American showman, famed for his extravagant musical productions

[3] *Sam Harris:* American theatrical producer

the theatre with the grandeur of the Mississippi at flood time, and when an office boy is needed, there is always a nephew on hand; if a secretary is wanted, a niece or a cousin magically appears. This may account in part for the fact that theatrical telephone messages are inevitably garbled, manuscripts go unread, and theatrical correspondence continues to be a whimsical affair that goes largely unanswered. But all this I did not know then. I persisted in believing the ad I dreamed of would certainly appear the following Sunday.

School closed and still I stubbornly waited, until it became imperative that I take whatever job I could get if I was going to work at all that summer. In desperation I even boldly considered the idea of marching into a theatrical office and asking point-blank for a job; but I lacked the courage and, as a matter of fact, I didn't even know where any of the offices were. By the time I was ready to concede defeat, all the best jobs were gone and I took the only job I could get. It was quite a distance from Broadway, and the heavy steel door I pushed open and closed fifty times a day as part of my job was a far cry from the stage door I had fondly hoped to pass through; but I was working "downtown" and a step nearer my goal. If I looked northward from 14th Street, as I stood on the steps of the subway station each night, I could see the golden glow of Times Square in the distance.

I worked in the storage vault of a large wholesale furrier, and my job was to open the vault as the hampers of wet skins were brought in and then hang the furs on racks to dry. It was tedious work, but it was cool inside the vault and I had ample time to read. It had another compensation, that job, and I took full advantage of it once I stoically accepted the fact that people were likely to hold their noses and walk rapidly away if they happened to pass within ten feet of me. They had good reason to. I possessed only one suit of clothes and that suit I wore to work every day. Not that it would have made much difference if I had owned a dozen suits and worn a different one each day, for after eight

3. What does the author mean by "the cult of toughness"? What does he say was the constant agony of his childhood?

4. What was the author's first hint that he had a talent for telling a story and holding the interest of an audience? How did he use this talent to gain power over the tough boys of the neighborhood?

5. What was the author's first summer job? Why was he unable to get the kind of summer job he really wanted? What criticism of the theater is he making by relating this fact?

6. What were the two compensations that came with the summer job?

Word Study

1. Refer to the selection for clues that may help to reveal the meaning of the italicized words. If you are not sure of the meaning of a word, use a dictionary to check your guess.

   "The prospect of . . . nudging closer to that small *shimmering* area where Broadway lay made life more endurable." (page 60)

   "All that winter I concocted *grandiose* dreams of getting a job. . . ." (page 60)

   ". . . my *olfactory* senses had been *anesthetized* by the daily smell of the vault. . . ." (page 62)

   "I pretended not to hear either the muttered threats or the *imprecations* of my fellow subway riders. . . ." (page 62)

2. The word *stoically* comes from the name of a school of Greek philosophers called Stoics. Find out who the Stoics were and what they believed in and see whether you can guess the meaning of *stoically*.

3. The word *nepotism* comes from the Latin noun *nepos* meaning "grandson" or "nephew." Tell what *nepotism* means in the sentence "Nepotism runs through the theatre with the grandeur of the Mississippi at floodtime. . . ."

4. The word *omnivorous* means "eating all things." The prefix *omni,* seen in many English words, comes from the Latin word *omnis* meaning "all." Find other English words with the prefix *omni* and tell what they mean.

Composition

1. Moss Hart chose to write his recollections in a pleasant, casual, and informal style. Discuss the impression you had of the author from the incidents he described and the words and tone he used to describe them.

2. At one point in the selection the author said, "I wonder if that toughness and competitiveness, which have become an ingrained part of our character as a people and a symbol of our way of life as a nation, are not a sign of weakness as well as of strength." Discuss this statement and tell why you agree or disagree with it.

3. Moss Hart aspired to a place of prominence in the theater. Discuss your own aspirations and give your reasons for wanting to pursue and realize them.

In his introduction to *Man-Eaters of Kumaon*, Jim Corbett states that tigers are not man-eaters by nature but become so by necessity. It is only when they are incapacitated by accidents or weakened by age that tigers become dangerous killers, resorting to human flesh because they are no longer able to catch other prey.

Here we see the author on the trail of a man-eating tiger that has already claimed 436 human victims. The setting is the Kumaon hills of the Himalayas in India.

THE CHAMPAWAT
MAN-EATER

Jim Corbett

I SPENT the following morning in going round the very extensive fruit orchard and tea garden and in having a bath at the spring, and at about midday the Tahsildar,[1] much to my relief, returned safely from Champawat.

I was standing talking to him while looking down a long sloping hill with a village surrounded by cultivated land in the distance, when I saw a man leave the village and start up the hill in our direction. As the man drew nearer I saw he was alternately running and walking, and was quite evidently the bearer of important news. Telling the Tahsildar I would return in a few minutes, I set off at a run down the hill, and when the man saw me coming he sat down to take breath. As soon as I was near enough to hear him he called out, "Come quickly, sahib, the man-eater has just killed a

[1] *Tahsildar:* chief revenue officer

girl." "Sit still," I called back, and turning ran up to the bungalow. I passed the news on to the Tahsildar while I was getting a rifle and some cartridges, and asked him to follow me down to the village.

The man who had come for me was one of those exasperating individuals whose legs and tongue cannot function at the same time. When he opened his mouth he stopped dead, and when he started to run his mouth closed; so telling him to shut his mouth and lead the way, we ran in silence down the hill.

At the village an excited crowd of men, women, and children awaited us and, as usually happens on these occasions, all started to talk at the same time. One man was vainly trying to quieten the babel. I led him aside and asked him to tell me what had happened. Pointing to some scattered oak trees on a gentle slope a furlong or so from the village, he said a dozen people were collecting dry sticks under the trees when a tiger suddenly appeared and caught one of their number, a girl sixteen or seventeen years of age. The rest of the party had run back to the village, and as it was known that I was staying at the bungalow a man had immediately been dispatched to inform me.

The wife of the man I was speaking to had been one of the party, and she now pointed out the tree, on the shoulder of the hill, under which the girl had been taken. None of the party had looked back to see if the tiger was carrying away its victim and, if so, in which direction it had gone.

Instructing the crowd not to make a noise, and to remain in the village until I returned, I set off in the direction of the tree. The ground here was quite open and it was difficult to conceive how an animal the size of a tiger could have approached twelve people unseen, and its presence not detected, until attention had been attracted by the choking sound made by the girl.

The spot where the girl had been killed was marked by a pool of blood and near it, and in vivid contrast to the crimson pool, was a broken necklace of brightly colored blue beads which the girl had been wearing. From this spot the track led up and round the shoulder of the hill.

The track of the tigress was clearly visible. On one side of it were great splashes of blood where the girl's head had hung down, and on the other side the trail of her feet. Half a mile up the hill I found the girl's sari,[1] and on the brow of the hill her skirt. Once again the tigress was carrying a naked woman, but mercifully on this occasion her burden was dead.

On the brow of the hill the track led through a thicket of blackthorn, on the thorns of which long strands of the girl's raven-black hair had caught. Beyond this was a bed of nettles through which the tigress had gone, and I was looking for a way round this obstruction when I heard footsteps behind me. Turning round I saw a man armed with a rifle coming towards me. I asked him why he had followed me when I had left instructions at the village that no one was to leave it. He said the Tahsildar had instructed him to accompany me, and that he was afraid to disobey orders. As he appeared determined to carry out his orders, and to argue the point would have meant the loss of valuable time, I told him to remove the heavy pair of boots he was wearing and, when he had hidden them under a bush, I advised him to keep close to me, and to keep a sharp lookout behind.

I was wearing a very thin pair of stockings, shorts, and a pair of rubber-soled shoes, and as there appeared to be no way round the nettles I followed the tigress through them —much to my discomfort.

Beyond the nettles the blood trail turned sharply to the left, and went straight down the very steep hill, which was densely clothed with bracken and ringals.[2] A hundred yards down, the blood trail led into a narrow and very steep watercourse, down which the tigress had gone with some difficulty,

[1] *sari:* a long garment worn by Indian women
[2] *ringals:* stunted bamboos

as could be seen from the dislodged stones and earth. I followed this watercourse for five or six hundred yards, my companion getting more and more agitated the further we went. A dozen times he caught my arm and whispered—in a voice full of tears—that he could hear the tiger, either on one side or the other, or behind us. Half-way down the hill we came on a great pinnacle of rocks some thirty feet high, and as the man had by now all the man-eater hunting he could stand, I told him to climb the rock and remain on it until I returned. Very gladly he went up, and when he straddled the top and signaled to me that he was all right I continued on down the watercourse, which, after skirting round the rock, went straight down for a hundred yards to where it met a deep ravine coming down from the left. At the junction was a small pool, and as I approached it I saw patches of blood on my side of the water.

The tigress had carried the girl straight down to this spot, and my approach had disturbed her at her meal. Splinters of bone were scattered round the deep pug[1] marks into which discolored water was slowly seeping and at the edge of the pool was an object which had puzzled me as I came down the watercourse, and which I now found was part of a human leg. In all the subsequent years I have hunted man-eaters I have not seen anything as pitiful as that young comely leg —bitten off a little below the knee as clean as though severed by the stroke of an axe—out of which the warm blood was trickling.

While looking at the leg I had forgotten all about the tigress until I suddenly felt that I was in great danger. Hurriedly grounding the butt of the rifle I put two fingers on the triggers, raising my head as I did so, and saw a little earth, from the fifteen-foot bank in front of me, come rolling down the steep side and plop into the pool. I was new to this game of man-eater hunting or I should not have exposed myself to an attack in the way I had done. My prompt action in pointing the rifle upwards had possibly saved my

[1] *pug:* footprint

life, and in stopping her spring, or in turning to get away, the tigress had dislodged the earth from the top of the bank.

The bank was too steep for scrambling, and the only way of getting up was to take it at a run. Going up the water-course a short distance I sprinted down, took the pool in my stride, and got far enough up the other side to grasp a bush and pull myself on to the bank. A bed of Strobilanthes, the bent stalks of which were slowly regaining their upright position, showed where, and how recently, the tigress had passed, and a little further on under an overhanging rock I found where she had left her kill when she came to have a look at me.

Her tracks now—as she carried away the girl—led into a wilderness of rocks, some acres in extent, where the going was both difficult and dangerous. The cracks and chasms between the rocks were masked with ferns and blackberry vines, and a false step, which might easily have resulted in a broken limb, would have been fatal. Progress under these conditions was of necessity slow, and the tigress was taking advantage of it to continue her meal. A dozen times I found where she had rested, and after each of these rests the blood trail became more distinct.

This was her four hundred and thirty-sixth human kill and she was quite accustomed to being disturbed at her meals by rescue parties, but this, I think, was the first time she had been followed up so persistently and she now began to show her resentment by growling. To appreciate a tiger's growl to the full it is necessary to be situated as I then was —rocks all round with dense vegetation between, and the imperative necessity of testing each footstep to avoid falling headlong into unseen chasms and caves.

I cannot expect you who read this at your fireside to appreciate my feelings at the time. The sound of the growling and the expectation of an attack terrified me at the same time as it gave me hope. If the tigress lost her temper sufficiently to launch an attack, it would not only give me an opportunity of accomplishing the object for which I had come, but it would enable me to get even with her for all the pain and suffering she had caused.

The growling, however, was only a gesture, and, when she found that instead of shooing me off it was bringing me faster on her heels, she abandoned it.

I had now been on her track for over four hours. Though I had repeatedly seen the undergrowth moving I had not seen so much as a hair of her hide, and a glance at the shadows climbing up on the opposite hillside warned me it was time to retrace my steps if I was to reach the village before dark.

The late owner of the severed leg was a Hindu, and some portion of her would be needed for the cremation, so as I passed the pool I dug a hole in the bank and buried the leg where it would be safe from the tigress, and could be found when wanted.

My companion on the rock was very relieved to see me. My long absence, and the growling he had heard, had convinced him that the tigress had secured another kill and his difficulty, as he quite frankly admitted, was how he was going to get back to the village alone.

I thought when we were climbing down the watercourse that I knew of no more dangerous proceeding than walking in front of a nervous man carrying a loaded gun, but I changed my opinion when on walking behind him he slipped and fell, and I saw where the muzzle of his gun—a converted .450 without a safety catch—was pointing. Since that day—except when accompanied by Ibbotson—I have made it a hard and fast rule to go alone when hunting man-eaters, for if one's companion is unarmed it is difficult to protect him, and if he is armed, it is even more difficult to protect oneself.

Arrived at the crest of the hill, where the man had hidden his boots, I sat down to have a smoke and think out my plans for the morrow.

The tigress would finish what was left of the kill during the night, and would to a certainty lie up among the rocks next day.

On the ground she was on there was very little hope of my being able to stalk her, and if I disturbed her without getting a shot, she would probably leave the locality and I should lose touch with her. A beat therefore was the only thing to do, provided I could raise sufficient men.

I was sitting on the south edge of a great amphitheatre of hills, without a habitation of any kind in sight. A stream entering from the west had fretted its way down, cutting a deep valley right across the amphitheatre. To the east the stream had struck solid rock, and turning north had left the amphitheatre by a narrow gorge.

The hill in front of me, rising to a height of some two thousand feet, was clothed in short grass with a pine tree dotted here and there, and the hill to the east was too precipitous for anything but a ghooral[1] to negotiate. If I could collect sufficient men to man the entire length of the ridge from the stream to the precipitous hill, and get them to stir up the tigress, her most natural line of retreat would be through the narrow gorge.

Admittedly a very difficult beat, for the steep hillside facing north, on which I had left the tigress, was densely wooded and roughly three-quarters of a mile long and half-a-mile wide; however, if I could get the beaters to carry out instructions, there was a reasonable chance of my getting a shot.

The Tahsildar was waiting for me at the village. I explained the position to him, and asked him to take immediate steps to collect as many men as he could, and to meet me at ten o'clock the following morning at the tree where the girl had been killed. Promising to do his best, he left for Champawat, while I climbed the hill to the bungalow.

[1] *ghooral:* a mountain goat

I was up at crack of dawn next morning, and after a substantial meal told my men to pack up and wait for me at Champawat, and went down to have another look at the ground I intended beating. I could find nothing wrong with the plans I had made, and an hour before my time I was at the spot where I had asked the Tahsildar to meet me.

That he would have a hard time in collecting the men I had no doubt, for the fear of the man-eater had sunk deep into the countryside and more than mild persuasion would be needed to make the men leave the shelter of their homes. At ten o'clock the Tahsildar and one man turned up, and thereafter the men came in twos, and threes, and tens, until by midday two hundred and ninety-eight had collected.

The Tahsildar had let it be known that he would turn a blind eye towards all unlicensed fire-arms, and further that he would provide ammunition where required; and the weapons that were produced that day would have stocked a museum.

When the men were assembled and had received the ammunition they needed I took them to the brow of the hill where the girl's skirt was lying, and pointing to a pine tree on the opposite hill that had been struck by lightning and stripped of bark, I told them to line themselves up along the ridge and, when they saw me wave a handkerchief from under the pine, those of them who were armed were to fire off their pieces, while the others beat drums, shouted, and rolled down rocks, and that no one was on any account to leave the ridge until I returned and personally collected him. When I was assured that all present had heard and understood my instructions, I set off with the Tahsildar, who said he would be safer with me than with the beaters whose guns would probably burst and cause many casualties.

Making a wide detour I crossed the upper end of the valley, gained the opposite hill, and made my way down to the blasted pine. From here the hill went steeply down and the Tahsildar, who had on a thin pair of patent leather shoes, said it was impossible for him to go any further. While he was removing his inadequate foot-gear to ease his blisters, the men on the ridge, thinking I had forgotten to give the pre-arranged signal, fired off their guns and set up a great shout. I was still a hundred and fifty yards from the gorge, and that I did not break my neck a dozen times in covering this distance was due to my having been brought up on the hills, and being in consequence as sure-footed as a goat.

As I ran down the hill I noticed that there was a patch of green grass near the mouth of the gorge, and as there was no time to look round for a better place, I sat down in the grass, with my back to the hill down which I had just come. The grass was about two feet high and hid half my body, and if I kept perfectly still there was a good chance of my not being seen. Facing me was the hill that was being beaten, and the gorge that I hoped the tigress would make for was behind my left shoulder.

Pandemonium had broken loose on the ridge. Added to the fusillade of guns was the wild beating of drums and the shouting of hundreds of men, and when the din was at its worst I caught sight of the tigress bounding down a grassy slope between two ravines to my right front, and about three hundred yards away. She had only gone a short distance when the Tahsildar from his position under the pine let off both barrels of his shot-gun. On hearing the shots the tigress whipped round and went straight back the way she had come, and as she disappeared into thick cover I threw up my rifle and sent a despairing bullet after her.

The men on the ridge, hearing the three shots, not unnaturally concluded that the tigress had been killed. They emptied all their guns and gave a final yell, and I was holding my breath and listening for the screams that would herald the tigress's arrival on the ridge, when she suddenly broke cover to my left front and, taking the stream at a bound, came straight for the gorge. The .500 modified cordite rifle, sighted at sea level, shot high at this altitude, and when the tigress stopped dead I thought the bullet had gone over her back, and that she had pulled up on finding her retreat cut off; as a matter of fact I had hit her all right, but a little far back. Lowering her head, she half turned towards me, giving me a beautiful shot at the point of her shoulder at a range of less than thirty yards. She flinched at this second shot but continued, with her ears laid flat and bared teeth, to stand her ground, while I sat with rifle to shoulder trying to think what it would be best for me to do when she charged, for the rifle was empty and I had no more cartridges. Three cartridges were all that I had brought with me, for I never thought I should get a chance of firing more than two shots, and the third cartridge was for—an emergency.

Fortunately the wounded animal most unaccountably decided against a charge. Very slowly she turned, crossed the stream to her right, climbed over some fallen rocks, and found a narrow ledge that went diagonally up and across the face of the precipitous hill to where there was a great flat projecting rock. Where this rock joined the cliff a small bush had found roothold, and going up to it the tigress started to strip its branches. Throwing caution to the winds I shouted to the Tahsildar to bring me his gun. A long reply was shouted back, the only word of which I caught was "feet." Laying down my rifle I took the hill at a run, grabbed the gun out of the Tahsildar's hands and raced back.

As I approached the stream the tigress left the bush and came out on the projecting rock towards me. When I was within twenty feet of her I raised the gun and found to my horror that there was a gap of about three-eighths of an inch between the barrels and the breech-lock. The gun had not burst when both barrels had been fired, and would probably not burst now, but there was danger of being blinded by a blow back. However, the risk would have to be taken, and, aligning the great blob of a bead that did duty as a sight on the tigress's open mouth, I fired. Maybe I bobbed, or maybe the gun was not capable of throwing the cylindrical bullet accurately for twenty feet; anyway, the missile missed the tigress's mouth and struck her on the right paw, from where I removed it later with my fingernails. Fortunately she was at her last gasp, and the tap on the foot was sufficient to make her lurch forward. She came to rest with her head projecting over the side of the rock.

From the moment the tigress had broken cover in her attempt to get through the gorge I had forgotten the beaters, until I was suddenly reminded of their existence by hearing a shout, from a short distance up the hill, of "There it is on the rock! Pull it down and let us hack it to bits." I could not believe my ears when I heard "hack it to bits," and yet I had heard aright, for others now had caught sight of the tigress and from all over the hillside the shout was being repeated.

The ledge by which the wounded animal had gained the protecting rock was fortunately on the opposite side from the beaters, and was just wide enough to permit my shuffling along it sideways. As I reached the rock and stepped over the tigress—hoping devoutly she was dead, for I had not had time to carry out the usual test of pelting her with stones—the men emerged from the forest and came running across the open, brandishing guns, axes, rusty swords, and spears.

At the rock, which was twelve to fourteen feet in height, their advance was checked, for the outer face had been worn smooth by the stream when in spate and afforded no foothold even for their bare toes. The rage of the crowd on seeing their dread enemy was quite understandable, for there was not a man among them who had not suffered at her hands. One man, who appeared demented and was acting as ringleader, was shouting over and over again as he ran to and fro brandishing a sword. "This is the *shaitan*[1] that killed my wife and my two sons." As happens with crowds, the excitement died down as suddenly as it has flared up, and to the credit of the man who had lost his wife and sons

[1] *shaitan:* an evil spirit

be it said that he was the first to lay down his weapon. He came near to the rock and said, "We were mad, sahib, when we saw our enemy, but the madness has now passed, and we ask you and Tahsildar sahib to forgive us." Extracting the unspent cartridge, I laid the gun across the tigress and hung down by my hands and was assisted to the ground. When I showed the men how I had gained the rock the dead animal was very gently lowered and carried to an open spot, where all could crowd round and look at her.

When the tigress had stood on the rock looking down at me I had noticed that there was something wrong with her mouth, and on examining her now I found that the upper and lower canine teeth on the right side of her mouth were broken, the upper one in half, and the lower one right down to the bone. This permanent injury to her teeth—the result of a gun-shot wound—had prevented her from killing her natural prey, and had been the cause of her becoming a man-eater.

The men begged me not to skin the tigress there, and asked me to let them have her until nightfall to carry through their villages, saying that if their womenfolk and children did not see her with their own eyes, they would not believe that their dread enemy was dead.

Two saplings were now cut and laid one on either side of the tigress, and with pugrees,[1] waistbands, and loincloths she was carefully and very securely lashed to them. When all was ready the saplings were manned and we moved to the foot of the precipitous hill; the men preferred to take the tigress up this hill, on the far side of which their villages lay, to going up the densely wooded hill which they had just beaten. Two human ropes were made by the simple expedient of the man behind taking a firm grip of the waistband, or other portion of clothing, of the man in front of him. When it was considered that the ropes were long and strong enough to stand the strain, they attached themselves

[1] *pugrees:* scarves wound round a hat to protect the head from the sun

to the saplings, and with men on either side to hold the feet of the bearers and give them foothold, the procession moved up the hill, looking for all the world like an army of ants carrying a beetle up the face of a wall. Behind the main army was a second and a smaller one—the Tahsildar being carried up. Had the ropes broken at any stage of that thousand-foot climb, the casualties would have been appalling, but the rope did not break. The men gained the crest of the hill and set off eastwards, singing on their triumphal march, while the Tahsildar and I turned west and made for Champawat.

Our way lay along the ridge and once again I stood among the blackthorn bushes on the thorns of which long tresses of the girl's hair had caught, and for the last time looked down into the amphitheatre which had been the scene of our recent exploit.

On the way down the hill the beaters had found the head of the unfortunate girl, and a thin column of smoke rising straight up into the still air from the mouth of the gorge showed where the relations were performing the last rites of the Champawat man-eater's last victim, on the very spot on which the man-eater had been shot.

After dinner, while I was standing in the courtyard of the Tahsil, I saw a long procession of pine torches winding its way down the opposite hillside, and presently the chanting of a hill song by a great concourse of men was borne up on the still night air. An hour later, the tigress was laid down at my feet.

It was difficult to skin the animal with so many people crowding round, and to curtail the job I cut the head and paws from the trunk and left them adhering to the skin, to be dealt with later. A police guard was then mounted over the carcass, and next day, when all the people of the countryside were assembled, the trunk, legs, and tail of the tigress were cut up into small pieces and distributed. These pieces of flesh and bone were required for the lockets which hill children wear round their necks, and the addition of a piece of tiger to the other potent charms is credited with giving the wearer courage, as well as immunity from the attacks of wild animals. The fingers of the girl, which the tigress had swallowed whole, were sent to me in spirits by the Tahsildar, and were buried by me in the Naini Tal lake close to the Nandadevi temples.

While I had been skinning the tigress the Tahsildar and his staff, assisted by the Headmen and graybeards of the surrounding villages and merchants of the Champawat bazaar, had been busy drawing up a program for a great feast and dance for the morrow, at which I was to preside. Round about midnight, when the last of the great throng of men had left with shouts of delight at being able to use roads and village paths that the man-eater had closed for four years, I had a final smoke with the Tahsildar, and telling him that I could not stay any longer and that he would have to take my place at the festivities, my men and I set off on our seventy-five-mile journey, with two days in hand to do it in.

At sunrise I left my men and, with the tigress's skin strapped to the saddle of my horse, rode on ahead to put in a few hours in cleaning the skin at Dabidhura, where I intended spending the night. When passing the hut on the hill of Pali it occurred to me that it would be some little satisfaction to the dumb woman to know that her sister had been avenged, so leaving the horse to browse—he had been bred near the snow-line and could eat anything from oak trees to nettles—I climbed the hill to the hut, and spread out the skin with the head supported on a stone facing the door. The children of the house had been round-eyed spectators of these proceedings and, hearing me talking to them, their mother, who was inside cooking, came to the door.

I am not going to hazard any theories about shock, and counter-shock, for I know nothing of these matters. All I know is that this woman, who was alleged to have been dumb a twelvemonth and who four days previously had made no attempt to answer my questions, was now running backwards and forwards from the hut to the road calling to her husband and the people in the village to come quickly and see what the sahib had brought. This sudden return of speech appeared greatly to mystify the children, who could not take their eyes off their mother's face.

I rested in the village while a dish of tea was being prepared for me and told the people who thronged round how the man-eater had been killed. An hour later I continued my journey and for half a mile along my way I could hear the shouts of goodwill of the men of Pali.

I had a very thrilling encounter with a leopard the following morning, which I only mention because it delayed my start from Dabidhura and put an extra strain on my small mount and myself. Fortunately the little pony was as strong on his legs as he was tough inside, and by holding his tail on the up-grades, riding him on the flat, and running behind him on the down-grades, we covered the forty-five miles to Naini Tal between 9 a.m. and 6 p.m.

At a durbar[1] held in Naini Tal a few months later Sir John Hewett, Lieutenant-Governor of the United Provinces, presented the Tahsildar of Champawat with a gun, and the man who accompanied me when I was looking for the girl, with a beautiful hunting-knife, for the help they had given me. Both weapons were suitably engraved and will be handed down as heirlooms in the respective families.

Questions and Comments

1. What signs left by the tiger make it possible for the author to trail it?

2. What does the author do with the severed leg of the Hindu girl? Why?

[1] *durbar:* a public audience

3. Why does the author prefer to be by himself when he is hunting man-eaters?

4. What plan of attack does the author devise to "trap" the tiger? Why does the Tahsildar go with the author instead of with the beaters?

5. Why do the beaters fire their guns prematurely?

6. What difficult choice is the author faced with when he aims the Tahsildar's gun at the tiger? What action does he decide to take? Why?

7. Why does one of the beaters beg to be forgiven by the author and the Tahsildar?

8. What explanation does the author give for the tiger's having become a man-eater?

9. What reason do the men have for wanting to carry the tiger through their villages?

10. Why does the author stop at the hut of the dumb woman? What effect does seeing the tiger skin have on the dumb woman?

Word Study

1. Try to determine the meaning of the italicized words from the context of the selection. Check your guesses with dictionary definitions.

"One man was vainly trying to quieten the *babel*. I led him aside. . . ." (page 66)

"A stream . . . had *fretted* its way down. . . ." (page 71)

". . . the hill to the east was too *precipitous*. . . ."(page 71)

"*Pandemonium* had broken loose on the ridge. Added to the *fusillade* of guns was the wild beating of drums. . . ." (page 73)

". . . the chanting of a hill song by a great *concourse* of men was borne up on the still night air." (page 77)

2. The trail led through *blackthorn, nettles,* and *bracken.* To what do the italicized words refer?

3. At what stage is a stream in *spate?*

4. The author is called "sahib." What does *sahib* mean?

5. The tiger appeared a *furlong* or so from the village. How far away was it?

6. What kind of theater is an *amphitheater?* What kind of rifle is a *cordite rifle?*

Composition

1. Explain how the author first created suspense in the selection and then made it gradually mount until the moment of the kill. Cite evidence from the selection to demonstrate your point.

2. Discuss your impression of the author from the style in which the selection is written, from the way that the author conducted himself during the hunt, and from the attitude he had toward the people around him.

3. Describe an incident in which someone you know or have read about revealed unusual courage. Try to explain the basis for such unusual courage in terms of the person involved and the situation with which he was confronted.

In times of great strife and danger, what makes some men cowards and other men heroes? What is the source of courage? Does it come from within? Is it possible that there is a source outside of ourselves that gives us inner strength?

Gawaine, the hero of this famous allegorical essay, is a fearless slayer of dragons who apparently derives his courage from a magic word. Read what happens to him when one day while facing a rip-snorting dragon he forgets his magic word.

THE FIFTY-FIRST DRAGON

Heywood Broun

OF all the pupils at the knight school Gawaine le Cœur-Hardy was among the least promising. He was tall and sturdy, but his instructors soon discovered that he lacked spirit. He would hide in the woods when the jousting class was called, although his companions and members of the faculty sought to appeal to his better nature by shouting to him to come out and break his neck like a man. Even when they told him that the lances were padded, the horses no more than ponies and the field unusually soft for late autumn, Gawaine refused to grow enthusiastic. The Headmaster and the Assistant Professor of Pleasaunce[1] were discussing the case one spring afternoon and the Assistant Professor could see no remedy but expulsion.

"No," said the Headmaster, as he looked out at the purple hills which ringed the school, "I think I'll train him to slay dragons."

"He might be killed," objected the Assistant Professor.

[1] *Pleasaunce:* that which awakens or causes pleasure

"So he might," replied the Headmaster brightly, but he added, more soberly, "We must consider the greater good. We are responsible for the formation of this lad's character."

"Are the dragons particularly bad this year?" interrupted the Assistant Professor. This was characteristic. He always seemed restive when the head of the school began to talk ethics and the ideals of the institution.

"I've never known them worse," replied the Headmaster. "Up in the hills to the south last week they killed a number of peasants, two cows and a prize pig. And if this dry spell holds there's no telling when they may start a forest fire simply by breathing around indiscriminately."

"Would any refund on the tuition fee be necessary in case of an accident to young Cœur-Hardy?"

"No," the principal answered, judicially, "that's all covered in the contract. But as a matter of fact he won't be killed. Before I send him up in the hills I'm going to give him a magic word."

"That's a good idea," said the Professor. "Sometimes they work wonders."

From that day on Gawaine specialized in dragons. His course included both theory and practice. In the morning there were long lectures on the history, anatomy, manners and customs of dragons. Gawaine did not distinguish himself in these studies. He had a marvelously versatile gift for forgetting things. In the afternoon he showed to better advantage, for then he would go down to the South Meadow and practise with a battle-ax. In this exercise he was truly impressive, for he had enormous strength as well as speed and grace. He even developed a deceptive display of ferocity. Old alumni say that it was a thrilling sight to see Gawaine charging across the field toward the dummy paper dragon which had been set up for his practice. As he ran he would brandish his ax and shout "A murrain on thee!" or some other vivid bit of campus slang. It never took him more than one stroke to behead the dummy dragon.

Gradually his task was made more difficult. Paper gave way to papier-mâché and finally to wood, but even the toughest of these dummy dragons had no terrors for Gawaine. One sweep of the ax always did the business. There were those who said that when the practice was protracted until dusk and the dragons threw long, fantastic shadows across the meadow Gawaine did not charge so impetuously nor shout so loudly. It is possible there was malice in this charge. At any rate, the Headmaster decided by the end of June that it was time for the test. Only the night before a dragon had come close to the school grounds and had eaten some of the lettuce from the garden. The faculty decided that Gawaine was ready. They gave him a diploma and a new battle-ax and the Headmaster summoned him to a private conference.

"Sit down," said the Headmaster. "Have a cigarette."

Gawaine hesitated.

"Oh, I know it's against the rules," said the Headmaster. "But after all, you have received your preliminary degree. You are no longer a boy. You are a man. Tomorrow you will go out into the world, the great world of achievement."

Gawaine took a cigarette. The Headmaster offered him a match, but he produced one of his own and began to puff away with a dexterity which quite amazed the principal.

"Here you have learned the theories of life," continued the Headmaster, resuming the thread of his discourse, "but after all, life is not a matter of theories. Life is a matter of facts. It calls on the young and the old alike to face these facts, even though they are hard and sometimes unpleasant. Your problem, for example, is to slay dragons."

"They say that those dragons down in the south wood are five hundred feet long," ventured Gawaine, timorously.

"Stuff and nonsense!" said the Headmaster. "The curate saw one last week from the top of Arthur's Hill. The dragon was sunning himself down in the valley. The curate didn't have an opportunity to look at him very long because he felt it was his duty to hurry back to make a report to me. He said the monster, or shall I say, the big lizard?—wasn't an inch over two hundred feet. But the size has nothing at all to do with it. You'll find the big ones even easier than the little ones. They're far slower on their feet and less aggressive, I'm told. Besides, before you go I'm going to equip you in such fashion that you need have no fear of all the dragons in the world."

"I'd like an enchanted cap," said Gawaine.

"What's that?" answered the Headmaster, testily.

"A cap to make me disappear," explained Gawaine.

The Headmaster laughed indulgently. "You mustn't believe all those old wives' stories," he said. "There isn't any such thing. A cap to make you disappear, indeed! What would you do with it? You haven't even appeared yet. Why, my boy, you could walk from here to London, and nobody would so much as look at you. You're nobody. You couldn't be more invisible than that."

Gawaine seemed dangerously close to a relapse into his old habit of whimpering. The Headmaster reassured him: "Don't worry; I'll give you something much better than an enchanted cap. I'm going to give you a magic word. All you have to do is to repeat this magic charm once and no dragon can possibly harm a hair of your head. You can cut off his head at your leisure."

He took a heavy book from the shelf behind his desk and began to run through it. "Sometimes," he said, "the charm is a whole phrase or even a sentence. I might, for instance, give you 'To make the'—No, that might not do. I think a single word would be best for dragons."

"A short word," suggested Gawaine.

"It can't be too short or it wouldn't be potent. There isn't so much hurry as all that. Here's a splendid magic word: 'Rumplesnitz.' Do you think you can learn that?"

Gawaine tried and in an hour or so he seemed to have the word well in hand. Again and again he interrupted the lesson to inquire, "And if I say 'Rumplesnitz' the dragon can't possibly hurt me?" And always the Headmaster replied, "If you only say 'Rumplesnitz,' you are perfectly safe."

Toward morning Gawaine seemed resigned to his career. At daybreak the Headmaster saw him to the edge of the forest and pointed him to the direction in which he should proceed. About a mile away to the southwest a cloud of steam hovered over an open meadow in the woods and the Headmaster assured Gawaine that under the steam he would find a dragon. Gawain went forward slowly. He wondered whether it would be best to approach the dragon on the run as he did in his practice in the South Meadow or to walk slowly toward him, shouting "Rumplesnitz" all the way.

The problem was decided for him. No sooner had he come to the fringe of the meadow than the dragon spied him and began to charge. It was a large dragon and yet it seemed decidedly aggressive in spite of the Headmaster's statement to the contrary. As the dragon charged it released huge clouds of hissing steam through its nostrils. It was almost as if a gigantic teapot had gone mad. The dragon came forward so fast and Gawaine was so frightened that he had time to say "Rumplesnitz" only once. As he said it, he swung his battle-ax and off popped the head of the dragon. Gawaine had to admit that it was even easier to kill a real dragon than a wooden one if only you said "Rumplesnitz."

Gawaine brought the ears home and a small section of the tail. His school mates and the faculty made much of him, but the Headmaster wisely kept him from being spoiled by insisting that he go on with his work. Every clear day Gawaine rose at dawn and went out to kill dragons. The Headmaster kept him at home when it rained, because he said the woods were damp and unhealthy at such times and that he didn't want the boy to run needless risks. Few good days passed in which Gawaine failed to get a dragon. On one particularly fortunate day he killed three, a husband and wife and a visiting relative. Gradually he developed a technique. Pupils who sometimes watched him from the hill-tops a long way off said that he often allowed the dragon to come within a few feet before he said "Rumplesnitz." He came to say it with a mocking sneer. Occasionally he did stunts. Once when an excursion party from London was watching him he went into action with his right hand tied behind his back. The dragon's head came off just as easily.

As Gawaine's record of killings mounted higher the Headmaster found it impossible to keep him completely in hand. He fell into the habit of stealing out at night and engaging in long drinking bouts at the village tavern. It was after such a debauch that he rose a little before dawn one fine August morning and started out after his fiftieth dragon. His head was heavy and his mind sluggish. He was heavy in other respects as well, for he had adopted the somewhat vulgar practice of wearing his medals, ribbons and all, when he went out dragon hunting. The decorations began on his chest and ran all the way down to his abdomen. They must have weighed at least eight pounds.

Gawaine found a dragon in the same meadow where he had killed the first one. It was a fair-sized dragon, but evidently an old one. Its face was wrinkled and Gawaine thought he had never seen so hideous a countenance. Much to the lad's disgust, the monster refused to charge and Gawaine was obliged to walk toward him. He whistled as he went. The dragon regarded him hopelessly, but craftily. Of course it had heard of Gawaine. Even when the lad raised his battle-ax the dragon made no move. It knew that there was no salvation in the quickest thrust of the head, for it had been informed that this hunter was protected by an enchantment. It merely waited, hoping something would turn up. Gawaine raised the battle-ax and suddenly lowered it again. He had grown very pale and he trembled violently. The dragon suspected a trick. "What's the matter?" it asked, with false solicitude.

"I've forgotten the magic word," stammered Gawaine.

"What a pity," said the dragon. "So that was the secret.

It doesn't seem quite sporting to me, all this magic stuff, you know. Not cricket, as we used to say when I was a little dragon; but after all, that's a matter of opinion."

Gawaine was so helpless with terror that the dragon's confidence rose immeasurably and it could not resist the temptation to show off a bit.

"Could I possibly be of any assistance?" it asked. "What's the first letter of the magic word?"

"It begins with an 'r,' " said Gawaine weakly.

"Let's see," mused the dragon, "that doesn't tell us much, does it? What sort of a word is this? Is it an epithet, do you think?"

Gawaine could do no more than nod.

"Why, of course," exclaimed the dragon, "reactionary Republican."

Gawaine shook his head.

"Well, then," said the dragon, "we'd better get down to business. Will you surrender?"

With the suggestion of a compromise Gawaine mustered up enough courage to speak.

"What will you do if I surrender?" he asked.

"Why, I'll eat you," said the dragon.

"And if I don't surrender?"

"I'll eat you just the same."

"Then it doesn't make any difference, does it?" moaned Gawaine.

"It does to me," said the dragon with a smile. "I'd rather you didn't surrender. You'd taste much better if you didn't."

The dragon waited for a long time for Gawaine to ask "Why?" but the boy was too frightened to speak. At last the dragon had to give the explanation without his cue line. "You see," he said, "if you don't surrender you'll taste better because you'll die game."

This was an old and ancient trick of the dragon's. By means of some such quip he was accustomed to paralyze his victims with laughter and then to destroy them. Gawaine was sufficiently paralyzed as it was, but laughter had no part in his helplessness. With the last word of the joke the dragon drew back his head and struck. In that second there flashed into the mind of Gawaine the magic word "Rumplesnitz," but there was no time to say it. There was time only to strike and, without a word, Gawaine met the onrush of the dragon with a full swing. He put all his back and shoulders into it. The impact was terrific and the head of the dragon flew away almost a hundred yards and landed in a thicket.

Gawaine did not remain frightened very long after the death of the dragon. His mood was one of wonder. He was enormously puzzled. He cut off the ears of the monster almost in a trance. Again and again he thought to himself, "I didn't say 'Rumplesnitz'!" He was sure of that and yet there was no question that he had killed the dragon. In fact, he had never killed one so utterly. Never before had he driven a head for anything like the same distance. Twenty-five yards was perhaps his best previous record. All the way back to the knight school he kept rumbling about in his mind seeking an explanation for what had occurred. He went to the Headmaster immediately and after closing the door told him what had happened. "I didn't say 'Rumplesnitz,' " he explained with great earnestness.

The Headmaster laughed. "I'm glad you've found out," he said. "It makes you ever so much more of a hero. Don't you see that? Now you know that it was you who killed all these dragons and not that foolish little word 'Rumplesnitz.' "

Gawaine frowned. "Then it wasn't a magic word after all?" he asked.

"Of course not," said the Headmaster, "you ought to be too old for such foolishness. There isn't any such thing as a magic word."

"But you told me it was magic," protested Gawaine. "You said it was magic and now you say it isn't."

"It wasn't magic in a literal sense," answered the Headmaster, "but it was much more wonderful than that. The word gave you confidence. It took away your fears. If I hadn't told you that you might have been killed the very first time. It was your battle-ax did the trick."

Gawaine surprised the Headmaster by his attitude. He was obviously distressed by the explanation. He interrupted a long philosophic and ethical discourse by the Headmaster with, "If I hadn't of hit 'em all mighty hard and fast any one of 'em might have crushed me like a, like a—" He fumbled for a word.

"Egg shell," suggested the Headmaster.

"Like a egg shell," assented Gawaine, and he said it many times. All through the evening meal people who sat near him heard him muttering, "Like a egg shell, like a egg shell."

The next day was clear, but Gawaine did not get up at dawn. Indeed, it was almost noon when the Headmaster found him cowering in bed, with the clothes pulled over his head. The principal called the Assistant Professor of Pleasaunce, and together they dragged the boy toward the forest.

"He'll be all right as soon as he gets a couple more dragons under his belt," explained the Headmaster.

The Assistant Professor of Pleasaunce agreed. "It would be a shame to stop such a fine run," he said. "Why, counting that one yesterday, he's killed fifty dragons."

They pushed the boy into a thicket above which hung a meager cloud of steam. It was obviously quite a small dragon. But Gawaine did not come back that night or the next. In fact, he never came back. Some weeks afterward brave spirits from the school explored the thicket, but they could find nothing to remind them of Gawaine except the metal parts of his medals. Even the ribbons had been devoured.

The Headmaster and the Assistant Professor of Pleasaunce agreed that it would be just as well not to tell the school how Gawaine had achieved his record and still less how he came to die. They held that it might have a bad effect on school spirit. Accordingly, Gawaine has lived in the memory of the school as its greatest hero. No visitor succeeds in leaving the building today without seeing a great shield which hangs on the wall of the dining hall. Fifty pairs of dragons' ears are mounted upon the shield and underneath in gilt letters is "Gawaine le Cœur-Hardy," followed by the simple inscription, "He killed fifty dragons." The record has never been equaled.

Questions and Comments

1. When you first meet Gawaine at the knight school, what kind of student is he?

2. What does the Headmaster decide will be good for Gawaine? What reason does the Headmaster have for taking this course of action?

3. What is the magic word? What effect does it have on Gawaine in his first encounter with a dragon?

4. How does Gawaine's growing fame and success as a dragon slayer affect his character?

5. What happens to Gawaine during his encounter with the fiftieth dragon? Why is he so troubled after slaying the fiftieth dragon?

6. What does the Headmaster reveal to Gawaine about the magic word? What effect does this knowledge have on him? What does this reveal about Gawaine?

7. Why does Gawaine's encounter with the fifty-first dragon end as it does? What point does the author illustrate by this ending?

8. Why do the Headmaster and the Assistant Professor decide to keep secret how Gawaine had achieved his record and how he had met his end?

9. What is the author's attitude toward the Headmaster and the Assistant Professor? Does the author poke fun at the teachers and the system of education at the school? Cite evidence from the selection to support your answer.

Word Study

1. In ancient times the expression "a murrain on thee" was a fairly common way of wishing someone bad luck. *Murrain* then referred to any disease or plague or pestilence. Look up the word and see what its meaning is today.

2. *Papier-mâché* is French for "chewed paper." Do you make papier-mâché figures by first chewing paper? Look the word up in a dictionary and tell what papier-mâché is.

3. When used as a verb *resigned* means "to have given up or left a job." What does the same word mean when used as an adjective in the sentence "Toward morning Gawaine seemed resigned to his career"?

4. Can you guess the meaning of the following words from their Latin origins? Use a dictionary to check your guesses.

   judicially—page 83 (The Latin word *judicium* means "judgment." What other English words have the same derivation?)

   protracted—page 84 (The Latin verb *trahere* means "to draw.")

   timorously—page 84 (The Latin noun *timor* means "fear.")

   curate—page 84 (The Latin noun *cura* means "care.")

Composition

1. "The Fifty-first Dragon" has been called an allegory. Tell what an allegory is and cite those aspects of this essay that seem to you to be allegorical in intention and treatment. Tell what the author allegorized.

2. Discuss what you feel is meant by the following famous words: "The only thing we have to fear is fear itself."

3. Give your opinion of the following statement: "There is no such thing as magic. Real power or ability must reside not in magic or in charms, but in ourselves."

Having received his medical degree from the University of Glasgow, A. J. Cronin served for a year as ship's doctor on the *Rawalpindar*. From this fascinating, exotic experience, he next turned to the comparatively drab routine of his new position as assistant to the doctor of Tannochbrae, a small village in Scotland. His first case turned out to be an emergency that called for all the skill, courage, and resourcefulness at his command.

from ADVENTURES
IN TWO WORLDS

A. J. Cronin

SCOTLAND again, and real Scots weather—sad contrast to the sunny skies and spicy breezes of the tropics. On the deserted little platform of Dundonald Junction I stood in the blinding wind and rain, wondering if I should take a cab. Economy denied the cab, dignity demanded it—not my own dignity, but that of my new position.

At length I beckoned to the red-faced cabby in the long green coat, who, from beside the one flyblown four-wheeler that graced the station exit, had been considering me for the last three minutes with a stealthy, speculative eye.

"How much to Tannochbrae village? Dr. Cameron's house."

Auld Geordie cautiously came over. None of your southern alacrity, none of that "Cab, sir!" nonsense about Geordie. He knew his worth, did old Geordie Dewar, and never sold himself for less.

"How much luggage have ye got?" he parried, though the luggage was plainly seen—one portmanteau upon the pavement, and a small black Gladstone bag, a very new bag, which I gripped in my right hand. Then he added:

"You'll be Cameron's new assistant, I'm thinking?"

"Just so!"

"Two shillings to you, then—Doctor."

He threw a cunning emphasis upon the title, but for all that I kept my head and said sternly:

"I mean the short cut." I who had never been in Tannochbrae before! "Not the long way you proposed to wander round with me!"

"As Goad's my Maker. . . ." protested Geordie.

A lively argument ensued, at the end of which a compromise—one shilling and "the price of a pint"—was effected with expressions of good will on both sides.

The portmanteau was slung upon the roof, old Geordie climbed rheumily upon the box, and I was rattled off along the stony moorland road.

At the end of the voyage home, Captain Hamble had pressed me to remain with him on the *Rawalpindar* but at the same time had honestly advised me against lapsing into a routine which, to his knowledge, had turned many an eager and ambitious young man into a lazy and lackadaisical ship's surgeon. The captain had been extremely kind to me and in Calcutta had taken me ashore many times to lunch at the Grand Hotel and to see the sights—the great temples and gilded palaces, the teeming bazaars where sacred cattle roamed and ravaged the stalls at will, the gorgeous botanical gardens filled with exotic birds and blossoms, the grisly burning ghats[1] that lined the waters of the Hoogly. All this had fascinated me, had stirred within me a longing to record my impressions of so exciting a scene. Yet I was fully aware of the sound sense in Hamble's warning, and hearing from a

[1] *burning ghats:* spaces in the ghats (stairways descending to a river) where the Hindus cremated the dead

classmate at the University that there was an assistantship vacant in Tannochbrae—"Not much, mind you. . . . Regular country practice . . . , and he's a hard nut, old Cameron, though a rare good sort at heart"—I had, not without reluctance, quitted my berth in the ship.

So here I was, hunched in this mouldy four-wheeler, clattering down the cobbled street of a small West Highland village. Halfway down we swung to the right, into the drive of Arden House, a soundly built white stone dwelling with a coach house at the side and a semicircular spread of lawn in front.

The rain dripped miserably as I sprang up the front steps and rang the bell. After a minute, the door opened and the housekeeper, a thin, elderly woman, dressed entirely in black, confronted me. Her hair was tightly drawn, her person spotless, and in her bleak face was stamped authority, mingled with a certain grudging humanity; she had the look, indeed, of one tempted terribly to smile, who guards perpetually against a single sign of levity, lest it ruin her self-esteem.

For a few seconds she inspected me, my bag, my hat, even my boots; then, with a slight elevation of her brows, my luxurious background of horse and cab.

"Ye've a cab!" she observed severely, as though I had arrived in the state coach drawn by four cream horses. A pause. "Well! I suppose you'd better come in. Don't forget to wipe your feet."

I dutifully wiped my feet and "came in," feeling that I had made a bad beginning.

"The doctor's out," she announced. "He's fair run off his legs, poor man, since the last assistant left. Aah! He was no good, that one—no good ataaal!" And with a faint shake of her head, as though, in her considered judgement, I would not prove much better, she left me marooned on the hearthrug.

Somehow I had to smile. Then I glanced round the big, comfortable room—the dining room, it was—with warm red

curtains and Turkey-red carpet, a blazing coal fire, and furniture of sound mahogany. No aspidistra,[1] thank God! A big
bowl of apples on the dresser, a full glass barrel of biscuits,
and whisky in the square-cut decanter. No pictures, no
photographs, but, of all things, three yellow violins hanging
on the walls. A good—oh, a decent room to live in. I was
warming myself pleasantly at the blaze when the door was
flung open and Cameron came stamping in.

"That's right," said Cameron, without a handshake or a
word of preamble, "warm your backside at the fire while I
work myself to death outside. Dammit to hell! I thought
Stirrock said ye would be here this mornin'. Janet! Janet!"—at
the pitch of his lungs—"For God's sake bring in our tea."

He was a medium-sized, oldish man with a face beaten
bright crimson by Scots weather and Scots whisky, and a
pugnacious little grey imperial, now dewed with raindrops.
He stooped slightly, so that his head had a forward, belligerent thrust. He wore gaiters, cord breeches, and a big, baggy
tweed jacket of a nondescript, vaguely greenish colour, the
side pockets stuffed to the bursting point with everything
from an apple to a gum-elastic catheter.[2] About him there
hung invariably the odour of drugs, carbolic, and strong tobacco.

Obtaining a good three-quarters of the fire, he inspected
me sideways and asked abruptly:

"Are ye strong? Sound in wind and limb?"

"I hope so!"

"Married?"

"Not yet."

"Thank God! Can ye play the fiddle?"

"No!"

"Neither can I—but I can make them bonny. Do ye smoke
a pipe?"

"I do!"

---

[1] *aspidistra:* member of the lily family, cultivated as a house plant
[2] *catheter:* a tube used to drain fluids from body cavities

"Humph! Do ye drink whisky?"

My dander had been rising under this interrogation. I don't like you, I thought, as I looked at the odd, unprofessional figure beside me, and I never will. I answered surlily:

"I drink what I like, and when I like!"

The spark of a smile gleamed in Cameron's sardonic eye.

"It might be worse," he murmured, and then: "Sit in and have your tea."

Janet had swiftly and silently set the table—cake, buns, toast, preserve, brown bread, home-baked scones, cheese, and bannocks[1]—and now, with the big brown teapot, she brought in a huge dish of cold ham and poached eggs.

"There's no falderals in this house," Cameron explained briefly as he poured the tea—he had beautiful hands, I noticed, hard-skinned, yet supple. "Breakfast, middle-day dinner, high tea, and supper—plain food and plenty. We work our assistant here, but—by your leave—we don't starve him."

We were well through the meal when Janet came in with more hot water. Only then did she say impassively:

"There's a man been waiting this last half hour—young Lachlan Mackenzie, him that has the steading[2] up Inverbeg way. His bairn's badly, he makes out."

Cameron arrested a piece of oatcake halfway to his mouth to let out his favourite oath:

"Dammit to hell!" he cried, "and me up at Inverbeg this mornin' and passed his very door. Th' infernal eediot! I'll wager the child's been sick for days. Do they all think I'm made of steel?" He checked himself. Then, with a sigh which seemed to let off all his boiling steam, he added in quite a different voice, "All right, Janet. All right. Let him come in here the now."

In a moment Mackenzie stood in the doorway, cap in hand —a poor, shiftless-looking crofter,[3] very much abashed by his

---

[1] *bannocks:* thin cakes made of meal
[2] *steading:* a farmhouse
[3] *crofter:* one who cultivates a small tenant farm

surroundings, and terribly nervous under the doctor's inter-
rogating eye.

"It's the boy, Doctor," he muttered, twisting his cap. "The
wife thinks it's the croup."

"How long has he been poorly, Lachlan?"

This friendly use of his name gave the young fellow confidence.

"Two days, Doctor—but we didna' think it was the
croup. . . ."

"Ay, ay, Lachlan. The croup! Just so, just so." A pause.
"How did ye get in?"

"I just walkit in, Doctor—it's no that far."

Not far! It was seven miles from Inverbeg to Tannochbrae.

Cameron rubbed his cheek slowly.

"All right, Lachlan man! Don't you worry. Away with
Janet now and have your tea while the gig's bein' got round."

Silence in the dining room when he had gone. Cameron
reflectively stirred his tea. Almost apologetically he said:

"I can't be hard on a poor devil like that. It's a weakness I
never seem to get over. He owes me for his wife's last con-
finement—he'll never pay it. But I'll get out the gig, drive
seven miles, see the child, drive seven miles back. And what
do you think I'll mark against him in the book? One and six
—if I don't forget. And what does it matter if I do forget?
He'll never pay me a red bawbee[1] in any case. Oh, dammit
to hell! What a life for a man who loves fiddles!"

Silence again; then I ventured:

"Shall I do the call?"

Cameron took a long pull at his tea. The bright satire was
back in his eye as he said:

"That's a braw[2] wee black bag ye've got—ay, I see it on
the sofa—brand-new and shiny, with your stethoscope and all
the new contrivances inside, bonny and complete. No wonder

[1] *bawbee:* an old Scotch coin, also a colloquial expression for a halfpenny
[2] *braw:* Scotch for "fine" or "fine-looking"

ye're fair itchin' to use it." He looked me straight in the face. "All right! Ye can go. But let me warn you, my lad, in a practice like mine it's not the bag that matters—it's the man!" He got up. "Do the call then, and I'll do the surgery. Take some antitoxin with you to be safe. It's on the right-hand shelf as you go in the back room. Here! I'll show ye. I'm not wantin' you to drive seven miles to find out that croup is liable to mean diphtheria."

The gig was waiting outside the front porch, with Lachlan already in the back, and Jamie, the groom, standing ready with the waterproof sheet. We set off through the wet, blustery night.

In the village the rain fell heavily enough, but when we crossed the bridge and breasted the hill it broke upon us in torrents. The wind drove full into our teeth like a hurricane.

Fifteen minutes, and I was half drenched; my hat saturated, trickles of water oozing down my neck, and my precious bag, which I held upon my knees, streaming like a wet seal. I wanted to curse the weather, the practice, and Cameron; but I shut my teeth and said nothing.

It was bad, bad going. The road was dark, too, the gig lamps so blurred by a film of mud that Jamie had difficulty in keeping the horse upon the road. Away to the right, behind massed firs, were the lights of Darroch, vague, unfriendly; and to the left, lying like a great dark beast, the amorphous bulk of the Ardfillan Hills.

We went on through the pitch blackness and the rain in silence. Then from ahead came the quick lapping of water against some hidden shore.

"The loch!" said Jamie, by way of explanation. They were the only words spoken during the journey.

The unseen road wound now by this angry, unseen water. Then, three miles on, we bore sharply to the left and stopped finally at a small steading where a single illuminated window seemed somehow swamped and hopeless in the great void of sodden blackness.

As we climbed out of the gig, Lachlan's wife opened the door. She looked no more than a girl despite her clumsy sacking apron and uncouth brogues. A coil of hair fell carelessly down her neck, and her big eyes were dark and youthful against the anxious pallor of her face. She helped me out of my wet coat in silence; then, though she still said not a word, her worried eye indicated the kitchen bed. I walked over to it, my boots squelching on the stone-flagged floor.

A little boy of three lay tossing under a single blanket, his brow damp with sweat, his face completely livid as he gasped for breath. I asked for a spoon, but did not use it; instead, with my finger I depressed the child's tongue. Yes! The whole of the fauces[1] covered with thick, greenish-white membrane. Laryngeal[2] diphtheria!

"I've made him some gruel, Doctor," the mother murmured, "but he doesna' . . . doesna' seem to fancy it."

"He can't swallow," I said.

Because I was nervous my voice sounded unsympathetic, even harsh.

"Is he bad, then, Doctor?" she whispered, with a hand at her breast.

Bad! I thought, with my fingers on the pulse. She doesn't dream how bad he is! Bending down, I made a complete and careful examination. There was no doubt at all—the child was dying. What a horrible position, I thought again, that this should be my first case.

I went to my bag, opened it, filled my big syringe with 8,000 units of antidiphtheritic serum.[3] The child barely moaned as the needle sank into his thigh and the serum slowly filtered in. To gain time I went back to the fire. Jamie and Lachlan were in the room now, too, for it was the only warm place in the house. They stood together by the door. I could feel their eyes on me, watchful, expectant, together

---

[1] *fauces:* the cavity at the back of the mouth
[3] *Laryngeal:* pertaining to the larynx or the cavity at the upper end of the human windpipe, which contains the vocal chords
[3] *antidiphtheritic serum:* a serum used to counteract diphtheria

with the terrified eyes of the mother. I was the centre of
that humble room. They looked to me to do something for
the child.

What was I to do? I knew very well what I should do. But
I was afraid. I returned to the bed. If anything, the boy was
worse. In half an hour, before the serum could act, he would
be dead from obstruction of the windpipe. Another wave of
fear came over me. I had to make up my mind. Now—at
once—or it would be too late.

Automatically I faced round. I felt myself so young, so
utterly inept and inexperienced in the face of the great
elemental forces which surged within the room. I said in a
manner wholly unimpressive:

"The boy has diphtheria. The membrane is blocking the
larynx. There's only one thing to do. Operate. Open the windpipe below the obstruction."

The mother wrung her hands, and screamed:

"Oh, no, Doctor, no!"

I turned to Jamie.

"Lift the boy onto the table."

There was a second's hesitation; then slowly Jamie went
over and lifted the almost senseless child on to the scrubbed
pine table. But at that Lachlan broke down.

"I canna' stand it! I canna' stand it!" He cried weakly, and
looked around desperately for an excuse. "I'll away and put
the horse in the stable."

Blubbering, he rushed out.

Now the mother had recovered herself. Pale as a ghost,
her hands clenched fiercely, she looked at me.

"Tell me what to do, and I'll do it."

"Stand there and hold his head back tight!"

I swabbed the skin of the child's throat with iodine. I took
a clean towel and laid it across those glazing eyes. The case
was far beyond an anaesthetic; madness to think of using it.
Jamie was holding the oil lamp near. Setting my teeth, I
picked up the lancet. I made the incision with a steady hand,
but I felt my legs trembling beneath me. A deep incision, but

not deep enough. I must go deeper, deeper—go boldly in, yet watch all the time for the jugular vein. If I cut that vein . . . ! I widened the incision, using the blunt end of the scalpel, searching desperately for the white cartilage of the trachea.[1] The child, roused by pain, struggled like a fish in a strangling net. God! would I never find it? I was muddling hopelessly, messing about—I knew it—the child would die; they would say that I had killed him. I cursed myself in spirit. Beads of sweat broke out on my brow, as I remembered, suddenly, MacEwen's fatal words: *"You will never be a surgeon."*

The child's breathing was terrible now, thin, infrequent; the whole of his tiny thorax[2] sucked and sobbed over each frightful, useless breath. The neck veins were engorged, the throat livid, the face blackening. Not a minute longer, I thought! He's finished, and so am I. For one sickening instant I had a quick vision of all the operations I had known—of the cold, immaculate precision of the Infirmary theatre, and then, by frightful contrast, this struggling, desperate thing dying under my knife upon a kitchen table by the flare of an oil lamp, while the wind howled and stormed outside. Oh, God, I prayed, help me, help me now.

I felt my eyes misting. A great emptiness possessed my whole being. And then under my searching knife the thin white tube sprang into view. Swiftly I incised it, and in the instant the child's gasping ceased. Instead, a long clear breath of air went in through the opening. Another—another. The cyanosis[3] vanished, the pulse strengthened. Swept by a terrific reaction, I felt that I was going to collapse. Afraid to move, I kept my head down to hide the smarting tears that sprang into my eyes. I've done it, I thought; oh, God, I've done it after all!

[1] *trachea:* the windpipe

[2] *thorax:* section of the body containing the lungs

[3] *cyanosis:* a condition in which the skin turns blue due to inadequate oxygenation of the blood

Later I slipped the tiny silver tracheotomy[1] tube into the opening. I washed the blood from my hands, lifted the boy back to bed. The temperature had fallen a point and a half. As I sat by the bedside, watching, cleaning the tube of mucus, I felt a queer, benign interest in the child—I studied his little face, no longer strange to me.

From time to time the mother replenished the fire so silently she was like a shadow in the room. Jamie and Lachlan were asleep upstairs. At five in the morning I gave another 4,000 units of serum. At six the child was sleeping, far less restive than before. At seven I rose and stretched myself. Smiling, I said:

"He'll do now, I expect!" And I explained to the mother the method of cleaning out the tube. "In ten days it'll all be healed up good as new."

Now there was no terror in her eyes, but a gratitude— moving and inarticulate—like the gratitude of some dumb creature to a god.

The horse was harnessed, the gig brought round. We all drank a cup of tea standing. The rain had stopped long since. And at half past seven Jamie and I were off, striking through the pale glory of the morning. Strangely, Jamie was no longer taciturn; he had a word for this and that—a word of comradeship which fell graciously upon my ears.

It was close on nine when, tired, unshaven, and clutching the mud-splashed bag, I stumbled into the dining room of Arden House. Cameron was there, fresh as a new pin, whistling a little tune softly, between his teeth—he had an exasperating habit of whistling in the morning!—as he inspected a dish of bacon and eggs.

He looked me up and down; then with a dry twinkle in his eye, before I could speak, he declared:

"There's one guid thing has happened anyway! Ye've taken the newness off your bag."

[1] *tracheotomy:* the operation of cutting into the trachea

Questions and Comments

The selection you have just read is from A. J. Cronin's autobiography, *Adventures in Two Worlds*. Mr. Cronin, who gave up his medical practice to become a writer, is the author of many novels, including *The Citadel* and *The Keys of the Kingdom*.

1. Why had Captain Hamble advised the author against remaining on the *Rawalpindar* as ship's doctor?

2. What questions does Dr. Cameron ask the author during their initial interview? What is the author's reaction to the questioning?

3. Who is Lachlan Mackenzie? Why does he appear at Dr. Cameron's house?

4. What is Dr. Cameron's feeling about the author's black bag? What does the doctor mean when he says "in a practice like mine it's not the bag that matters—it's the man"?

5. What situation is the author confronted with at the Mackenzie cottage? What does his diagnosis disclose?

6. What emergency operation must the author perform? What words come into his mind as he performs the operation?

7. What feelings about his patient does the author experience after the operation that he did not feel before it?

8. What is the significance of Dr. Cameron's concluding remark at the end of the selection?

Word Study

1. Explain how the names *portmanteau* and *Gladstone bag* came to be applied to suitcases and how *imperial* came to be applied to a beard.

2. Show that you know to what the following nouns refer: *decanter* (whisky in the square-cut decanter), *gaiters* (Dr.

Cameron wore them), *scones* (home-baked scones), *bairn* (Lachlan Mackenzie's bairn), *croup* (Mrs. Mackenzie thought the child had the croup), *brogues* (Mrs. Mackenzie wore them), *gruel* (Mrs. Mackenzie had made some for the child).

3. *Fol-de-rol* is a refrain in some old songs. What does *falderals* (an alternate spelling of *folderols*) mean as used in Dr. Cameron's speech "There's no falderals in this house"?

4. Give the meaning of the following words, using clues in the context wherever possible: *alacrity* (no Southern alacrity about the cabby—page 93, *lackadaisical* (a lazy and lackadaisical ship's surgeon—page 94, *levity* (guards against a single sign of levity—page 95), *pugnacious* (a pugnacious little grey imperial—page 96), *dander* (dander had been rising under the interrogation—page 97), *sardonic* (Cameron's sardonic eye—page 97), *amorphous* (the amorphous bulk of the Ardfillan Hills—page 99), *livid* (his face completely livid—page 100), *inept* (so young, so utterly inept and inexperienced—page 101), *benign* (a queer, benign interest in the child—page 103), *taciturn* (Jamie was no longer taciturn—page 103).

Composition

1. The author of this selection has a faculty for making clear, sharp, thumbnail character sketches. Select one which you consider to be particularly effective. Indicate the dominant impression you get of the character and point to details which strengthen this impression.

2. In times of emergency and crisis people are often put to severe tests. Describe an incident in which a person you know or have read about was confronted with a crisis. Tell what the crisis was and how the person coped with it.

Stephen Leacock, one of the world's best-known humorists, was for many years a professor of political economy at McGill University in Montreal. Of this dual role the London *Times* commented that Leacock always had a cap and gown in his closet as well as a cap and bells and frequently wore both outfits at once. Here when we see him launching on his financial career, it is obvious which outfit he has left in the closet.

MY FINANCIAL CAREER

Stephen Leacock

WHEN I go into a bank I get rattled. The clerks rattle me; the wickets rattle me; the sight of the money rattles me; everything rattles me.

The moment I cross the threshold of a bank and attempt to transact business there, I become an irresponsible idiot.

I knew this beforehand, but my salary had been raised to fifty dollars a month and I felt that the bank was the only place for it.

So I shambled in and looked timidly round at the clerks. I had an idea that a person about to open an account must needs consult the manager.

I went up to a wicket marked "Accountant." The accountant was a tall, cool devil. The very sight of him rattled me. My voice was sepulchral.

"Can I see the manager?" I said, and added solemnly, "alone." I don't know why I said "alone."

"Certainly," said the accountant, and fetched him.

The manager was a grave, calm man. I held my fifty-six dollars clutched in a crumpled ball in my pocket.

"Are you the manager?" I said. God knows I didn't doubt it.

"Yes," he said.

"Can I see you," I asked, "alone?" I didn't want to say "alone" again, but without it the thing seemed self-evident.

The manager looked at me in some alarm. He felt that I had an awful secret to reveal.

"Come in here," he said, and led the way to a private room. He turned the key in the lock.

"We are safe from interruption here," he said; "sit down."

We both sat down and looked at each other. I found no voice to speak.

"You are one of Pinkerton's men, I presume," he said.

He had gathered from my mysterious manner that I was a detective. I knew what he was thinking, and it made me worse.

"No, not from Pinkerton's," I said, seeming to imply that I came from a rival agency.

"To tell the truth," I went on, as if I had been prompted to lie about it, "I am not a detective at all. I have come to open an account. I intend to keep all my money in this bank."

The manager looked relieved but still serious; he concluded now that I was a son of Baron Rothschild[1] or a young Gould.[2]

"A large account, I suppose," he said.

"Fairly large," I whispered. "I propose to deposit fifty-six dollars now and fifty dollars a month regularly."

The manager got up and opened the door. He called to the accountant.

"Mr. Montgomery," he said unkindly loud, "this gentleman is opening an account, he will deposit fifty-six dollars. Good morning."

I rose.

---

[1] *Baron Rothschild:* member of a family of financiers and bankers
[2] *Gould:* Jay Gould was a nineteenth-century American financier associated with railroads.

A big iron door stood open at the side of the room.

"Good morning," I said, and stepped into the safe.

"Come out," said the manager coldly, and showed me the other way.

I went up to the accountant's wicket and poked the ball of money at him with a quick convulsive movement as if I were doing a conjuring trick.

My face was ghastly pale.

"Here," I said, "deposit it." The tone of the words seemed to mean, "Let us do this painful thing while the fit is on us."

He took the money and gave it to another clerk.

He made me write the sum on a slip and sign my name in a book. I no longer knew what I was doing. The bank swam before my eyes.

"Is it deposited?" I asked in a hollow, vibrating voice.

"It is," said the accountant.

"Then I want to draw a cheque."

My idea was to draw out six dollars of it for present use. Someone gave me a cheque-book through a wicket and someone else began telling me how to write it out. The people in the bank had the impression that I was an invalid millionaire. I wrote something on the cheque and thrust it in at the clerk. He looked at it.

"What! are you drawing it all out again?" he asked in surprise. Then I realised that I had written fifty-six instead of six. I was too far gone to reason now. I had a feeling that it was impossible to explain the thing. All the clerks had stopped writing to look at me.

Reckless with misery, I made a plunge.

"Yes, the whole thing."

"You withdraw your money from the bank?"

"Every cent of it."

"Are you not going to deposit any more?" said the clerk, astonished.

"Never."

An idiot hope struck me that they might think something had insulted me while I was writing the cheque and that I had changed my mind. I made a wretched attempt to look like a man with a fearfully quick temper.

The clerk prepared to pay the money.

"How will you have it?" he said.

"What?"

"How will you have it?"

"Oh"—I caught his meaning and answered without even trying to think—"in fifties."

He gave me a fifty-dollar bill.

"And the six?" he asked dryly.

"In sixes," I said.

He gave it me and I rushed out.

As the big door swung behind me I caught the echo of a roar of laughter that went up to the ceiling of the bank. Since then I bank no more. I keep my money in cash in my trousers pocket and my savings in silver dollars in a sock.

Questions and Comments

1. What device used by the author in the first paragraph sets the tone of the entire sketch? How would you characterize the tone?

2. Why does Leacock assume a somewhat mysterious manner when he approaches the accountant? How does this manner affect the accountant?

3. Into what chain of errors does Leacock's first question lead? Show that each step in the comedy is a natural result of the preceding one.

4. Exaggeration often is the basis of humor. Is this the case in "My Financial Career"? If not, what is the basis for the humor?

Word Study

1. In "So I shambled in and looked timidly at the clerks" *shambled* is a verb, used very effectively. *Shambles* may be used as a noun. The noun *shambles* comes from an obsolete English word for meat market. How do you account for the present meaning of the word?

2. Use the word *sepulchral* (as in "My voice was sepulchral") in a sentence of your own that clearly shows you know the meaning of the word.

Composition

1. Write an essay on the subject "My Most Embarrassing Moment." Try to avoid describing your feelings directly but rather let the situation itself reveal your mental state.

2. Relate your own first venture into an unfamiliar environment, contrasting your own feelings of anticipation and the actual facts of your reception.

"I went to the woods because I wished to live deliberately, to front only the essential facts of life, and see if I could not learn what it had to teach, and not, when I came to die, discover that I had not lived." These are words from Thoreau's famous book, *Walden* (1854), which grew out of Thoreau's two years of primitive existence at Walden Pond, near his birthplace, Concord, Massachusetts. The selection here is taken from *Walden*.

THE BATTLE OF THE ANTS

Henry David Thoreau

I WAS witness to events of a less peaceful character. One day when I went out to my wood-pile, or rather my pile of stumps, I observed two large ants, the one red, the other much larger, nearly half an inch long, and black, fiercely contending with one another. Having once got hold they never let go, but struggled and wrestled and rolled on the chips incessantly. Looking farther, I was surprised to find that the chips were covered with such combatants, that it was not a *duellum,* but a *bellum,* a war between two races of ants, the red always pitted against the black, and frequently two red ones to one black. The legions of these Myrmidons[1] covered all the hills and vales in my wood-yard, and the ground was already strewn with the dead and dying, both red and black. It was the only battle which I have ever witnessed, the only battle-field I ever trod while the battle was raging; internecine war; the red republicans on the one hand, and the black imperialists on the other. On every side they were engaged in deadly combat, yet without any noise that I could hear, and human soldiers never fought so resolutely.

[1] *Myrmidons:* followers of Achilles in the Trojan War

I watched a couple that were fast locked in each other's embraces, in a little sunny valley amid the chips, now at noonday prepared to fight till the sun went down, or life went out. The smaller red champion had fastened himself like a vise to his adversary's front, and through all the tumblings on that field never for an instant ceased to gnaw at one of his feelers near the root, having already caused the other to go by the board; while the stronger black one dashed him from side to side, and, as I saw on looking nearer, had already divested him of several of his members. They fought with more pertinacity than bull-dogs. Neither manifested the least disposition to retreat. It was evident that their battle-cry was Conquer or die. In the meanwhile there came along a single red ant on the hillside of this valley, evidently full of excitement, who either had despatched his foe, or had not yet taken part in the battle; probably the latter, for he had lost none of his limbs; whose mother had charged him to return with his shield or upon it. Or perchance he was some Achilles, who had nourished his wrath apart, and had now come to avenge or rescue his Patroclus.[1] He saw this unequal combat from afar,—for the blacks were nearly twice the size of the red,—he drew near with rapid pace till he stood on his guard within half an inch of the combatants, then, watching his opportunity, he sprang upon the black warrior, and commenced his operations near the root of his right fore-leg, leaving the foe to select among his own members; and so there were three united for life, as if a new kind of attraction had been invented which put all other locks and cements to shame. I should not have wondered by this time to find that they had their respective musical bands stationed on some eminent chip, and playing their national airs the while, to excite the slow and cheer the dying combatants. I was myself excited somewhat even as if they had

---

[1] *Patroclus:* friend of Achilles. While Achilles was sulking after a quarrel with Agamemnon, Patroclus wore the armor of Achilles into battle.

been men. The more you think of it, the less the difference. And certainly there is not the fight recorded in Concord history, at least, if in the history of America, that will bear a moment's comparison with this, whether for the numbers engaged in it, or for the patriotism and heroism displayed. For numbers and for carnage it was an Austerlitz or Dresden.[1] Concord Fight![2] Two killed on the patriots' side, and Luther Blanchard wounded! Why here every ant was a Buttrick,—"Fire! for God's sake fire!"—and thousands shared the fate of Davis and Hosmer. There was not one hireling there. I have no doubt that it was a principle they fought for, as much as our ancestors, and not to avoid a three-penny tax on their tea; and the results of this battle will be as important and memorable to those whom it concerns as those of the battle of Bunker Hill, at least.

I took up the chip on which the three I have particularly described were struggling, carried it into my house, and placed in under a tumbler on my window-sill, in order to see the issue. Holding a microscope to the first-mentioned red ant, I saw that, though he was assiduously gnawing at the near fore-leg of his enemy, having severed his remaining feeler, his own breast was all torn away, exposing what vitals he had there to the jaws of the black warrior, whose breast-plate was apparently too thick for him to pierce; and the dark carbuncles of the sufferer's eyes shone with ferocity such as war only could excite. They struggled half an hour longer under the tumbler, and when I looked again the black soldier had severed the heads of his foes from their bodies, and the still living heads were hanging on either side of him like ghastly trophies at his saddle-bow, still apparently as firmly fastened as ever, and he was endeavoring with feeble struggles, being without feelers and with only the remnant of a

---

[1] *Austerlitz or Dresden:* great battles, victories of Napoleon

[2] *Concord Fight:* At Concord's North Bridge, April 19, 1775, the militiamen Isaac Davis and Joseph Hosmer were killed and Luther Blanchard was wounded. Major John Buttrick gave the command to fire on the British troops.

leg, and I know not how many other wounds, to divest himself of them; which at length, after half an hour more, he accomplished. I raised the glass, and he went off over the window-sill in that crippled state. Whether he finally survived that combat, and spent the remainder of his days in some Hotel des Invalides,[1] I do not know; but I thought that his industry would not be worth much thereafter. I never learned which party was victorious, nor the cause of the war; but I felt for the rest of that day as if I had had my feelings excited and harrowed by witnessing the struggle, the ferocity and carnage, of a human battle before my door.

Questions and Comments

1. Thoreau's friend Ralph Waldo Emerson said of Thoreau, "He knew the country like a fox or bird and passed through it as freely by paths of his own. . . . He saw as with a microscope, heard as with an ear trumpet, and his memory was a photographic register of all he saw and heard." Do you agree with this comment on Thoreau's powers of observation? Give evidence from the selection in support of your answer.

2. How does Thoreau make the comparison of the fight of the three ants with an incident on a human battlefield?

3. How does Thoreau make the comparison of the battle of the two forces of ants with a battle of two opposing human forces?

4. Thoreau felt that his feelings had been both excited and harrowed by the struggle he had witnessed. Which passages in the selection show the excitement of battle?

5. What seems to be Thoreau's attitude toward war? Give evidence in support of your answer.

[1] *Hotel des Invalides:* Paris building, a home for war veterans. Napoleon's tomb is on the grounds.

Word Study

1. The word *internecine* (internecine war) can mean "marked by great slaughter or mutual destruction" or "involving conflict within a group." What does the word mean as used in this selection?

2. One kind of *carbuncle* is a painful infection like a boil. What kind of carbuncle does Thoreau mean when he talks about "the dark carbuncles of the sufferer's eyes"?

3. Refer to the selection and give the meaning of the italicized words as revealed by the context. Use a dictionary to check your guesses.

   "The smaller red champion had fastened himself like a *vise* to his adversary's front. . . ." (page 112)

   "They fought with . . . *pertinacity.* . . ." (page 112)

   "For numbers and for *carnage* it was an Austerlitz or Dresden." (page 113)

   ". . . he was *assiduously* gnawing at the near fore-leg of his enemy. . . ." (page 113)

   ". . . he was endeavoring with feeble struggles . . . to *divest* himself of them. . . ." (page 114)

Composition

1. Give your own observations of something in nature—either peaceful events or, like the battle of the ants, less peaceful events.

2. Write a short paper on the subject "Lessons Nature Can Teach Us."

3. Explain the following quotation from *Walden* and tell whether you think it can be followed today or should be followed: "Simplicity, simplicity, simplicity! I say, let your affairs be as two or three, and not a hundred or a thousand; instead of a million count half a dozen, and keep your accounts on a thumb-nail."

Although John J. Rowlands spent several years prospecting for gold and silver in the country south of Hudson Bay, he would probably agree that Cache Lake itself was the richest discovery he ever made. In this selection from *Cache Lake Country,* Mr. Rowlands tells of his Thoreau-like existence in the north woods.

PORTAGE TO CONTENTMENT

John J. Rowlands

On most maps Cache Lake is only a speck hidden among other blue patches big enough to have names, and unless you know where to look you will never find it. But a place like Cache Lake is seldom discovered on a map. You just come on it—that is if you are lucky. Most men who travel the north woods sooner or later happen on a lake or stream that somehow they cannot forget and always want to go back to. Generally they never do go back.

Cache Lake lies deep in a wilderness of spruce and pine which, except for a timber cruiser[1] like myself and maybe a trapper now and then, few white men know. But the Indians find it good game country, and so do the big gray timber wolves that run its hills. So like many other worth-while things, there's no easy trail to Cache Lake, for it is protected by distance, mile after forgotten mile of woods and water, and it is still clean and clear and safe from civilization.

Strange it is how things work out sometimes. A man starts out for a place in mind, but before he gets there he comes

[1] *timber cruiser:* one who inspects forests, estimating the value of timber

on something more to his liking than he thought a spot ever could be. That's how it was with Cache Lake. I was working north through a chain of lakes and streams to look over some timber for the lumber company. I had never been in the region before, but knew in a general way where I was heading. It was in the Snow Goose Lake country and I figured I would go up the Manitoupeepagee River and make myself a camp handy to the district I had to look over. A trapper told me I would find Wabun Lake a likely place for living. Just by way of remarking, Wabun is Indian for "east" or "dawn."

The time was early September, which is one of the best months for traveling in the north when the days are clear and sunny and the nights sharp with frost to make a fire feel good and remind you that fall is coming on. I stopped one night at the south end of Snow Goose Lake, where the Indians camp in the summer, and at dawn I started on. At that time of day the water is apt to be quiet and since my canoe with outfit and supplies was riding almost to the gunwales, the smoother the water the easier it was for me.

You leave the north end of Snow Goose Lake by a narrow creek or thoroughfare, a dark and deep neck of still water with muskeg and tamarack on the west side and heavy spruce on the east where the ground rises. It was so quiet I could hear the drops from the paddle hitting the water. The map showed that the waterway linked Snow Goose Lake with a small lake which had no name, so I didn't think much about it. Lake Wabun was a day's paddling ahead with some tracking up the river to boot, and my mind was set on getting there as soon as I could make it.

After I cleared the thoroughfare and came out on the small lake, I stopped paddling like a fellow will when he sees new water for the first time. The sun had come up and mist hung motionless like a big cobweb just above the surface. "Ghosts' breath" we called it when we were young. Over to my right, to the eastward, the shore was lined with jack pines and in one place close down by the water I could see a natural clearing. On the west was part of the great swamp I had passed coming up from Snow Goose Lake, but going north on that side the land lifted and the white boles of big canoe birches showed on the slopes of a low ridge.

I have seen maybe a thousand northern lakes, and they all look alike in many ways, but there was something different about that little lake that held me hard. I sat there perhaps half an hour, like a man under a spell, just looking it over. This lake gave me the queer feeling that I had been there before. The tall pine tops were moving in the first soft breeze of morning and as the mist drifted away dark shadows began to edge across the water into the woods just as they had somewhere, sometime long ago. Then, as the sun cleared the hills and turned the still black water into shining gold, I remembered. This was the lake of my boyhood dreams! This was the lake I used to picture when I camped with my chum by a little millpond near a meadow on a farm. We made believe it was a lake in the far northern wilderness. The cows that came down to drink were deer and moose; the dogs that barked were wolves, and the perch we caught were fighting trout. Our flat-bottomed boat was a birch bark canoe.

Then I remembered the little brook that hustled into one end of the pond and now as I looked toward the north I saw the froth of white water at the far end where the Manitou-peepagee comes down over a rock-spiked forty-foot pitch. This was my lake at last, even to the black duck that came out of the shadows of a cove to fly clear against the sky and drop down on rigid wings with feet outstretched for a landing. In our millpond it was a kingfisher.

Then, for no reason that I understood, I paddled ashore, built a fire and made myself a pail of tea. And there was the big tree, not the elm that stood by the old millpond, but a tall white pine just where it ought to be. I knew then I had found the place I had always wanted to be.

After a while I headed on my way, but, when I pulled out for the carry at the head of the lake and looked back, I knew I would one day return. The fact is, I was back in a week and I pitched my tent in the clearing and worked out of Cache Lake on my job of cruising the timber country. The longer I stayed the better I liked the lake and after a while I began thinking about giving it a name, for by then I had a feeling that it belonged to me. It could be called a lot of pleasant names and all of them would fit, but I liked "Cache" because here was stored the best the north had to give: fine timber to build a cabin and keep a man warm, fish and game and berries for food, and the kind of peace and contentment that is found only in the woods. Where you store your belongings in the north, the things you can't live without, that's a cache. I could think of no better name.

Cache Lake brought me luck, for I hadn't been there long when I learned that Chief Tibeash, a Cree Indian I had known years before when my father and I came north to fish, was living on Shining Tree Lake about two miles from my camp. It was a meeting, I can tell you, for I had lost track of the Chief when we moved to another part of the country and many a time after I came back to the north again I had tried to get trace of him. But Indians don't leave forwarding addresses.

I was young and green when I first met the Chief and in those days I thought I knew the ways of the woods, but it didn't take me long to realize that I couldn't see much more than a puppy when his eyes open. Not until I traveled the woods with the Chief for several summers did I know the real meaning of a newly bent blade of grass, a broken twig, or water slowly oozing into a hoof-print in the mud. I hadn't learned to see an animal standing motionless in the woods, much less catch the quick movement at the moment of its escape. But the Chief saw it all. With him I learned to use my eyes and my nose and my ears in ways only the woods people know. Here in the clean air of the forest the sense of smell becomes keen and in time you learn to detect many things, lynx and bear, moose and other animals, by their scents. Gradually the eyes learn to see and the ears to hear, for every sound in the wilderness has a meaning, be it the faint rustle of a deer mouse in dry grass or the quavering howl of a timber wolf.

Chief Tibeash is not the kind of Indian you might picture. He is small and lean and his muscles are as tough and strong as a rawhide thong. The warm brown of dry pine spills is the color of his skin, and the many fine lines about his eyes come from years of squinting across glaring snow and ice and shining water. You might expect his eyes to be dark, but they are gray and keen. If you could summon his ancestors back it wouldn't surprise me if you would find among the darker skins a fine looking *voyageur*[1] with gray eyes. The Chief figures he is about seventy now. His mother told him that he was born in "the winter of the deep snows," which could be any one of many winters up here, so he can't be sure. But his age doesn't matter, for he is faster on the trail and can last longer in a canoe than many a younger man. He still takes a hundred-pound pack over a five-mile portage without stopping to rest.

It was the Chief who showed me how to handle a canoe like an Indian with the short stroke that begins at the waist and ends with a thrust from the shoulders and never tires. The proudest moment of my early years in the woods was when I was taken for an Indian because of the way I worked my paddle. I learned to live in shelters made from what came to hand in the woods and to know and use the natural foods of the wilderness. It was the Chief who helped me to make my first hunting sled and taught me to drive a dog team. I helped him tan deer and moose hides and make them into moccasins. Now I was back with him again as though there had been no space of years since I had seen Chief Tibeash.

---

[1] *voyageur:* a man employed by a fur company to transport goods and men to and from remote stations, principally by boat

When I finished cruising the timber and started out to make my report to the company, I promised the Chief I would come back someday, but right then I didn't know just when it would be. Well, when the company people got my report they asked me how I would like to make a permanent camp on Cache Lake and keep watch over the timber country. It didn't take me more than two breaths to say I would take the job and be glad to have it. All I asked was that they send in tools, spikes, and tar paper roofing to build a log cabin, and supplies to keep me fit through the winter. That they did with a large hand, including good windows for the cabin, two stoves and plenty of pipe.

The stuff came in three freight canoes and the six young fellows that brought it stayed on to help me build the cabin, for by then it was late October and we had no time to lose before the snow came. The way those men went to work getting out logs, singing and yelling as they cut, was a caution. We used white pine for the walls and tamarack for the roof timbers. Green logs mean you must watch the chinking, for they open up as they dry, but winter was coming and we couldn't wait for them to season, a process which takes at least six months.

While the boys cut and placed the logs the Chief and I brought in plenty of sphagnum moss and gray clay for chinking, and in two weeks the cabin was closed in with the roof on. I found enough down timber that was dry to make the floor of hand-squared logs. A pretty sight it is to watch a man, who knows how to use an adz, square a timber almost as straight as if it was sawed. They did a fine job of fitting.

The boys stayed on to cut twenty cords of firewood, for no man in his right mind faces a north woods winter without having his wood cut and stacked. Mostly wood is cut in the winter and yarded to season until the fall. In that way you can take your time and choose the weather. But cutting wood day by day to keep warm when the temperature drops to the bottom of the thermometer is something I don't like to think about. When the crew left, all the Chief and I had to do was to finish the inside of my home and make it snug with bunks, tables, and chairs.

The site I chose for my cabin is on a knoll and from my window I can look out across the lake and over the ridge to hills far beyond. Tall jack pines lift high above my roof, and down in the marshy ground along the lake's edge to the south fish-net willows grow side by side with alder and high bush cranberries.

One of the things that means a lot to me at Cache Lake is my spring which lies back a little way in the woods just north of the cabin. I have always had a soft spot in my heart for springs. In a great valley I have run across a spring forty feet wide with water bubbling up under pressure. I have even cooked eggs in a pool so hot the water would scald you, and on one occasion I saw a spring of cold, sweet water in a hollow in the rocks on a tiny island far out in the ocean. But above all I love the little springs that are hidden in the moist and shadowed places in the north woods.

Paths to springs are not laid out by men. They choose their own way, twisting between trees, side-stepping rocks, and skirting marshy places. So it is with the path to my spring, for roots, lightly covered by moss, lie in wait to catch your toe, and when bruised on hot summer days give off the pleasant scent of spruce or balsam sap. You walk on through a patch of sphagnum moss, soft and heavy with water, and if you look you find the little star-shaped tufts that grow between the rocks, green on top and brown below. Everywhere balsam and spruce seedlings, some of them only a few inches high, are fighting their way toward the sky that shows in little patches through the tops of the trees high above, but in this struggle for survival only a few will grow up to feel the warmth of the sun. And overhead from the dead branches long whisps of gray moss hang like the beards of old, old men.

Suddenly from under your feet a bird startles up into the air and is gone before you hardly have a chance to see it, although there is no mistaking the sound of a partridge, and maybe a little further on a fool hen will lumber into the air and light on a low spruce limb where you could knock it over if you wanted to. I have flushed hundreds of partridges in my day but my heart always jumps when they whirr off the ground.

A great dead pine blown over by winter winds years ago lies part way into the spring, and in the dark cavern under its roots where the soil still clings, a hole shows where a chipmunk makes its home. All about it are ferns—thin, pale fronds that reach up only a few inches—and a little way beyond, where there is too much shade for their good, are a few thin raspberry bushes.

Going to my spring you walk from open pine woods into a quiet world of green shadows and broken sunbeams where life begins with little seedlings and ends in sodden boles resting under blankets of moss, slowly sinking into the dark soil from which they once lifted their heads to the sun. There is beauty even in decay.

The first sign that you are close to the spring is a granite boulder which shoulders its way out of the moss. Here, close to one side of the big stone, you come upon a pool, clear, cool, and sweet. When your eyes get used to looking down you see grains of white sand jumping up like little fountains where the water comes in. The stream that carries the run-off is only a few inches wide, but further along it nourishes skunk cabbage and marsh plants as it makes its way toward the lake below.

Then if you glance up and away to the east where the ground begins to rise again you think you are looking into a smoky haze, but it is only the gray trunks of the spruce standing close in the dim light. And when you turn back, if it happens to be early June, lady's-slippers will be growing in a cool, shady place that gets just a little sun. And in mid-summer on the higher ground where the pine needles are deep, Indian pipes stand like little groups of ivory statues.

I had been living on Cache Lake for several years when one June day the plane that the company kept to patrol the timber limits dropped down on the lake and brought in a young fellow who was making his living by drawing and photographing wild animals and birds. And a first rate artist he was. His name was Henry—we called him Hank—and the letter he brought from the company asked me to be neighborly and make him at home for as long as he wanted to stay. I was glad to have this new friend who came loaded with drawing paper, pencils and ink, several cameras, and gear enough to keep him going for a long time.

The Chief took a strong liking to Hank and the three of us had a good summer. It was so good Hank decided he would stay on, so the Chief and I turned to and helped him build a cabin over on Beaver Tail Lake, which is about two miles to the east of me, and a mighty sightly place.

The Cache Lake country is a land of rolling hills, none of them very high, with more lakes and streams than can easily be counted. It is a country of heavy forest, broken by muskegs and swamps where the black spruce grows. There is fine timber, white pine the best of all, and big hemlocks with the twigs on top that usually point to the east. Hundreds of square miles are covered with banksian pine, which we call jack pine, and others know as Labrador or Hudson Bay pine. It is one of the trees that comes back after a forest fire, for they say its seeds sprout faster if the cones have been scorched. And everywhere you go there is plenty of spruce and balsam, that good tree which provides man with a bed to sleep on and gum to heal wounds or to cover the seams of birch bark canoes.

Up on the sandy ridge the quaking aspen grows, and when the soft breeze blows on the leaves they make a whispering sound. The Chief calls them "the trees that talk to themselves." And on the slopes of these whispering hills you find poplar and white birch, "the ladies of the woods." The Indians call it canoe birch, for it provides them with bark for canoes and from it they also make good paddles, snowshoe frames, and sleds. In the swamps, some of them many miles across and lonely, the feathery tamarack stand in close ranks, and there is no finer cover for deer and moose than the cedar that grows in the lowland.

Up in the northwest is Faraway See Hill, the highest point of land anywhere around here. It was used by the Indians as a lookout for generations, for Cache Lake lies on one of the ancient highways of the north, and from my cabin on the knoll I like to look down on the lake and imagine the scenes of the old days when big canoes and dog trains passed this way and became part of the rich history of the great fur trade of the north country.

After I had been living at Cache Lake about two years, a geologist came by and stopped in for the night as men do up here. They always know they are welcome. He was making a study of the minerals of the country and knew a lot about how these northern lakes and rivers were formed. I took him up on Faraway See Hill and, looking down on Cache Lake, he told me he was sure that my lake had been formed by beaver works hundreds, maybe thousands, of years ago, and that the narrows between Cache Lake and Snow Goose Lake was where the great beaver dams had been built centuries before.

When the ice went out a year ago and scarred the banks in the narrows I found an old, yellowed beaver tooth sticking out of the soil. Likely as not, he told me, if I dug deep I would find the sticks of the beaver dam preserved in the mud and water.

Long before men ever thought of flood control, which you hear so much about today, beavers were at work. Behind their dams the soil brought down by the water settled in the low places and began to build up rich land. The fact is, my friend said, some of the finest farming land on this continent was made by beavers. Until I began studying their history I had never heard that beavers were plentiful ages ago in Europe and Asia. The kind we have in this country is a close relative of the European species and they tell me our beaver is even kin to the squirrel family.

From that welcome day in spring when the rivers break the icy thongs of winter, and flow free and wild, until the last leaf skitters down in late October, Cache Lake country is a land of ever-changing color and activity. The sifting rains of April release again the scents of rich earth, brown wood, and sodden leaves, and soon fresh grass shows in the clearings and the buds on the trees burst their winter sheaths. The Canada geese and the ducks, heading north, drop down to feed in the lakes that steal their color from the sharp blue sky. Then the singing birds come back from the south. May brings the peepers singing in the swamps and birds getting ready to nest in June, when the young animals will be out exploring their new world for the first time. Summer comes with a rush, bringing long, hot days to help plant life blossom and ripen its seeds. The mosquitoes and black flies are at their worst when July comes along, and you know August is here when the drowsy warmth of dog days raises the acid odor of rotting pine spills while heat waves dance in the hazy woods. It is not a pleasant smell to some to be sure, for it's the odor of rotting vegetation turning back to the earth from which it first came.

Almost before you know it the blueberries are ripening in the clearings and in other places, especially where the land has been cut over, raspberries hang like rubies in the sunlight. About that time, if you know where to look, juicy blackberries can be found too.

Late in August when the leaves of the poplars stir with the sound of a host of fluttering wings, you may feel the first cool breath of early autumn in the night air. Now the summer foliage slowly turns to crimson and gold, a violet haze dims the far hills and the blue lakes turn to silver.

To me there is something almost comical about the first flurry of snow that comes usually in September. It's the way the clumsy big flakes float down, dipping and rising as if afraid to hit the ground. But they are not timid very long. In another month the snow has gained experience and the flakes, small and solid, drive down in close slanting lines, sure of where they are going and the job they have to do in the winter months ahead.

I like the feeling of danger in the cold autumn air that carries a quiet warning that winter is on the way and that time is running short. You would best be prepared for Pawatchicananum, the Whirlwind Moon of December, and Kushapawasticanum, January's Moon of the Great Cold, and Kichi, the Big Moon that rides the February sky.

There's no mistaking the signs of the first heavy storm of December. An old friend of mine used to say: "Snow like meal, snow a great deal." And that is pretty nearly always true, for when I hear the peculiar whispering of fine snow sifting down through the still air when the temperature is up around the freezing mark, I stack more wood on the porch and get ready to hole up for a few days. As the storm tucks the woods under its heavy white blanket the temperature is apt to fall, and when the weather clears it may be far below zero.

Some folks say the north is savage and a heartless country. In a way that is true, for winter shows little feeling for the man who takes no steps to prepare for its heavy snow and ice and the fury of its bitter winds. Here in the big winds the strong win and the weak lose, which, to be fair to the north, is the way folks everywhere work out life among themselves.

The white silence that closes down on the woods in winter like some kind of fog is strangely different from the hush of summer, when there are soft sounds that cannot be denied even though it may seem quiet. But when deep snow blankets the land and ice holds it in its rigid grip, there are few things left from which sound can escape except the wild creatures and the cracking of frost in the trees. So when the brittle silence of winter is broken by a noise it seems louder and is the more startling.

The Old Lady in the Clouds[1] is generous when she starts plucking her geese and in normal years we are likely to have five feet of snow in the woods where the wind can't blow it away or pack it hard. And in low and sheltered places I have seen it actually twenty feet deep. On the waterways where the strong winds keep it moving the snow is seldom very deep and its surface, beaten hard by the winds, is fine for traveling.

After a heavy storm with little wind, snow burdens the trees and great snow bosses[2] form between the branches of the spruce and balsam, while the slender cedar saplings in the swamps give up the fight and bow their heads to the ground. Many of them never quite straighten out again. Every stump becomes a gigantic white toadstool and in some open places the wind makes beautiful ripples on the snow like the marks of waves on a sandy beach. Along the streams where rabbits girdle the willows, the marks of their sharp teeth may be ten feet above the ground when spring carries the snow away.

Questions and Comments

1. What kind of work does the author say he was involved in when he discovered Cache Lake?

2. What is the feeling the author experiences as he views the lake? What is his explanation of this feeling?

3. Why does the author call the lake that he discovers Cache Lake?

4. Why does the author say that Cache Lake brought him luck?

[1] *The Old Lady in the Clouds:* the heroine of a popular tale of the Plains Indians of North America
[2] *bosses:* smooth mounds

5. Who is the Chief? What does the author say he learned from the Chief?

6. The author says, "Paths to springs are not laid out by men." What does he mean?

7. Why does a geologist come to Cache Lake? What is his explanation of the formation of Cache Lake?

8. Why does the author say that Cache Lake is "a land of ever changing color and activity"?

9. Why does the author agree that the North can be a "savage and a heartless country"?

Word Study

1. It would be hard to visualize a nature scene like that described on page 117——"a dark and deep neck of still water with *muskeg* and *tamarack* on the west side and heavy *spruce* on the east where the ground rises"——without knowing what muskeg, tamarack, and spruce are. Other nature nouns in the selection that possibly may be unfamiliar are *boles* (the white boles of big canoe birches); *kingfisher* (the duck of Cache Lake replaced the kingfisher of the millpond at home); *spills* (the Chief's skin was the color of dry pine spills); *sphagnum moss* (good for chinking); *skunk cabbage, lady's slipper,* and *Indian pipes* (all signs of spring); *banksian pine* (a jack pine); *peepers* (that sing in the swamps). Show that you can identify what the italicized words name.

2. What part of a canoe are its *gunwales?* Look up the word and show the relationship between *gun* and *gunwales.*

3. The boys that helped the author build his cabin used an *adz* to "square a timber almost as straight as if it was sawed." Exactly what is an adz?

4. The same boys cut twenty *cords* of firewood for the author. How big a pile of firewood did they provide?

Composition

1. At one point in the selection the author compares the mist hanging from trees to big cobwebs. Much of the poetic effect of this selection is created by the author's use of apt and often strikingly beautiful comparisons. Point out several such comparisons and discuss the effect you feel the author was striving for through his use of them.

2. The author says that in the North, like everywhere else, "the strong win and the weak lose." Discuss your opinion of this belief and tell why you do or do not agree with the author.

3. Compare the relative merits of living in a city and living in an isolated spot like Cache Lake. State your own preference and the reasons for your choice.

Aviator, writer, philosopher—Antoine de Saint-Exupéry has given to the world a vivid account of his experiences as a flier. Several volumes resulted from his adventures as a mail pilot—*Southern Mail, Night Flight,* and *Wind, Sand and Stars. Flight to Arras* grew out of his World War II service with the French Air Force. He died while on a flying expedition during that war.

This poetic description of a violent storm which Saint-Exupéry encountered over the Patagonian Argentine, a barren region between the Andes Mountains and the Atlantic Ocean, is from *Wind, Sand and Stars.*

THE ELEMENTS

Antoine de Saint-Exupéry

I HAD taken off from the field at Trelew and was flying down to Comodoro-Rivadavia, in the Patagonian Argentine. Here the crust of the earth is as dented as an old boiler. The high-pressure regions over the Pacific send the winds past a gap in the Andes into a corridor fifty miles wide through which they rush to the Atlantic in a strangled and accelerated buffeting that scrapes the surface of everything in their path. The sole vegetation visible in this barren landscape is a plantation of oil derricks looking like the after-effects of a forest fire. Towering over the round hills on which the winds have left a residue of stony gravel, there rises a chain of prow-shaped, saw-toothed, razor-edged mountains stripped by the elements down to the bare rock.

For three months of the year the speed of these winds at ground level is up to a hundred miles an hour. We who flew

the route knew that once we had crossed the marshes of Trelew and had reached the threshold of the zone they swept,
we should recognize the winds from afar by a grey-blue tint
in the atmosphere at the sight of which we would tighten
our belts and shoulder-straps in preparation for what was
coming. From then on we had an hour of stiff fighting and
of stumbling again and again into invisible ditches of air.
This was manual labor, and our muscles felt it pretty much
as if we had been carrying a longshoreman's load. But it
lasted only an hour. Our machines stood up under it. We had
no fear of wings suddenly dropping off. Visibility was generally good, and not a problem. This section of the line was
a stint, yes; it was certainly not a drama.

But on this particular day I did not like the color of the
sky.

The sky was blue. Pure blue. Too pure. A hard blue sky
that shone over the scraped and barren world while the
fleshless vertebrae of the mountain chain flashed in the sunlight. Not a cloud. The blue sky glittered like a new-honed
knife. I felt in advance the vague distaste that accompanies
the prospect of physical exertion. The purity of the sky upset me. Give me a good black storm in which the enemy is
plainly visible. I can measure its extent and prepare myself
for its attack. I can get my hands on my adversary. But
when you are flying very high in clear weather the shock of
a blue storm is as disturbing as if something collapsed that
had been holding up your ship in the air. It is the only time
when a pilot feels that there is a gulf beneath his ship.

Another thing bothered me. I could see on a level with
the mountain peaks not a haze, not a mist, not a sandy fog,
but a sort of ash-colored streamer in the sky. I did not like
the look of that scarf of filings scraped off the surface of the
earth and borne out to sea by the wind. I tightened my leather
harness as far as it would go and I steered the ship with one
hand while with the other I hung on to the longeron[1] that

---

[1] *longeron:* part of the framing of the fuselage

ran alongside my seat. I was still flying in remarkably calm air.

Very soon came a slight tremor. As every pilot knows, there are secret little quiverings that foretell your real storm. No rolling, no pitching. No swing to speak of. The flight continues horizontal and rectilinear. But you have felt a warning drum on the wings of your plane, little intermittent rappings scarcely audible and infinitely brief, little cracklings from time to time as it there were traces of gunpowder in the air.

And then everything round me blew up.

Conerning the next couple of minutes I have nothing to say. All that I can find in my memory is a few rudimentary notions, fragments of thoughts, direct observations. I cannot compose them into a dramatic recital because there was no drama. The best I can do is to line them up in a kind of chronological order.

In the first place, I was standing still. Having banked right in order to correct a sudden drift, I saw the landscape freeze abruptly where it was and remain jiggling on the same spot. I was making no headway. My wings had ceased to nibble into the outline of the earth. I could see the earth buckle, pivot—but it stayed put. The plane was skidding as if on a toothless cogwheel.

Meanwhile I had the absurd feeling that I had exposed myself completely to the enemy. All those peaks, those crests, those teeth that were cutting into the wind and unleashing its gusts in my direction, seemed to me so many guns pointed straight at my defenseless person. I was slow to think, but the thought did come to me that I ought to give up altitude and make for one of the neighboring valleys where I might take shelter against a mountainside. As a matter of fact, whether I liked it or not I was being helplessly sucked down towards the earth.

Trapped this way in the first breaking waves of a cyclone about which I learned, twenty minutes later, that at sea level it was blowing at the fantastic rate of one hundred and fifty miles an hour, I certainly had no impression of tragedy. Now, as I write, if I shut my eyes, if I forget the plane and the flight and try to express the plain truth about what was happening to me, I find that I felt weighed down, I felt like a porter carrying a slippery load, grabbing one object in a jerky movement that sent another slithering down, so that, overcome by exasperation, the porter is tempted to let the whole load drop. There is a kind of law of the shortest distance to the image, a psychological law by which the event to which one is subjected is visualized in a symbol that represents its swiftest summing up: I was a man who, carrying a pile of plates, had slipped on a waxed floor and let his scaffolding of porcelain crash.

I found myself imprisoned in a valley. My discomfort was not less, it was greater. I grant you that a down current has never killed anybody, that the expression "flattened out by a down current" belongs to journalism and not to the language of flyers. How could air possibly pierce the ground? But here I was in a valley at the wheel of a ship that was three-quarters out of my control. Ahead of me a rocky prow swung to left and right, rose suddenly high in the air for a second like a wave over my head, and then plunged down below my horizon.

Horizon? There was no longer a horizon. I was in the wings of a theatre cluttered up with bits of scenery. Vertical, oblique, horizontal, all of plane geometry was awhirl. A hundred transversal valleys were muddled in a jumble of perspectives. Whenever I seemed about to take my bearings a new eruption would swing me round in a circle or send me tumbling wing over wing and I would have to try all over again to get clear of all this rubbish. Two ideas came into my mind. One was a discovery: for the first time I understood the cause of certain accidents in the mountains when no fog was present to explain them. For a single second, in a waltzing landscape like this, the flyer had been unable to distinguish between vertical mountainsides and horizontal planes. The other idea was a fixation: The sea is flat: I shall not hook anything out at sea.

I banked—or should I use that word to indicate a vague and stubborn jockeying through the east-west valleys? Still nothing pathetic to report. I was wrestling with chaos, was wearing myself out in a battle with chaos, struggling to keep in the air a gigantic house of cards that kept collapsing despite all I could do. Scarcely the faintest twinge of fear went through me when one of the walls of my prison rose suddenly like a tidal wave over my head. My heart hardly skipped a beat when I was tripped up by one of the whirling eddies of air that the sharp ridge darted into my ship. If I felt anything unmistakably in the haze of confused feelings and notions that came over me each time one of these powder magazines blew up, it was a feeling of respect. I respected that sharp-toothed ridge. I respected that peak. I respected that dome. I respected that transversal valley opening out into my valley and about to toss me God knew how violently as soon as its torrent of wind flowed into the one on which I was being borne along.

What I was struggling against, I discovered, was not the wind but the ridge itself, the crest, the rocky peak. Despite my distance from it, it was the wall of rock I was fighting with. By some trick of invisible prolongation, by the play of a secret set of muscles, this was what was pummeling me. It was against this that I was butting my head. Before me on the right I recognized the peak of Salamanca, a perfect cone which, I knew, dominated the sea. It cheered me to think I was about to escape out to sea. But first I should have to wrestle with the gale off that peak, try to avoid its down-crushing blow. The peak of Salamanca was a giant. I was filled with respect for the peak of Salamanca.

There had been granted me one second of respite. Two seconds. Something was collecting itself into a knot, coiling itself up, growing taut. I sat amazed. I opened astonished eyes. My whole plane seemed to be shivering, spreading outward, swelling up. Horizontal and stationary it was, yet lifted before I knew it fifteen hundred feet straight into the air in a kind of apotheosis. I who for forty minutes had not been able to climb higher than two hundred feet off the ground was suddenly able to look down on the enemy. The plane quivered as if in boiling water. I could see the wide waters of the ocean. The valley opened out into this ocean, this salvation.—And at that very moment, without any warning whatever, half a mile from Salamanca, I was suddenly struck straight in the midriff by the gale off that peak and sent hurtling out to sea.

There I was, throttle wide open, facing the coast. At right angles to the coast and facing it. A lot had happened in a single minute. In the first place, I had not flown out to sea. I had been spat out to sea by a monstrous cough, vomited out of my valley as from the mouth of a howitzer.[1] When, what seemed to me instantly, I banked in order to put myself where I wanted to be in respect of the coast-line, I saw that the coast-line was a mere blur, a characterless strip of blue; and I was five miles out to sea. The mountain range stood up like a crenelated fortress against the pure sky while the cyclone crushed me down to the surface of the waters. How hard that wind was blowing I found out as soon as I tried to climb, as soon as I became conscious of my disastrous mistake: throttle wide open, engines running at my maximum, which was one hundred and fifty miles an hour, my plane hanging sixty feet over the water, I was unable to budge. When a wind like this one attacks a tropical forest it swirls through the branches like a flame, twists them into corkscrews, and uproots giant trees as if they were radishes. Here, bounding off the mountain range, it was leveling out the sea.

Hanging on with all the power in my engines, face to the coast, face to that wind where each gap in the teeth of the range sent forth a stream of air like a long reptile, I felt

[1] *howitzer:* a short cannon that can be fired at a high angle of elevation

as if I were clinging to the tip of a monstrous whip that was cracking over the sea.

In this latitude the South American continent is narrow and the Andes are not far from the Atlantic. I was struggling not merely against the whirling winds that blew off the east-coast range, but more likely also against a whole sky blown down upon me off the peaks of the Andean chain. For the first time in four years of airline flying I began to worry about the strength of my wings. Also, I was fearful of bumping the sea—not because of the down currents which, at sea level, would necessarily provide me with a horizontal air mattress, but because of the helplessly acrobatic positions in which this wind was buffeting me. Each time that I was tossed I became afraid that I might be unable to straighten out. Besides, there was a chance that I should find myself out of fuel and simply drown. I kept expecting the gasoline pumps to stop priming, and indeed the plane was so violently shaken up that in the half-filled tanks as well as in the gas lines the gasoline was sloshing round, not coming through, and the engines, instead of their steady roar, were sputtering in a sort of dot-and-dash series of uncertain growls.

I hung on, meanwhile, to the controls of my heavy transport plane, my attention monopolized by the physical struggle and my mind occupied by the very simplest thoughts. I was feeling practically nothing as I stared down at the imprint made by the wind on the sea. I saw a series of great white puddles, each perhaps eight hundred yards in extent. They were running towards me at a speed of one hundred and fifty miles an hour where the down-surging windspouts broke against the surface of the sea in a succession of horizontal explosions. The sea was white and it was green—white with the whiteness of crushed sugar and green in puddles the color of emeralds. In this tumult one wave was indistinguishable from another. Torrents of air were pouring down upon the sea. The winds were sweeping past in giant gusts as when, before the autumn harvests, they blow a great flowing change of color over a wheatfield. Now and again the water went incongruously transparent between the white pools, and I could see a green and black sea-bottom. And then the great glass of the sea would be shattered anew into a thousand glittering fragments.

It seemed hopeless. In twenty minutes of struggle I had not moved forward a hundred yards. What was more, with flying as hard as it was out here five miles from the coast, I wondered how I could possibly buck the winds along the shore, assuming I was able to fight my way in. I was a perfect target for the enemy there on shore. Fear, however, was out of the question. I was incapable of thinking. I was emptied of everything except the vision of a very simple act. I must straighten out. Straighten out. Straighten out.

There were moments of respite, nevertheless. I dare say those moments themselves were equal to the worst storms I had hitherto met, but by comparison with the cyclone they were moments of relaxation. The urgency of fighting off the wind was not quite so great. And I could tell when these intervals were coming. It was not I who moved towards those zones of relative calm, those almost green oases clearly painted on the sea, but they that flowed towards me. I could read clearly in the waters the advertisement of a habitable province. And with each interval of repose the power to feel and to think was restored to me. Then, in those moments, I began to feel I was doomed. Then was the time that little by little I began to tremble for myself. So much so that each time I saw the unfurling of a new wave of the white offensive I was seized by a brief spasm of panic which lasted until the exact instant when, on the edge of that bubbling cauldron, I bumped into the invisible wall of wind. That restored me to numbness again.

Up! I wanted to be higher up. The next time I saw one of those green zones of calm it seemed to me deeper than before and I began to be hopeful of getting out. If I could climb high enough, I thought, I would find other currents in which I could make some headway. I took advantage of the truce to essay a swift climb. It was hard. The enemy had not weakened. Three hundred feet. Six hundred feet. If I could get up to three thousand feet I was safe, I said to myself. But there on the horizon I saw again that white pack unleashed in my direction. I gave it up. I did not want them at my throat again; I did not want to be caught off balance. But it was too late. The first blow sent me rolling over and over and the sky became a slippery dome on which I could not find a footing.

One has a pair of hands and they obey. How are one's orders transmitted to one's hands?

I had made a discovery that horrified me: my hands were numb. My hands were dead. They sent me no message. Probably they had been numb a long time and I had not noticed it. The pity was that I had noticed it, had raised the question. That was serious.

Lashed by the wind, the wings of the plane had been dragging and jerking at the cables by which they were controlled from the wheel, and the wheel in my hands had not ceased jerking a single second. I had been gripping the wheel with all my might for forty minutes, fearful lest the strain snap the cables. So desperate had been my grip that now I could not feel my hands.

What a discovery! My hands were not my own. I looked at them and decided to lift a finger: it obeyed me. I looked away and issued the same order: now I could not feel whether the finger had obeyed or not. No message had reached me. I thought: "Suppose my hands were to open: how would I know it?" I swung my head round and looked again: my hands were still locked round the wheel. Nevertheless, I was afraid. How can a man tell the difference between the sight of a hand opening and the decision to open that hand, when there is no longer an exchange of sensations between the hand and the brain? How can one tell the difference between an image and an act of the will? Better stop thinking of the picture of open hands. Hands live a life of their own. Better not offer them this monstrous temptation. And I began to chant a silly litany which went on uninterruptedly until this flight was over. A single thought. A single image. A single phrase tirelessly chanted over and over again: "I shut my hands. I shut my hands. I shut my hands." All of me was condensed into that phrase and for me the white sea, the whirling eddies, the saw-toothed range ceased to exist. There was only "I shut my hands." There was no danger, no cyclone, no land unattained. Somewhere there was a pair of rubber hands which, once they let go the wheel, could not possibly come alive in time to recover from the tumbling drop into the sea.

I had no thoughts. I had no feelings except the feeling of being emptied out. My strength was draining out of me and so was my impulse to go on fighting. The engines continued their dot-and-dash sputterings, their little crashing noises that were like the intermittent cracklings of a ripping canvas. Whenever they were silent longer than a second I felt as if a heart had stopped beating. There! that's the end. No, they've started up again.

The thermometer on the wing, I happened to see, stood at twenty below zero, but I was bathed in sweat from head to foot. My face was running with perspiration. What a dance! Later I was to discover that my storage batteries had been jerked out of their steel flanges and hurtled up through the roof of the plane. I did not know then, either, that the ribs on my wings had come unglued and that certain of my steel cables had been sawed down to the last thread. And I continued to feel strength and will oozing out of me. Any minute now I should be overcome by the indifference born of utter weariness and by the mortal yearning to take my rest.

What can I say about this? Nothing. My shoulders ached Very painfully. As if I had been carrying too many sacks too heavy for me. I leaned forward. Through a green transparency I saw sea-bottom so close that I could make out all the details. Then the wind's hand brushed the picture away.

In an hour and twenty minutes I had succeeded in climbing to nine hundred feet. A little to the south—that is, on my left—I could see a long trail on the surface of the sea, a sort of blue stream. I decided to let myself drift as far down as that stream. Here where I was, facing west, I was as good as motionless, unable either to advance or retreat. If I could reach that blue pathway, which must be lying in the shelter of something not the cyclone, I might be able to move in slowly to the coast. So I let myself drift to the left. I had the feeling, meanwhile, that the wind's violence had perhaps slackened.

It took me an hour to cover the five miles to shore. There in the shelter of a long cliff I was able to finish my journey south. Thereafter I succeeded in keeping enough altitude to fly inland to the field that was my destination. I was able to stay up at nine hundred feet. It was very stormy, but nothing like the cyclone I had come out of. That was over.

On the ground I saw a platoon of soldiers. They had been sent down to watch for me. I landed near by and we were a whole hour getting the plane into the hangar. I climbed out of the cockpit and walked off. There was nothing to say. I was very sleepy. I kept moving my fingers, but they stayed numb. I could not collect my thoughts enough to decide whether or not I had been afraid. Had I been afraid? I couldn't say. I had witnessed a strange sight. What strange sight? I couldn't say. The sky was blue and the sea was white. I felt I ought to tell someone about it since I was back from so far away! But I had no grip on what I had been through. "Imagine a white sea . . . very white . . . whiter still." You cannot convey things to people by piling up adjectives, by stammering.

You cannot convey anything because there is nothing to convey. My shoulders were aching. My insides felt as if they had been crushed in by a terrible weight. You cannot make drama out of that, or out of the cone-shaped peak of Salamanca. That peak was charged like a powder magazine; but if I said so people would laugh. I would myself. I respected the peak of Salamanca. That is my story. And it is not a story.

Questions and Comments

Like a poet, Saint-Exupéry uses brilliant and startlingly original comparisons to discover the beautiful in the commonplace and the terrifying in the ordinary. Take, for example, his emotionally chilling description of a chain of mountains as "prow-shaped, saw-toothed, razor-edged." His comparisons enable us to see fierce winds as swirling flames, the foam of ocean waves as crushed white sugar, the green of the ocean as emeralds, and the sky as a slippery dome.

Saint-Exupéry relates the unfamiliar to the familiar. For example, he compares the feeling of being at the controls of an airplane during a cyclone to the sensation of a porter carrying a slippery load of luggage, or a man slipping on a waxed floor while carrying a pile of porcelain plates.

The poetic images and comparisons help the reader see and feel what Saint-Exupéry himself experienced—and give the selection its dramatic impact.

1. What words in the first paragraph help to give an ominous tone to the selection?

2. What is the author ordinarily prepared for in the region in which he is flying? What does he see that disturbs him on this particular day? Why does he say "Give me a good black storm"?

3. What does the author compare himself to when he tries to express the "plain truth" about what was happening to him? What feeling experienced by the author does the comparison help to convey to the reader?

4. While the author is being buffeted, tossed, and tumbled about by the cyclone, two ideas come into his mind. The first he calls a "discovery" and the second he calls a "fixation." What does he mean by each of these terms?

5. The author says, "The valley opened out into this ocean, this salvation." Why is the statement an ironical one? What is the effect of the sentence that follows it?

6. The author observes directly the effect of the ordeal on his own body, his own physical condition. How do such observations help to convey the impression of the cyclone's violence? Point out several such passages.

7. What discovery does the author make about his hands? What does he mean by "They sent me no message"? How is he able to test and prove this fact?

8. As he clings to his wheel, what phrase does he chant over and over again? What effect does the chanting have on his sense of peril?

9. In the next to the last paragraph the author asks the question "Had I been afraid?" From his description of the ordeal, do you think he was afraid? If not, what emotions do you think he was experiencing? Cite evidence from the text to support your answer.

10. When the author says "I was back from so far away," is he talking about mileage? What does he mean?

Word Study

1. The author uses many terms from the world of plane geometry to describe what he was seeing as his plane tumbled wing over wing. Explain the meaning of the italicized words in the following excerpt from the selection: "I was in the wings of a theater cluttered up with bits of scenery. *Vertical, oblique, horizontal,* all of plane geometry was awhirl. A hundred *transversal* valleys were muddled in a jumble of *perspectives.*"

2. The word *chronological* comes from two Greek words, *chronos* meaning "time" and *logos* meaning "word" or "account." What are some other words we have formed from *chronos?* From *logos?*

3. The word *apotheosis* has been formed from the Greek word *theos* meaning "god." Explain the meaning of *apotheosis*

(lifted fifteen hundred feet straight into the air in a kind of apotheosis). What are some other words we have formed from *theos?*

4. Give the meaning of these flying terms: *bank, roll, pitch, drift.*

5. Tell the meaning of the italicized words: *residue* (the winds left a residue of gravel), *honed* (a new-honed knife), *intermittent* (intermittent rappings scarcely audible and infinitely brief), *rudimentary* (a few rudimentary notions), *crenelated* (a crenelated fortress), *incongruously* (the water went incongruously transparent), *litany* (chant a silly litany), *flanges* (the storage batteries had been jerked out of their steel flanges).

Composition

1. When a writer describes inanimate objects in terms of human characteristics, the technique is called *personification.* The author of this selection repeatedly refers to the cyclone as if it were human. He calls it the "enemy." Discuss the author's use of personification and tell what human characteristics you feel the author attributed to the cyclone.

2. Perhaps you have been caught in a sudden storm, awesome in its suddenness and violence. Describe the event and your reactions.

3. Before telling the story given here, the author makes this statement: "The reason why writers fail when they attempt to evoke horror is that horror is something invented after the fact, when one is re-creating the experience over again in the memory. Horror does not manifest itself in the world of reality." Tell whether or not you agree with this statement, if possible giving an illustration from your own experience.

Acts of courage fill us with admiration and may inspire us. When great courage is revealed in a very young person, it can become even more memorable.

At the age of sixteen John Gunther, Jr. was stricken with an incurable brain tumor. Weak, partially disabled, and suffering from the pain of his affliction, Johnny was nevertheless determined to attend his graduation exercises at Deerfield Academy. Within a month after his graduation, he died.

The following selection is a father's portrayal of one of the most triumphant yet heartbreaking moments in the tragically brief life of his son.

from DEATH BE NOT PROUD

John Gunther

WE DROVE to Deerfield on May 27, and Johnny graduated on June 4, though he had not been to school for fourteen months. The days passed in a proud procession, and I think probably it was the happiest week of his life.

It seemed chilly when we started, and Johnny, as always extracting compensation out of any ill fortune, said, "Well, at least we don't have a heat wave." We passed through Hartford and he asked, "Were you here when you did your research?—I wouldn't dream of asking how long you stayed, probably half an hour." I was full of nerves as we got near Deerfield with its stiff old houses and great fanlike elms, and impatiently I asked him if I had overshot the side road and did he recognize any landmarks. He replied gently, "You know I don't see well out of my left eye."

Then without the slightest self-consciousness he took his place in his class. He sat between old friends in the dining hall (the instructors had warned them) and Frances whispered that they should inconspicuously cut his meat if necessary. The boys stared at him for a second as if he were a ghost—of course his hair had not grown back fully after the last operation and he wore a white turban—and then accepted his appearance without question.

Every evening after dinner an informal ceremony takes place at Deerfield which is one of the distinguishing marks of this magnificent school; each boy from Freshman to Senior meets with Mr. Boyden, and the roll of the entire school is called. The boys are heaped together on the floor. Usually there is a casualty or two—some youngsters hurt in a football game—for whom there are big leather chairs. Johnny eased himself into one of these, and his name was called in the roll exactly as if he had never been absent for a moment. Then he limped slowly and proudly to the Senior Dorm where he would have been living this past year, and looked at what should have been his room with a piercing yearning. Boys were moving back and forth in the orderly bustle that precedes commencement. Johnny had the attitude of one who is both a participant in and a spectator of a great event. Mr. Boyden crept up to us and asked if we were sure he would not get too tired. Then he joined calmly in a bull session.

It was decided that he should sleep in the infirmary—a building he knew only too exasperatingly well. The next morning we came to pick him up at what we thought was a reasonable hour. But he had left the building before eight, alone, and was at that moment taking the final exam in chemistry! He passed it B Minus—though he had never taken a regular chemistry course in his life.

Later that day I bumped into him accidentally on the bright sunlit grass as he dragged himself from behind a hedge in shadow. His left shoulder sagged; his arm hung almost useless; his mouth was twisted with effort; the left side of his lip sank down; his eyes were filmy; he was happy. "Oh, pardon me, sir," Johnny said. He had not recognized me, and thought that I was some master he did not know.

Everybody tried hard to keep him from being too active. But he said, "Walking around this way helps the wound heal." Frances told him to sit around in the sun—how they both loved the sun!—and get brown and he answered, "All you are interested in, Mother, is my color!" When he had trouble with knife and fork one evening, he told her in exquisite parody of what she often said, "Be patient. Believe in calmness and Nirvana." It was a lovely day the next day and Johnny spent an hour learning some calculus from a fellow student. He worked out the equations on the bottom of a paper plate during a picnic lunch in the soft grass. Frances remonstrated that he might be getting tired. He replied briefly, "There's no future to just sitting."

The day before graduation was strenuous, with a lunch for the parents at noon and then a baseball game which Johnny watched with serious interest for about four innings. The dress-up banquet that night, to celebrate among other things Mr. Boyden's forty-fifth year as headmaster, lasted three hours; Johnny did not miss a minute of it. He tramped across the lawn afterward, with his classmate Henry Eisner holding his hand, for the off-the-record talk Mr. Boyden gives each graduating class. Then the class, standing under the trees in a night grown chilly, serenaded the Boydens on the front porch. Johnny, on the outskirts of the massed pack of boys, looked suddenly exhausted, and I slipped away from the adults to join him inconspicuously, standing just behind him. He did not mind, though as a rule he loathed having us anywhere near him at school. I was afraid he might fall. Then I heard his light, silvery tenor chime in with the other voices. The song floated across the lawn and echoed back. We hiked to the infirmary and Johnny ran into a classmate who had won an award. "Congratulations!" he snapped briskly.

The next morning the boys assembled early for the quarter-mile walk to the white-frame Deerfield church, arranging themselves four abreast in order of their height. I did not think Johnny could manage such a march. He shook us off and disappeared. The procedure is that the boys, reaching the church, line up behind the pews, and then walk one by one down the center aisle, as each name is called. Mr. Flynt, the president of the board of trustees, then shakes hands with each boy, giving him his diploma in the left hand. We explained that Johnny might not be able to grasp the smooth roll of diploma with his left fingers, and asked Mr. Flynt to try to slip it into the right hand instead. The boys began to march in slowly, and though Johnny should have been conspicuous with his white bandage, we did not see him and I was in an agony fearing that he had fallen out. Mr. Boyden, sweeping the assembly with his all-embracing sharp affectionate glance, caught Frances's eye and nodded to her reassuringly. One by one the names were called out, and each boy disassociated himself from the solid group and marched forward alone. The call was alphabetical, and by the time the G's were reached we were limp with suspense, since we did not know for sure that Johnny had even got into the church. As each boy passed down the aisle, there was applause, perfunctory for some, pronounced for others. Gaines, Gillespie, Goodwin, Griffin, Gunther. Slowly, very slowly, Johnny stepped out of the mass of his fellows and trod by us, carefully keeping in the exact center of the long aisle, looking neither to the left nor the right, but straight ahead, fixedly, with the white bandage flashing in the light through the high windows, his chin up, carefully, not faltering, steady, but slowly, so very slowly. The applause began and then rose and the applause became a storm, as every single person in that old church became whipped up, tight and tense, to see if he would make it. The applause became a thunder, it rose and soared and banged, when Johnny finally reached the pulpit. Mr. Flynt carefully tried to put the diploma in his right hand, as planned. Firmly Johnny took it from the right hand to left, as was proper, and while the whole audience rocked now with release from tension, and was still wildly, thunderously applauding, he passed around to the side and, not seeing us, reached his place among his friends.

That evening we talked of Harvard. Some of the boys were getting their admission notices, and Johnny, now that he had actually been graduated, wondered when his would come. He was impatient. He had a great sense of the passage of time.

Everything that Johnny suffered was in a sense repaid by the few heroic moments of that walk down the center aisle of that church. This was his triumph and indominable summation. Nobody who saw it will ever forget it, or be able to forget the sublime strength of will and character it took.

Questions and Comments

1. What remarks of Johnny's in the second paragraph reveal his optimism?

2. What is the reaction of Johnny's friends when he makes his appearance in the dining hall? What aspects of his appearance made them react in this way?

3. The author accidentally bumps into Johnny one day on the campus. What is so touching about this accidental meeting of father and son?

4. At one point, Johnny remarks, "There's no future to just sitting." In view of the circumstances, what does this reveal about Johnny?

5. What is the effect on spectators as Johnny walks down the aisle of the Deerfield church to accept his diploma?

6. The author refers to Johnny's acceptance of the diploma as his son's "triumph and indomitable summation." What does he mean?

Word Study

1. Try to determine the meaning of the italicized words from the context. Check your guesses with dictionary definitions.

   ". . . Frances whispered that they should *inconspicuously* cut his meat if necessary." (page 146)

   "Frances *remonstrated.* . . ." (page 147)

   "As each boy passed down the aisle, there was applause, *perfunctory* for some, pronounced for others." (page 148)

2. Nirvana is a part of Buddhism doctrine. If necessary, look up *Nirvana* and also *parody* in a dictionary so that you can explain the meaning of the following passage: "When he had trouble with knife and fork one evening, he told her in exquisite parody of what she often said, 'Be patient. Believe in calmness and Nirvana.' "

Composition

1. Discuss the tone of this selection and show how the author carefully chose the tone that he felt was most suited to the subject matter of the selection.

2. From a number of remarks made by John Gunther, Jr., the author is able to reveal a good deal about the boy's character. Write a character sketch of John using several of these remarks as a basis for your opinion.

3. Speaking of his son's courageous behavior, the author says that it required "sublime strength of will and character." Give an illustration of similar great courage shown by someone you either know or have read about.

Bad luck affects people in many different ways. Some people are crushed by it; others attain spectacular heights in spite of it. Al Capp, the creator of one of America's best-loved and most widely read comic strips, *Li'l Abner,* suffered a tragic accident at the age of nine. He tells about it in the following selection and explains how, in the years that followed, he learned to live with his handicap.

MY WELL-BALANCED LIFE
ON A WOODEN LEG

Al Capp

I BECAME a candidate for a wooden leg on Aug. 21, 1919, when I was 9 years old. That day my father, a vague and unworldly man, gave me 50¢ to get a haircut: 35¢ for the haircut, 5¢ for a tip, 10¢ for trolley fare. At least that was the way he figured it. I, a calculating and worldly kid, figured it a little differently. I had seen a tantalizing offer on a sign in a downtown New Haven window: "Prof. Amoroso, Barber Academy—Haircuts 15 cents—No Tipping." By hitching a ride on the back of an ice wagon I could step into Professor Amoroso's with 50¢ and, with luck, step out again with most of the money (and possibly some of my scalp) intact. Clutching that 50¢ piece, blinded with dreams of riches and power, I hopped off the ice cart in front of the barber academy—and directly in the path of a huge old-fashioned trolley car. I was caught under the wheels and before the car could be stopped my left leg was severed at the thigh.

During the ride to the hospital and later while I was under anaesthetic, I never once unclutched that half dollar. My mother finally took it from me. For years afterward she kept that coin, the kind of melancholy memento that only mothers understand, in the drawer of her sewing machine. I used to find her now and then, staring into the open drawer and quietly weeping. (A dozen years later, during the Depression and a particularly severe family financial crisis, she opened the drawer again, stared at the coin for the last time, and marched to the grocery store with it.)

Losing a leg at 9 is not all loss. For one thing it made me a celebrity among the other kids, to whom I had previously been merely another vague and grubby menace. True, I was not much good at baseball, wrestling or apple-orchard raiding, but then I never had been much good at them, and now I was spared the embarrassment of displaying my awkwardness. As for grownups, suddenly they noticed spiritual qualities in me as a slow-moving, one-legged boy which had been totally hidden from them when I was a hooting, howling, fast-moving two-legger. Gifts poured in from formerly unenchanted, unprofitable and unheard-of relatives. Yes, at 9, I reveled in the drama and distinction of that shocking pinned-up pants leg and those swagger crutches. With two legs I had been a nobody. With one leg I was somebody.

Then came the day that had been hailed so glowingly by my doctor, my parents and the local wooden leg salesman—the day when I could strap on my new leg and walk around again like everyone else. It was one of the most shattering letdowns of my life. I damn well did *not* walk around like everyone else. I went through weeks of stumbling, of toppling, of aching, cursing and weeping before I mastered the gadget. And still I did not walk around like everyone else. I walked like everyone else who had a wooden leg. I swayed and I dragged.

For a while the other kids were even more fascinated by the wooden leg than they had been by the absence of the real one, and that made a satisfyingly unique figure of me for as long as it lasted. But the novelty wore off and the years wore on. I became a teen-ager with all the routine problems of teen-agers—and one special problem: namely, how to get myself treated by girls in their teens as though I did not have a special problem.

A teen-ager wants more than anything else in life to look, act and be treated like all other teen-agers. On the first two counts I did fine. I am sure that I looked and behaved as oddly as all the other teen-agers at Central High School in Bridgeport, Conn., where I then lived. But I got different and special treatment, especially from the girls, and that made life hell for me. My rooster roughness and rowdiness was forgiven with sweet understanding, when what I wanted was the same thrilled contempt that was accorded two-legged rowdies for the same behavior.

So I took to hanging out on street corners. Every afternoon I would leave the high school world, limp a half-dozen blocks along Main Street, and prop myself against the corner of D. M. Read's store at the city's busiest intersection. I was then in a different world, and I was then a different guy. As long as I stayed in one place, the girls I stared at and whistled at treated me like any other street-corner wise guy —with the exaggerated disdain that a nicely behaved girl uses to tell a boy on a street corner who is not behaving very nicely that she would not dream of acknowledging him because she is terribly interested in him. If a girl did look back invitingly, I would look away, pleased but immobile. On a good afternoon there might be as many as a dozen look-backs and look-aways before the streets thinned out. I would go home delighted, having had a remarkable few hours of being treated ordinarily.

Then one day three teen-age girls stopped for traffic in what was then called a roadster, and I aimed a brassy leer their way. Two of them turned up their noses. But the third and prettiest smiled at me—and then, to my joy and dismay, dropped her school pad over the side and motioned me with an inviting smile to pick up the pad and, possibly, her too. My triumph filled me with panic. If I moved she'd find out. So I stared stonily in the other direction until at last they were forced to move on. When I turned back the pad still lay in the street. I limped over and snatched it up. Inside was a girl's name and address. The address was in Brooklawn, then the best residential section of Bridgeport, an area of great houses, all with verandas—and all with steps.

Now to a man who has lost his leg above the knee, steps are an endless horror. On level ground he can make reasonable progress, striding forward with his good leg and rhythmically swinging the wooden one up behind. On steps, however, he must rise on the good leg, stop, pull up the wooden one, rise again with the good leg—pull and stop, pull and stop. It is a slow and unappealing process, the only experience with my wooden leg that irritates me to this day. When I was a boy, it was a humiliation I'd go to any length to avoid.

But I wanted to meet that girl. I phoned her. She had driven off before I could return the pad, I explained gravely, but I would be glad to deliver it to her tonight. She said that was awfully nice of me and maybe if I had no other plans I could have lemonade with her—say at 7 o'clock? She would be waiting on the porch.

At a quarter to 7 I hurried up the walk to her house. I was deliberately early: if I reached the veranda before her, she would find me seated and would not see me climbing the stairs, or even walking. My plan worked fine, and when she opened the door a few minutes before 7, I was waiting. There was a long pause.

"I'm sorry," she said at last from the doorway. "But I can't see you tonight. I have to go away. Thank you for returning the pad. Please leave it on the chair." She turned back in, and the door closed behind her.

I dropped the pad and hurried down the stairs and away as fast as I could. I never saw her again. It would have been

too much for both of us to bear, for we had both been playing the same game. I had arrived early so she would not see
me walk. She had planned to be waiting on the porch so I
would not see her walk. For in the instant of her turning
away at the door, I had seen the stiffening of her shoulder,
the outthrust movement of her hip—the sure signs that she,
too, of all the sad, shy girls on earth, had an artificial leg.

In time much of my embarrassment about the leg passed.
I discovered that there are three types of wooden leg wear-
ers: one large group, one small group—and me. The great
majority of people with artificial limbs are reasonable people
who treat these appendages with common civility and understanding and give them routine care. They do not deliberately abuse their wooden legs, but they do not go out of their
way to pamper them.

Then there is a small, fanatically dedicated group of
people who regard themselves as appendages to their wooden
legs. They devote their lives to coddling these hunks of wood
and tin. They study body balance and coordination. They
twist their bodies—and their minds—all out of shape to serve
it. I once knew a quiet, bookish, tolerably interesting young
man who lost his leg. Suddenly he changed. Formerly un-
athletic, he now devoted his life to proving that he was as
good a man as anyone with two legs. He challenged his
friends to foot races. He danced like a maniac. He charged
and snorted around like a crazed Arabian steed. He became a crashing bore.

Then there is the third group: me, I buy, use and enjoy
all the marvelous gadgets of the 20th Century, but I believe
their purpose is to serve and understand me, not that mine
is to serve and understand them. So when any gadget which I
have bought, used and enjoyed but do not understand
breaks down, from tie clasp to Cadillac, I abandon it. In the
case of my wooden leg, which I cannot abandon, I ignore it.
The most I will do is pick up any important parts that drop
off and, if I have time, take them around to the nearest
garage for a quick repair job. Otherwise I leave my wooden

leg to shift for itself. It it wants to come where I am going, all it has to do is follow me.

One result of this sort of stern handling is that I am a free man instead of a slave to a gadget. Another is that now and then I become the central figure of bloodcurdling spectacles, when my leg suddenly and totally disintegrates. Sometimes the result is pure slapstick, such as the time when the collapse of my leg kept me, an eager 18-year-old, from making a pass at another 18-year-old of the opposite sex. Sometimes the result is merely pleasant, such as the time in Washington a few years ago when the leg broke down just in time to keep me from hearing a speech by Allen Dulles.

The romantic fiasco occurred while I was living in Boston as a pure but impatient art student at the Museum School. One day I was tipped off by a fellow student, a cad and *bon vivant*[1] who had learned much about life in his travels (mainly after dark, from the girls' dormitory to Reservoir Park in his Marmon roadster), that a quiet, hitherto-unnoticed female art student named Norma necked. Now it was not clear to me what this meant exactly, or where exactly it ended, but I was pretty sure it did not end with a wholesome handshake, the way all of my dates had panned out up to then. So I made a date with Norma. I discovered that she lived in Lynn, a suburb of Boston which was reached by a series of trolley routes and finally by a bus. On the way out I discovered that the last bus going in the other direction came by at 12 sharp. After that there was nothing. I had to make hay by midnight if I was going to catch that bus.

Norma's parents, well mannered but totally out of touch with the dreams of youth, stayed around, fed me lemonade and cookies, and jabbered until after 11, and then with a reminder that tomorrow was a school day for both of us now frantic children, went upstairs to bed.

It was 11:15. I put my arm around Norma. She said, "Let's go out to the porch." We both rose. Then I sat down. Norma

[1] *bon vivant:* one who loves good living

looked at me, puzzled. Then she explained, "It's darker on the porch."

I remained sitting. I had to. My wooden leg was jammed —immovably locked at the knee. I looked all right sitting. Standing, I looked like a crane.

Both Norma and I, frenzied by the inexorable approach of that bus, tugged at that leg, pounded it, yanked it. Aroused by the commotion, Norma's father came down and went at it with a screwdriver and hammer with such vigor that in no time at all the knee joint was separated from the thigh joint, the ankle joint was separated from the knee joint, and the whole mass, including me, was spread in lunatic disorder on the parlor floor.

The bus had long since gone, and so had our golden chance. Norma flounced off to bed and her parents bedded me down on the parlor sofa. The next morning her father gathered my ankle and my knee, my nuts and my bolts, drove them and me in to Boston, and deposited the lot at a wooden leggery.

I called Norma again about three years later, when I had a car and could be sure of getting myself home, intact or in sections, come what may. I could tell that Norma's father, who answered the phone, remembered me, because he said, "Oh, yes, you're the boy who came apart—uh—just a minute, I'll call her to the phone." I then heard Norma being called, my name spoken, and her voice: "Oh, no! Not *him!* Say I've just gone out. We can't go through that again!"

It was 30 years later when my good old unreliable leg rescued me from Allen Dulles. A man who said he was in the State Department called me from Washington. "Mr. Capp," he said, "the President has noticed the increasing hostility toward America all over the world. To counter it he has decided to launch a People-to-People campaign—our people talking plain American sense to the plain people of the rest of the world. He has decided to appoint 41 leaders of American industry and thought as chairmen of committees to carry out this program. The President wants to know if you will accept the chairmanship of the Cartoonists' Committee."

Well, first we had to be checked for security, and then we 41 certified leaders of American industry and thought were invited to Washington to attend a top-secret, high-level briefing on the world situation, beginning with the President at the White House, running through a luncheon with Vice President Nixon, and winding up with a speech at 4 o'clock by Mr. Dulles.

By 4 o'clock we were 41 mighty disturbed leaders of American industry and thought. We had been given the inside dope. We had been told the appalling news that the Communist Conspiracy and the Free World were locked in a mighty struggle for men's minds and, what was even more appalling, we had been told in exactly those words.

As we entered the meeting room to hear the director of our Central Intelligence Agency, I was walking with a large leader of either American industry or thought, I forget which, named Gene Tunney.[1] Suddenly I know I had better not take another step—I had better grab something solid. So I grabbed Gene Tunney. He looked at me, astonished. I looked astonished at my left pants leg. It was empty, flapping in the breeze, and dripping nuts and bolts. A yard behind, teetering crazily on the carpet, was the naked lower half of my wooden leg, still, of course, gruesomely garbed in shoe and sock.

Forty horrified patriots rushed to my rescue. "Capp has broken his leg," went the cry. "Send for an ambulance!"

"The hell with that," I said. "All I need is a broom to sweep up all this loose stuff, a bag to put it in, and a ride to the nearest garage."

The man at the garage said he could screw me together in a few minutes. "Take your time," I said. And so this story

[1] *Gene Tunney:* prizefighter who became world heavyweight champion by defeating Jack Dempsey in 1926

has a happy ending. When I sauntered back into the meeting room, the speech was over. I was, however, provided with a copy of it. Allen Dulles had not minced words. He had stated that the Communist Conspiracy and the Free World were locked in a mighty struggle for men's minds.

As you sway through life on a wooden leg, an odd and blessed thing happens. The rest of the world becomes accustomed, and then forgets that you have one, just as it becomes accustomed to, and then forgets the color of your eyes or whether you wear a vest. And you become accustomed to the limitations of one-legged life, such as not being able to pole-vault or drive a shift car, or being limited to half as much athlete's foot as other people have. But to children a wooden leg is eternally a surprise and a delight. Strange children gape unabashed, ask questions, and fool with it to see how it works. And when the wooden leg is actually in their own family, it is a sparkling source of entertainment.

When my own children were small they used to come into my bedroom while I dressed and fight for the privilege of pulling Poppa's "broken leg" out from under the bed and handing it to him, just as my grandchildren do now. And I have been asked the same questions by two generations of wide-eyed, fascinated little girls.

"Does it hurt, Poppa (or Grandpa)?"

"No, it feels good. See, no matter how hard I hit it with this shoehorn, it doesn't hurt a bit."

Or, in mock terror: "Poppa! You're not going to stick that tack into your leg!"

"I certainly am. It's the best way to keep a sock up on a leg like this one. Garters slip."

For 25 years tiny daughters and granddaughters of mine have been trying to walk like me and have carefully followed me around with one little leg held stiff. My son's reaction was more matter of fact. As a very little boy, he was interested in the mechanics of my leg. When I explained how it worked he instantly lost interest. And small wonder, since the most modern wooden leg is more primitive than a child's simple mechanical toy.

Strange children, like my own children, have always been perfectly straightforward and unembarrassed about my leg. I have responded in kind. "What's the matter with your darn old leg?" they ask.

"It's a wooden leg," I explain.

"Kin I see it?"

I raise my trouser leg a bit and then I go on. It's the best way to handle it, I explain to my startled friends.

But sometimes it is not the best way. One day, walking through Harvard Square in Cambridge, I approached a small boy sitting on the sidewalk, tinkering with a bicycle. He looked up at me without interest and then down with sudden fascination at my left leg.

He rose, staring, to get a better view. It was a creepy sensation, but I just kept walking. As I came up to him he said without lifting his eyes, "Why do you walk so funny?"

I explained why.

"Kin I see it?" said the boy.

I lifted my pants leg and showed it to him. He then went back to his bicycle and I went on with my walk.

The next morning there was the boy again, this time without the bicycle but with another boy. They were waiting for me. "Show it to him," said my friend. I showed it to both of them.

"Let's see you walk on it some more," they said.

"Sure," I said. They followed me for a while, then vanished.

The next morning there were four of them. I tried to turn down a side street, but they spotted me.

"There he is!" yelled my little nemesis. They all dashed after me. Quite a few people glanced our way.

"Show it to them!" screeched the leading little monster. dancing around me.

"Scat!" I said.

"Lift up your pants," he shouted, "and show us all your wooden leg!"

"Some other time," I managed a smile. "I'm in kind of a hurry, fellas."

"LIFT UP YOUR PANTS," they all roared, "AND SHOW US ALL YOUR WOODEN LAAAIG!"

"YOU ALL GET THE HELL OUT OF HERE," I bellowed, "OR I'LL KICK YOU WITH IT."

Nobody talks to Cambridge kids like that and ever sees them again.

Adults, on the other hand, are embarrassed if they are caught looking at my wooden leg. If they are strangers, they look guiltily away. If they are not, they hastily talk about something else. But nobody ever handled the situation with greater aplomb than the waiter to whom I gave my breakfast order as I lay in bed one morning in the Savoy Hotel in London. As he was taking my order, he caught sight of the shoed and stockinged leg that peeped out from under the bed. He stared. Suddenly he realized that I was watching him. He finished writing down the order, then looked me straight in the eye and said, "Very good, sir. And what will the other gentleman have?"

Questions and Comments

1. What were the circumstances under which the author lost his leg?

2. What does the author mean when he says, "Losing a leg at 9 is not all loss"? What did he gain?

3. What does the author refer to as one of the most shattering letdowns of his life?

4. What is the author's "special problem" with regard to teenage girls? What action does he take to overcome it?

5. How does the author get the name and address of the girl in the car? Why is he upset at the prospect of going to her home?

6. Why does the girl refuse to meet the author when he arrives at her house? Why does he make no further effort to see her?

7. What does the author mean when he describes himself as a "free man" rather than a "slave to a gadget"? What does this attitude reveal to you about the character of the author?

8. What is the "odd and blessed thing" that the author claims happens after you have worn a wooden leg for a while?

9. What is the general reaction of children to the author's wooden leg? How does their reaction differ from that of an adult?

Word Study

1. In the first paragraph the author says, "I had seen a tantalizing offer on a sign in a downtown New Haven window." The word *tantalize* has an interesting mythological background. Find the meaning of this word and the mythological tale from which it comes.

2. Some people coddle their wooden legs. How is the meaning of *coddle* as used here related to its meaning as in "coddle eggs"?

3. The author refers to a screeching little monster as his "little nemesis." What does *nemesis* mean? Who was Nemesis in Greek mythology?

4. Try to guess the meaning of the italicized words from the context of the selection. Check your guesses with dictionary definitions.

"If a girl did look back invitingly, I would look away, pleased but *immobile*." (page 153)

"The great majority of people with wooden legs are reasonable people who treat these *appendages* with common civility. . . ." (page 155)

". . . I become the central figure of bloodcurdling spectacles, when my leg suddenly and totally *disintegrates*." (page 156)

"The romantic *fiasco* occurred while I was living in Boston. . . . (page 156)

"Norma *flounced off* to bed. . . ." (page 157)

"Strange children gape *unabashed*. . . ." (page 159)

"But nobody ever handled the situation with greater *aplomb* than the waiter. . . ." (page 160)

Composition

1. Part of the charm of this selection is the casual and humorous way the author treats an unfortunate situation. Cite examples from the selection which reveal the author's approach to his disability and explain how this approach influences the overall tone of the selection.

2. Give your opinion of this statement: "A teen-ager wants more than anything else in life to look, act and be treated like all other teen-agers."

3. Describe how a person you know or have read about attempted to cope with a disability. Explain what you feel to have been the major contributing factor to this person's victory or defeat in his struggle with the disability.

In the following essay, Robert Benchley presents several of his ideas on that necessary evil known as "an appointment with the dentist." Don't be at all surprised if at one or two points in your reading you find yourself squirming and twitching with pangs of self-recognition.

THE TOOTH, THE WHOLE TOOTH, AND NOTHING BUT THE TOOTH

Robert Benchley

SOME well-known saying (it doesn't make much difference what) is proved by the fact that everyone likes to talk about his experiences at the dentist's. For years and years little articles like this have been written on the subject, little jokes like some that I shall presently make have been made, and people in general have been telling other people just what emotions they experience when they crawl into the old red plush guillotine.

They like to explain to each other how they feel when the dentist puts "that buzzer thing" against their bicuspids, and, if sufficiently pressed, they will describe their sensations on mouthing a rubber dam.

"I'll tell you what I hate," they will say with great relish, "when he takes that little nut-pick and begins to scrape. Ugh!"

"Oh, I'll tell you what's worse than that," says the friend, not to be outdone, "when he is poking around careless-like, and strikes a nerve. Wow!"

And if there are more than two people at the experience-meeting, everyone will chip in and tell what he or she considers to be the worst phase of the dentist's work, all present enjoying the narration hugely and none so much as the narrator who has suffered so.

This sort of thing has been going on ever since the first mammoth gold tooth was hung out as a bait to folks in search of a good time. (By the way, when *did* the present obnoxious system of dentistry begin? It can't be so very long ago that the electric auger was invented, and where would a dentist be without an electric auger? Yet you never hear of Amalgam Filling Day, or any other anniversary in the dental year. There must be a conspiracy of silence on the part of the trade to keep hidden the names of the men who are responsible for all this.)

However many years it may be that dentists have been plying their trade, in all that time people have never tired of talking about their teeth. This is probably due to the inscrutable workings of Nature who is always supplying new teeth to talk about.

As a matter of fact, the acutal time and suffering in the chair is only a fraction of the gross expenditure connected with the affair. The preliminary period, about which nobody talks, is much the worse. This dates from the discovery of the wayward tooth and extends to the moment when the dentist places his foot on the automatic hoist which jacks you up into range. Giving gas for tooth-extraction is all very humane in its way, but the time for anaesthetics is when the patient first decides that he must go to the dentist. From then on, until the first excavation is started, should be shrouded in oblivion.

There is probably no moment more appalling than that in which the tongue, running idly over the teeth in a moment of care-free play, comes suddenly upon the ragged edge of a space from which the old familiar filling has disappeared. The world stops and you look meditatively up to the corner of the ceiling. Then quickly you draw your tongue away, and try to laugh the affair off, saying to yourself:

"Stuff and nonsense, my good fellow! There is nothing the matter with your tooth. Your nerves are upset after a hard day's work, that's all."

Having decided this to your satisfaction, you slyly, and with a poor attempt at being casual, slide the tongue back along the line of adjacent teeth, hoping against hope that it will reach the end without mishap.

But there it is! There can be no doubt about it this time. The tooth simply has got to be filled by someone, and the only person who can fill it with anything permanent is a dentist. You wonder if you might not be able to patch it up yourself for the time being,—a year or so—perhaps with a little spruce-gum and a coating of new-skin. It is fairly far back, and wouldn't have to be a very sightly job.

But this has an impracticable sound, even to you. You might want to eat some peanut-brittle (you never can tell when someone might offer you peanut-brittle these days), and the new-skin, while serviceable enough in the case of cream soups and custards, couldn't be expected to stand up under heavy crunching.

So you admit that, since the thing has got to be filled, it might as well be a dentist who does the job.

This much decided, all that is necessary is to call him up and make an appointment.

Let us say that this resolve is made on Tuesday. That afternoon you start to look up the dentist's number in the telephone-book. A great wave of relief sweeps over you when you discover that it isn't there. How can you be expected to make an appointment with a man who hasn't got a telephone? And how can you have a tooth filled without making an appointment? The whole thing is impossible, and that's all there is to it. God knows you did your best.

On Wednesday there is a slightly more insistent twinge, owing to bad management of a sip of ice-water. You decide that you simply must get in touch with that dentist when you get back from lunch. But you know how those things are. First one thing and then another came up, and a man came in from Providence who had to be shown around the office, and by the time you had a minute to yourself it was five o'clock. And anyway, the tooth didn't bother you again. You wouldn't be surprised if, by being careful, you could get along with it as it is until the end of the week when you will have more time. A man has to think of his business, after all, and what is a little personal discomfort in the shape of an unfilled tooth to the satisfaction of work well done in the office?

By Saturday morning you are fairly reconciled to going ahead, but it is only a half day and probably he has no appointments left, anyway. Monday is really the time. You can begin the week afresh. After all, Monday is really the logical day to start in going to the dentist.

Bright and early Monday morning you make another try at the telephone-book, and find, to your horror, that some time between now and last Tuesday the dentist's name and number have been inserted into the directory. There it is. There is no getting around it: "Burgess, Jas. Kendal, DDS. . . . Courtland—2654." There is really nothing left to do but to call him up. Fortunately the line is busy, which gives you a perfectly good excuse for putting it over until Tuesday. But on Tuesday luck is against you and you get a clear connection with the doctor himself. An appointment is arranged for Thursday afternoon at 3:30.

Thursday afternoon, and here it is only Tuesday morning! Almost anything may happen between now and then. We might declare war on Mexico, and off you'd have to go, dentist appointment or no dentist appointment. Surely a man couldn't let a date to have a tooth filled stand in the way of his doing his duty to his country. Or the social revolution might start on Wednesday, and by Thursday the whole town might be in ashes. You can picture yourself standing, Thursday afternoon at 3:30, on the ruins of the City Hall, fighting off marauding bands of Reds, and saying to yourself, with a sigh of relief: "Only to think! At this time I was to have been climbing into the dentist's chair!" You never can tell when your luck will turn in a thing like that.

But Wednesday goes by and nothing happens. And Thursday morning dawns without even a word from the dentist saying that he has been called suddenly out of town to lecture before the Incisor Club. Apparently, everything is working against you.

By this time, your tongue has taken up a permanent resting-place in the vacant tooth, and is causing you to talk indistinctly and incoherently. Somehow you feel that if the dentist opens your mouth and finds the tip of your tongue in the tooth, he will be deceived and go away without doing anything.

The only thing left is for you to call him up and say that you have just killed a man and are being arrested and can't possibly keep your appointment. But any dentist would see through that. He would laugh right into his transmitter at you. There is probably no excuse which it would be possible to invent which a dentist has not already heard eighty or ninety times. No, you might as well see the thing through now.

Luncheon is a ghastly rite. The whole left side of your jaw has suddenly developed an acute sensitiveness and the disaffection has spread to the four teeth on either side of the original one. You doubt if it will be possible for him to touch it at all. Perhaps all he intends to do this time is to look at it anyway. You might even suggest that to him. You could very easily come in again soon and have him do the actual work.

Three-thirty draws near. A horrible time of day at best. Just when a man's vitality is lowest. Before stepping in out of the sunlight into the building in which the dental parlor is, you take one look about you at the happy people scurrying by in the street. Carefree children that they are! What do they know of Life? Probably that man in the silly-looking hat never had trouble with so much as his baby-teeth. There they go, pushing and jostling each other, just as if within ten feet of them there was not a man who stands on the brink of the Great Misadventure. Ah well! Life is like that!

Into the elevator. The last hope is gone. The door clangs and you look hopelessly about you at the stupid faces of your fellow passengers. How can people be so clownish? Of course, there is always the chance that the elevator will fall and that you will all be terribly hurt. But that is too much to expect. You dismiss it from your thoughts as too impractical, too visionary. Things don't work out as happily as that in real life.

You feel a certain glow of heroic pride when you tell the operator the right floor number. You might just as easily have told him a floor too high or too low, and that would, at least, have caused delay. But after all, a man must prove himself a man and the least you can do is to meet Fate with an unflinching eye and give the right floor number.

Too often has the scene in the dentist's waiting-room been described for me to try to do it again here. They are all alike. The antiseptic smell, the ominous hum from the operating-rooms, the ancient *Digests,* and the silent, sullen group of waiting patients, each trying to look unconcerned and cordially disliking everyone else in the room,—all these have been sung by poets of far greater lyric powers than mine. (Not that I really think that they *are* greater than mine, but that's the customary form of excuse for not writing something you haven't got time or space to do. As a matter of fact, I think I could do it much better than it has ever been done before).

I can only say that, as you sit looking, with unseeing eyes, through a large book entitled, "The War in Pictures," you would gladly change places with the most lowly of God's creatures. It is inconceivable that there should be anyone worse off than you, unless perhaps it is some of the poor wretches who are waiting with you.

That one over in the arm-chair, nervously tearing to shreds a copy of "The Dental Review and Practical Inlay

Worker." She may have something frightful the trouble with her. She couldn't possibly look more worried. Perhaps it is very, very painful. This thought cheers you up considerably. What cowards women are in times like these!

And then there comes the sound of voices from the next room.

"All right, Doctor, and if it gives me any more pain shall I call you up? . . . Do you think that it will bleed much more? . . . Saturday morning, then, at eleven. . . . Good bye, Doctor."

And a middle-aged woman emerges (all women are middle-aged when emerging from the dentist's office) looking as if she were playing the big emotional scene in "John Ferguson."[1] A wisp of hair waves dissolutely across her forehead between her eyes. Her face is pale, except for a slight inflammation at the corners of her mouth, and in her eyes is that far-away look of one who has been face to face with Life. But she is through. She should care how she looks.

The nurse appears, and looks inquiringly at each one in the room. Each one in the room evades the nurse's glance in one last, futile attempt to fool someone and get away without seeing the dentist. But she spots you and nods pleasantly. God, how pleasantly she nods! There ought to be a law against people being as pleasant as that.

"The doctor will see you now," she says.

The English language may hold a more disagreeable combination of words than "The doctor will see you now." I am willing to concede something to the phrase "Have you anything to say before the current is turned on." That may be worse for the moment, but it doesn't last so long. For continued, unmitigating depression, I know nothing to equal "The doctor will see you now." But I'm not narrow-minded about it. I'm willing to consider other possibilities.

Smiling feebly, you trip over the extended feet of the man next to you, and stagger into the delivery-room, where amid a ghastly array of death-masks of teeth, blue flames waving

---

[1] *"John Ferguson"*: a play written by the Irish dramatist, St. John Ervine

eerily from Bunsen burners, and the drowning sound of perpetually running water which chokes and gurgles at intervals, you sink into the chair and close your eyes.

.　.　.　.　.

But now let us consider the spiritual exaltation that comes when you are at last let down and turned loose. It is all over, and what did it amount to? Why, nothing at all. A-ha-ha-ha-ha-ha! Nothing at all.

You suddenly develop a particular friendship for the dentist. A splendid fellow, really. You ask him questions about his instruments. What does he use this thing for, for instance? Well, well, to think of a little thing like that making all that trouble. A-ha-ha-ha-ha-ha! . . . And the dentist's family, how are they? Isn't that fine!

Gaily you shake hands with him and straighten your tie. Forgotten is the fact that you have another appointment with him for Monday. There is no such thing as Monday. You are through for today, and all's right with the world.

As you pass out through the waiting-room, you leer at the others unpleasantly. The poor fishes! Why can't they take their medicine like grown people and not sit there moping as if they were going to be shot?

Heigh-ho! Here's the elevator-man! A charming fellow! You wonder if he knows that you have just had a tooth filled. You feel tempted to tell him and slap him on the back. You feel tempted to tell everyone out in the bright, cheery street. And what a wonderful street it is too! All full of nice, black snow and water. After all, Life is sweet!

And then you go and find the first person whom you can accost without being arrested and explain to him just what it was that the dentist did to you, and how you felt, and what you have got to have done next time.

Which brings us right back to where we were in the beginning, and perhaps accounts for everyone's liking to divulge their dental secrets to others. It may be a sort of hysterical relief that, for the time being, it is all over with.

Questions and Comments

1. In his discussion of dental care, what does the author mean
   by a "preliminary period"? What is his feeling about this
   period?

2. What thoughts come immediately to the author's mind
   when he discovers that his tooth needs filling?

3. What are some of the methods the author resorts to in order
   to avoid going to the dentist?

4. At one point, the author says that "all women are middle-
   aged when emerging from the dentist's office." What does
   he mean?

5. What change immediately takes place in the author's general outlook the moment he is released from the dentist's
   chair? What are his new feelings about the dentist?

6. According to the author, what is the first thing a person
   does after a visit to the dentist?

Word Study

1. Teeth called *bicuspids* have two points (in Latin *bi* means
   "two" and *cuspid* "point"), and teeth called *incisors* have
   sharp, cutting edges (in Latin *caedere* means "cut"). Which
   of your teeth are bicuspids and which incisors?

2. In a parenthetical aside the author says "By the way, when
   did the present *obnoxious* system of dentistry begin? It
   can't be so very long ago that the electric *auger* was invented. . . . Yet you never hear of *Amalgam* Filling Day, or
   any other anniversary in the dental year." What do the
   italicized words mean?

3. The author refers to the dentist's chair as "the old red
   plush guillotine." Who was Joseph Guillotin, the man responsible for our word *guillotine?*

4. Give the meaning of the italicized words, using clues in the context of the selection wherever possible. Check your guesses in a dictionary.

"A wisp of hair waves *dissolutely* across her forehead. . . ." (page 170)

"For continued, *unmitigating* depression, I know nothing to equal 'The doctor will see you now.' " (page 170)

"And then you go and find the first person whom you can *accost* without being arrested. . . ." (page 171)

"Which . . . perhaps accounts for everyone's liking to *divulge* their dental secrets to others." (page 171)

Composition

1. While dealing with serious aspects of life, humorists like Robert Benchley and Al Capp maintain a funny, if not hilarious, approach to their subject matter. Compare both humorists and explain how each achieved his funniest touches in their respective selections.

2. Most people have been guilty at one time or another of putting off unpleasant chores. Describe an incident in which you deliberately delayed doing a job that you would eventually have to do. Describe some of the methods you used to avoid the job. Tell what consequences, if any, resulted from your delaying.

Samuel Clemens was well qualified to write knowledgeably about riverboats and rivermen. He served for a period of four years as a pilot on the Mississippi River. It was the fulfillment of a boyhood dream. As a matter of fact, his penname, Mark Twain, is a depth call of the Mississippi pilots signifying "two fathoms of water."

He tried his hand at a variety of occupations—as a printer, silver prospector, reporter and city editor for a Nevada newspaper—before he became one of the world's best-loved and most-quoted humorists.

His earliest work, consisting mainly of elaborate hoaxes and tall stories, was characteristic of frontier humor. One of his tall stories, "The Celebrated Jumping Frog of Calaveras County," made him a nationally famous humorist overnight. Of his books, *Tom Sawyer* and *Huckleberry Finn* have achieved the greatest acclaim, the latter having been described by some critics as one of the finest novels ever written by an American. The following selection comes from *Life on the Mississippi*.

SOUNDING

Mark Twain

WHEN the river is very low, and one's steamboat is "drawing all the water" there is in the channel—or a few inches more, as was often the case in the old times—one must be painfully circumspect in his piloting. We used to have to "sound" a number of particularly bad places almost every trip when the river was at a very low stage.

Sounding is done in this way: The boat ties up at the shore, just above the shoal crossing; the pilot not on watch takes his "cub" or steersman and a picked crew of men (sometimes an officer also), and goes out in the yawl—provided the boat has not that rare and sumptuous luxury, a regularly devised "sounding-boat"—and proceeds to hunt for the best water, the pilot on duty watching his movements through a spy-glass, meantime, and in some instances assisting by signals of the boat's whistle, signifying "try higher up" or "try lower down"; for the surface of the water, like an oil-painting, is more expressive and intelligible when inspected from a little distance than very close at hand. The whistle signals are seldom necessary, however; never, perhaps, except when the wind confuses the significant ripples upon the water's surface. When the yawl has reached the shoal place, the speed is slackened, the pilot begins to sound the depth with a pole ten or twelve feet long, and the steersman at the tiller obeys the order to "hold her up to starboard"; or "let her fall off to larboard";* or "steady—steady as you go."

When the measurements indicate that the yawl is approaching the shoalest part of the reef, the command is given to "Ease all!" Then the men stop rowing and the yawl drifts with the current. The next order is, "Stand by with the buoy!" The moment the shallowest point is reached, the pilot delivers the order, "Let go the buoy!" and over she goes. If the pilot is not satisfied, he sounds the place again; if he finds better water higher up or lower down, he removes the buoy to that place. Being finally satisfied, he gives the order, and all the men stand their oars straight up in the air, in line; a blast from the boat's whistle indicates that the signal has been seen; then the men "give way" on their oars and lay the yawl alongside the buoy; the steamer comes creeping carefully down, is pointed straight at the buoy, husbands her power for the coming struggle, and presently, at the critical moment, turns on all her steam and goes grinding and wallowing over the buoy and the sand, and gains the deep water beyond. Or maybe she doesn't; maybe she "strikes and swings." Then she has to while away several hours (or days) sparring herself off.

* *author's note:* The term "larboard" is never used at sea, now, to signify the left hand; but was always used on the river in my time.

Sometimes a buoy is not laid at all, but the yawl goes ahead, hunting the best water, and the steamer follows along in its wake. Often there is a deal of fun and excitement about sounding, especially if it is a glorious summer day, or a blustering night. But in winter the cold and the peril take most of the fun out of it.

A buoy is nothing but a board four or five feet long, with one end turned up; it is a reversed schoolhouse bench, with one of the supports left and the other removed. It is anchored on the shoalest part of the reef by a rope with a heavy stone made fast to the end of it. But for the resistance of the turned-up end of the reversed bench, the current would pull the buoy under water. At night, a paper lantern with a candle in it is fastened on top of the buoy, and this can be seen a mile or more, a little glimmering spark in the waste of blackness.

Nothing delights a cub so much as an opportunity to go out sounding. There is such an air of adventure about it; often there is danger; it is so gaudy and man-of-war-like to sit up in the stern-sheets and steer a swift yawl; there is something fine about the exultant spring of the boat when an experienced old sailor crew throw their souls into the oars; it is lovely to see the white foam stream away from the bows; there is music in the rush of the water; it is deliciously exhilarating, in summer, to go speeding over the breezy expanses of the river when the world of wavelets is dancing in the sun. It is such grandeur, too, to the cub, to get a chance to give an order; for often the pilot will simply say, "Let her go about!" and leave the rest to the cub, who instantly cries, in his sternest tone of command, "Ease, starboard! Strong on the larboard! Starboard, give way! With a will, men!" The cub enjoys sounding for the further reason that the eyes of the passengers are watching all the yawl's movements with absorbing interest, if the time be daylight; and if it be night, he knows that those same wondering eyes are fastened upon the yawl's lantern as it glides out into the gloom and dims away in the remote distance.

One trip a pretty girl of sixteen spent her time in our pilot-house with her uncle and aunt, every day and all day long. I fell in love with her. So did Mr. Thornburg's cub, Tom G. Tom and I had been bosom friends until this time; but now a coolness began to arise. I told the girl a good many of my river adventures, and made myself out a good deal of a hero; Tom tried to make himself appear to be a hero, too, and succeeded to some extent, but then he always had a way of embroidering. However, virtue is its own reward, so I was a barely perceptible trifle ahead in the contest. About this time something happened which promised handsomely for me: the pilots decided to sound the crossing at the head of 21.[1] This would occur about nine or ten o'clock at night, when the passengers would be still up; it would be Mr. Thornburg's watch, therefore my chief would have to do the sounding. We had a perfect love of a sounding-boat—long, trim, graceful, and as fleet as a greyhound; her thwarts were cushioned; she carried twelve oarsmen; one of the mates was always sent in her to transmit orders to her crew, for ours was a steamer where no end of "style" was put on.

We tied up at the shore above 21, and got ready. It was a foul night, and the river was so wide, there, that a landsman's uneducated eyes could discern no opposite shore through such a gloom. The passengers were alert and interested; everything was satisfactory. As I hurried through the engine-room, picturesquely gotten up in storm toggery, I met Tom, and could not forbear delivering myself of a mean speech:

"Ain't you glad *you* don't have to go out sounding?"

Tom was passing on, but he quickly turned, and said:

"Now just for that, you can go and get the sounding-pole yourself. I was going after it, but I'd see you in Halifax, now, before I'd do it."

"Who wants you to get it? I don't. It's in the sounding-boat."

[1] *21:* The various islands in the river were numbered. This is island 21.

"It ain't either. It's been new-painted; and it's been up on the ladies' cabin-guards two days, drying."

I flew back, and shortly arrived among the crowd of watching and wondering ladies just in time to hear the command:

"Give way, men!"

I looked over, and there was the gallant sounding-boat booming away, the unprincipled Tom presiding at the tiller, and my chief sitting by him with the sounding-pole which I had been sent on a fool's errand to fetch. Then that young girl said to me:

"Oh, how awful to have to go out in that little boat on such a night! Do you think there is any danger?"

I would rather have been stabbed. I went off, full of venom, to help in the pilot-house. By and by the boat's lantern disappeared, and after an interval a wee spark glimmered upon the face of the water a mile away. Mr. Thornburg blew the whistle in acknowledgment, backed the streamer out, and made for it. We flew along for a while, then slackened steam and went cautiously gliding toward the spark. Presently Mr. Thornburg exclaimed:

"Hello, the buoy lantern's out!"

He stopped the engines. A moment or two later he said:

"Why, there it is again!"

So he came ahead on the engines once more, and rang for the leads. Gradually the water shoaled up, and then began to deepen again! Mr. Thornburg muttered:

"Well, I don't understand this. I believe that buoy has drifted off the reef. Seems to be a little too far to the left. No matter, it is safest to run over it, anyhow."

So, in that solid world of darkness we went creeping down on the light. Just as our bows were in the act of plowing over it, Mr. Thornburg seized the bell-ropes, rang a startling peal, and exclaimed:

"My soul, it's the sounding-boat!"

A sudden chorus of wild alarms burst out far below—a pause—and then a sound of grinding and crashing followed. Mr. Thornburg exclaimed:

"There! the paddle-wheel has ground the sounding-boat to lucifer matches! Run! See who is killed!"

I was on the main-deck in the twinkling of an eye. My chief and the third mate and nearly all the men were safe. They had discovered their danger when it was too late to pull out of the way; then, when the great guards overshadowed them a moment later, they were prepared and knew what to do; at my chief's order they sprang at the right instant, seized the guard, and were hauled aboard. The next moment the sounding-yawl swept aft to the wheel and was struck and splintered to atoms. Two of the men and the cub Tom were missing—a fact which spread like wildfire over the boat. The passengers came flocking to the forward gangway, ladies and all, anxious-eyed, white-faced, and talked in awed voices of the dreadful thing. And often and again I heard them say, "Poor fellows! poor boy, poor boy!"

By this time the boat's yawl was manned and away, to search for the missing. Now a faint call was heard, off to the left. The yawl had disappeared in the other direction. Half the people rushed to one side to encourage the swimmer with their shouts; the other half rushed the other way to shriek to the yawl to turn about. By the callings the swimmer was approaching, but some said the sound showed failing strength. The crowd massed themselves against the boiler-deck railings, leaning over and staring into the gloom; and every faint and fainter cry wrung from them such words as "Ah, poor fellow, poor fellow! is there *no* way to save him?"

But still the cries held out, and drew nearer, and presently the voice said pluckily:

"I can make it! Stand by with a rope!"

What a rousing cheer they gave him! The chief mate took his stand in the glare of a torch-basket, a coil of rope in his hand, and his men grouped about him. The next moment the swimmer's face appeared in the circle of light, and in another one the owner of it was hauled aboard, limp and drenched, while cheer on cheer went up. It was that devil Tom.

The yawl crew searched everywhere, but found no sign of the two men. They probably failed to catch the guard, tumbled back, and were struck by the wheel and killed. Tom had never jumped for the guard at all, but had plunged head first into the river and dived under the wheel. It was nothing; I could have done it easy enough, and I said so; but everybody went on just the same, making a wonderful to-do over that ass, as if he had done something great. That girl couldn't seem to have enough of that pitiful "hero" the rest of the trip; but little I cared; I loathed her, anyway.

The way we came to mistake the sounding-boat's lantern for the buoy light was this: My chief said that after laying the buoy he fell away and watched it till it seemed to be secure; then he took up a position a hundred yards below it and a little to one side of the steamer's course, headed the sounding-boat up-stream, and waited. Having to wait some time, he and the officer got to talking; he looked up when he judged that the steamer was about on the reef; saw that the buoy was gone, but supposed that the steamer had already run over it; he went on with his talk; he noticed that the steamer was getting very close down to him, but that was the correct thing; it was her business to shave him closely, for convenience in taking him aboard; he was expecting her to sheer off, until the last moment; then it flashed upon him that she was trying to run him down, mistaking his lantern for the buoy light; so he sang out, "Stand by to spring for the guard, men!" and the next instant the jump was made.

Questions and Comments

If you liked this selection, you might want to read more of *Life on the Mississippi,* particularly Chapter IV "A Boy's Ambition," Chapter V "I Want to be a Cub-Pilot," and Chapter VIII "Perplexing Lessons."

1. What does the term "sounding" mean? What two methods of guiding the steamer through the shoals are described?

2. How does the author account for a cub's delight in going on a sounding expedition? To what extent is the cub's pleasure influenced by the interest of the spectators?

3. Why is the author particularly pleased by the necessity for sounding the crossing at the head of 21? How is he tricked? How could he have avoided the trick?

4. The author observes this particular sounding expedition first from the pilot-house and then from the main-deck. What does he report from each point?

5. How does the author's chief account for the accident?

6. Does the author really loathe the girl after the sounding episode? How do you account for his attitude?

Word Study

1. The author's note says that the term *larboard* is not now used to signify the left hand. What term is used instead? In the selection, what term is used to signify the right hand? What term is used to signify the rear of the steamer?

2. What kind of match is a lucifer match? Look up the word *lucifer* in a dictionary and report what you find.

3. When the river was low, one had to be *circumspect* in his piloting. The word comes from two Latin words—*circum* meaning "on all sides" and *spectus,* a form of the verb "to look." Explain the meaning of *circumspect.* What other words beginning with *circum* can you give?

4. The word *husband* is commonly used as a noun. What does it mean as a verb as in "the steamer . . . husbands her power for the coming struggle"?

Composition

1. Mark Twain was known as a humorist. Tell what touches of humor you found in the selection and at what human attitudes he was poking fun.

2. Discuss the author's feeling toward the Mississippi River and his job on the steamer-boat, giving examples from the selection to show his attitude.

3. Describe your own feeling toward a lake, a river, or the sea, if possible relating an incident to show your feeling—pleasure, excitement, perhaps dread.

It is very upsetting to discover unpleasant things about someone of whom you are very fond. In the following character sketch James Thurber tells of Doc Marlowe, a man who was a rather unusual mixture of good and bad.

DOC MARLOWE

James Thurber

I WAS too young to be other than awed and puzzled by Doc Marlowe when I knew him. I was only sixteen when he died. He was sixty-seven. There was that vast difference in our ages and there was a vaster difference in our backgrounds. Doc Marlowe was a medicine-show man. He had been a lot of other things, too: a circus man, the proprietor of a concession at Coney Island, a saloon-keeper; but in his fifties he had travelled around with a tent-show troupe made up of a Mexican named Chickalilli, who threw knives, and a man called Professor Jones, who played the banjo. Doc Marlowe would come out after the entertainment and harangue the crowd and sell bottles of medicine for all kinds of ailments. I found out all this about him gradually, toward the last, and after he died. When I first knew him, he represented the Wild West to me, and there was nobody I admired so much.

I met Doc Marlowe at old Mrs. Willoughby's rooming house. She had been a nurse in our family, and I used to go and visit her over weekends sometimes, for I was very fond of her. I was about eleven years old then. Doc Marlowe wore scarred leather leggings, a bright-colored bead vest that

183

he said he got from the Indians, and a ten-gallon hat with kitchen matches stuck in the band, all the way around. He was about six feet four inches tall, with big shoulders, and a long, drooping mustache. He let his hair grown long, like General Custer's.[1] He had a wonderful collection of Indian relics and six-shooters, and he used to tell me stories of his adventures in the Far West. His favorite expressions were "Hay, boy!" and "Hay, boy-gie!," which he used the way some people now use "Hot dog!" or "Doggone!" He told me once that he had killed an Indian chief named Yellow Hand in a tomahawk duel on horseback. I thought he was the greatest man I had ever seen. It wasn't until he died and his son came on from New Jersey for the funeral that I found out he had never been in the Far West in his life. He had been born in Brooklyn.

Doc Marlowe had given up the road when I knew him, but he still dealt in what he called "medicines." His stock in trade was a liniment that he had called Snake Oil when he travelled around. He changed the name to Blackhawk Liniment when he settled in Columbus. Doc didn't always sell enough of it to pay for his bed and board, and old Mrs. Willoughboy would sometimes have to "trust" him for weeks at a time. She didn't mind, because his liniment had taken a bad kink out of her right limb that had bothered her for thirty years. I used to see people whom Doc had massaged with Blackhawk Liniment move arms and legs that they hadn't been able to move before he "treated" them. His patients were day laborers, wives of streetcar conductors, and people like that. Sometimes they would shout and weep after Doc had massaged them, and several got up and walked around who hadn't been able to walk before. One man hadn't turned his head to either side for seven years before Doc soused him with Blackhawk. In half an hour he could move his head as easily as I could move mine. "Glory be to God!"

[1] *General Custer:* famous Indian fighter and Union general, who, because of his long blond hair, was called "Yellow Hair" by the Indians

he shouted. "It's the secret qualities in the ointment, my friend," Doc Marlowe told him, suavely. He always called the liniment ointment.

News of his miracles got around by word of mouth among the poorer classes of town—he was not able to reach the better people (the "tony folks," he called them)—but there was never a big enough sale to give Doc a steady income. For one thing, people thought there was more magic in Doc's touch than in his liniment, and, for another, the ingredients of Blackhawk cost so much that his profits were not very great. I know, because I used to go to the wholesale chemical company once in a while for him and buy his supplies. Everything that went into the liniment was standard and expensive (and well-known, not secret). A man at the company told me he didn't see how Doc could make much money on it at thirty-five cents a bottle. But even when he was very low in funds Doc never cut out any of the ingredients or substituted cheaper ones. Mrs. Willoughby had suggested it to him once, she told me, when she was helping him "put up a batch," and he had got mad. "He puts a heap of store by that liniment being right up to the mark," she said.

Doc added to his small earnings, I discovered, by money he made gambling. He used to win quite a few dollars on Saturday nights at Freck's saloon, playing poker with the marketmen and the railroaders who dropped in there. It wasn't for several years that I found out Doc cheated. I had never heard about marked cards until he told me about them and showed me his. It was one rainy afternoon, after he had played seven-up with Mrs. Willoughby and old Mr. Peiffer, another roomer of hers. They had played for small stakes (Doc wouldn't play cards unless there was some money up, and Mrs. Willoughby wouldn't play if very much was up). Only twenty or thirty cents had changed hands in the end. Doc had won it all. I remember my astonishment and indignation when it dawned on me that Doc had used the marked cards in playing the old lady and the old man.

"You didn't cheat *them,* did you?" I asked him. "Jimmy, my boy," he told me, "the man that calls the turn wins the money." His eyes twinkled and he seemed to enjoy my anger. I was outraged, but I was helpless. I knew I could never tell Mrs. Willoughby about how Doc had cheated her at seven-up. I liked her, but I liked him, too. Once he had given me a whole dollar to buy fireworks with on the Fourth of July.

I remember once, when I was staying at Mrs. Willoughby's, Doc Marlowe was roused out of bed in the middle of the night by a poor woman who was frantic because her little girl was sick. This woman had had the sciatica[1] driven out of her by his liniment, she reminded Doc. He placed her then. She had never been able to pay him a cent for his liniment or his "treatments," and he had given her a great many. He got up and dressed, and went over to her house. The child had colic, I suppose. Doc couldn't have had any idea what was the matter, but he sopped on liniment; he sopped on a whole bottle. When he came back home, two hours later, he said he had "relieved the distress." The little girl had gone to sleep and was all right the next day, whether on account of Doc Marlowe or in spite of him I don't know. "I want to thank you, Doctor," said the mother, tremulously, when she called on him that afternoon. He gave her another bottle of liniment, and he didn't charge her for it or for his "professional call." He used to massage, and give liniment to, a lot of sufferers who were too poor to pay. Mrs. Willoughby told him once that he was too generous and too easily taken in. Doc laughed—and winked at me, with the twinkle in his eye that he had had when he told me how he had cheated the old lady at cards.

Once I went for a walk with him out Town Street on a Saturday afternoon. It was a warm day, and after a while I said I wanted a soda. Well, he said, he didn't care if he took something himself. We went into a drugstore, and I ordered

---

[1] *sciatica:* severe pain of the hip and adjoining parts

a chocolate soda and he had a lemon phosphate. When we had finished, he said, "Jimmy, my son, I'll match you to see who pays for the drinks." He handed me a quarter and told me to toss the quarter and he would call the turn. He called heads and won. I paid for the drinks. It left me with a dime.

I was fifteen when Doc got out his pamphlets, as he called them. He had eased the misery of the wife of a small-time printer and the grateful man had given him a special price on two thousand advertising pamphlets. There was very little in them about Blackhawk Liniment. They were mostly about Doc himself and his "Life in the Far West." He had gone out to Franklin Park one day with a photographer—another of his numerous friends—and there the photographer took dozens of pictures of Doc, a lariat in one hand, a six-shooter in the other. I had gone along. When the pamphlets came out, there were the pictures of Doc, peering around trees, crouching behind bushes, whirling the lariat, aiming the gun. "Dr. H. M. Marlowe Hunting Indians" was one of the captions. "Dr. H. M. Marlowe after Hoss-Thieves" was another one. He was very proud of the pamphlets and always had a sheaf with him. He would pass them out to people on the street.

Two years before he died Doc got hold of an ancient, wheezy Cadillac somewhere. He aimed to start travelling around again, he said, but he never did, because the old automobile was so worn out it wouldn't hold up for more than a mile or so. It was about this time that a man named Hardman and his wife came to stay at Mrs. Willoughby's. They were farm people from around Lancaster who had sold their place. They got to like Doc because he was so jolly, they said, and they enjoyed his stories. He treated Mrs. Hardman for an old complaint in the small of her back and wouldn't take any money for it. They thought he was a fine gentleman. Then there came a day when they announced that they were going out to St. Louis, where they had a son. They talked some of settling in St. Louis. Doc Marlowe told them they ought to buy a nice auto cheap and drive out, instead of going by train—it wouldn't cost much and they could see the country, give themselves a treat. Now, he knew where they could pick up just such a car.

Of course, he finally sold them the decrepit Cadillac—it had been stored away somewhere in the back of a garage whose owner kept it there for nothing because Doc had relieved his mother of a distress in the groins, as Doc explained it. I don't know just how the garage man doctored up the car, but he did. It actually chugged along pretty steadily when Doc took the Hardmans out for a trial spin. He told them he hated to part with it, but he finally let them have it for a hundred dollars. I knew, of course, and so did Doc, that it couldn't last many miles.

Doc got a letter from the Hardmans in St. Louis ten days later. They had had to abandon the old junk pile in West Jefferson, some fifteen miles out of Columbus. Doc read the letter aloud to me, peering over his glasses, his eyes twinkling, every now and then punctuating the lines with "Hay, boy!" and "Hay, boy-gie!" "I just want you to know, Dr. Marlowe," he read, "what I think of low-life swindlers like you [Hay, boy!] and that it will be a long day before I put my trust in a two-faced lyer and imposture again [Hay, boy-gie!]. The garrage man in W. Jefferson told us your old rattletrap had been doctored up just to fool us. It was a low down dirty trick as no swine would play on a white man [Hay, boy!]." Far from being disturbed by the letter, Doc Marlowe was plainly amused. He took off his glasses after he finished it and laughed, his hand to his brow and his eyes closed. I was pretty mad, because I had liked the Hardmans, and because they had liked him. Doc Marlowe put the letter carefully back into its envelope and tucked it away in his inside coat pocket, as if it were something precious. Then he picked up a pack of cards and began to lay out a solitaire hand. "Want to set in a little seven-up game, Jimmy?" he asked me. I was furious. "Not with a cheater like you!" I shouted, and stamped out of the room, slamming the door. I could hear him chuckling to himself behind me.

The last time I saw Doc Marlowe was just a few days before he died. I didn't know anything about death, but I knew that he was dying when I saw him. His voice was very faint and his face was drawn; they told me he had a lot of pain. When I got ready to leave the room, he asked me to bring him a tin box that was on his bureau. I got it and handed it to him. He poked around in it for a while with unsteady fingers and finally found what he wanted. He handed it to me. It was a quarter, or rather it looked like a quarter, but it had heads on both sides. "Never let the other fella call the turn, Jimmy, my boy," said Doc, with a shadow of his old twinkle and the echo of his old chuckle. I still have the two-headed quarter. For a long time I didn't like to think about it, or about Doc Marlowe, but I do now.

Questions and Comments

James Thurber needs scarcely any introduction. Over the years, his stories, sketches, and cartoons have been delighting readers all over the world. Like all great humorists, Thurber was not primarily concerned with making people laugh. His writing is a criticism of life, designed to help people see their folly and foibles. Some of the all-time Thurber favorites are "The Secret Life of Walter Mitty," "The Night the Ghost Got In," and "The Catbird Seat." You will find many delightful examples of his work in his collection *Let Your Mind Alone,* from which the above selection is taken.

1. What did the author admire about Doc Marlowe? When did he learn most of the facts about Doc Marlowe's past?

2. Where did the author naturally assume Doc Marlowe was born? What did he find out after Doc Marlowe died?

3. How did Doc Marlowe make his living after he had given up the road? Why was he not more successful?

4. What suggestion did Mrs. Willoughby make to Doc Marlowe when they were making the liniment? What was his reaction to the suggestion? What point was the author making about Doc Marlowe by relating this incident?

5. How did the author react when he discovered that Doc Marlowe cheated at cards? What conflict did the author have within himself because of Doc Marlowe?

6. What is so amusing about Doc Marlowe's advertising pamphlets? About the incident with the Hardmans? Why are both of these incidents consistent with his character?

7. In addition to the two-headed quarter, what did Doc Marlowe give the author just before he died?

8. What is the author's tone or attitude toward Doc Marlowe? Cite evidence from the selection to support your answer. What does the last sentence tell you about the author's feelings toward Doc Marlowe?

Word Study

1. Refer to the selection and give the meaning of the italicized words as revealed by the context. Use a dictionary to check your guesses.

   "He had been the proprietor of a *concession* at Coney Island. . . ." (page 183)

   "Doc Marlowe would come out after the entertainment and *harangue* the crowd. . . ." (page 183)

   " 'It's the secret qualities in the ointment, my friend,' Doc Marlowe told him *suavely*." (page 185)

   " 'I want to thank you, Doctor,' said the mother *tremulously*. . . ." (page 186)

   "Of course, he finally sold them the *decrepit* Cadillac. . . ." (page 188)

2. Mr. Hardman made several spelling errors in his letter to Doc Marlowe. Find the spelling errors in this excerpt from the letter: ". . . it will be a long day before I put my trust in a two-faced lyer and imposture again. The garrage man in W. Jefferson told us your old rattletrap had been doctored up just to fool us."

Composition

1. The author's portrayal of Doc Marlowe is warm, human, and real because it shows both the good and the bad in the man. Discuss the way in which the author selected and presented his material in order to give flesh and dimension to his portrait.

2. Doc Marlowe's parting advice to the author was "Never let the other fella call the turn." Discuss what is meant by this and tell why you believe it is or is not a useful adage by which to live.

3. Write a character sketch of someone you know, keeping in mind that most people have failings as well as admirable characteristics. Try to explain both the failings and the virtues of this person.

In the year 430 B.C. the city of Athens was ravaged by a horrible plague. As the disease spread throughout the city, wreaking havoc, there was a consequent demoralization of the Athenians. Looting, violence, and general lawlessness became fairly commonplace. In this selection, the historian Thucydides vividly re-creates the devastation and horror of that terrible time.

THE PLAGUE OF ATHENS

Thucydides

SUCH was the funeral that took place during this winter, with which the first year of the war came to an end. In the first days of summer the Lacedæmonians[1] and their allies, with two-thirds of their forces as before, invaded Attica,[2] under the command of Archidamus, son of Zeuxidamus, king of Lacedæmon, and sat down and laid waste the country. Not many days after their arrival in Attica the plague first began to show itself among the Athenians. It was said that it had broken out in many places previously in the neighbourhood of Lemnos[3] and elsewhere; but a pestilence of such extent and mortality was nowhere remembered. Neither were the physicians at first of any service, ignorant as they were of the proper way to treat it, but they died themselves the most thickly, as they visited the sick most often; nor did any human art succeed any better. Supplications in the temples, divinations, and so forth were found equally futile, till the overwhelming nature of the disaster at last put a stop to them altogether.

[1] *Lacedæmonians:* Spartans
[2] *Attica:* a section of Greece whose chief towns were Athens, Piræus, and Eleusis
[3] *Lemnos:* a Greek island in the Aegean Sea

It first began, it is said, in the parts of Ethiopia above Egypt, and thence descended into Egypt and Libya[1] and into most of the king's country. Suddenly falling upon Athens, it first attacked the population in Piræus,[2]—which was the occasion of their saying that the Peloponnesians[3] had poisoned the reservoirs, there being as yet no wells there—and afterwards appeared in the upper city, when the deaths became much more frequent. All speculation as to its origin and its causes, if causes can be found adequate to produce so great a disturbance, I leave to other writers, whether lay or professional; for myself, I shall simply set down its nature, and explain the symptoms by which perhaps it may be recognised by the student, if it should ever break out again. This I can the better do, as I had the disease myself, and watched its operation in the case of others.

That year then is admitted to have been otherwise unprecedentedly free from sickness; and such few cases as occurred all determined in this. As a rule, however, there was no ostensible cause; but people in good health were all of a sudden attacked by violent heats in the head, and redness and inflammation in the eyes, the inward parts, such as the throat or tongue, becoming bloody and emitting an unnatural and fetid breath. These symptoms were followed by sneezing and hoarseness, after which the pain soon reached the chest, and produced a hard cough. When it fixed in the stomach, it upset it; and discharges of bile of every kind named by physicians ensued, accompanied by very great distress. In most cases also an ineffectual retching followed, producing violent spasms, which in some cases ceased soon after, in others much later. Externally the body was not very hot to the touch, nor pale in its appearance, but reddish, livid, and breaking out into small pustules and ulcers. But internally it burned so that the patient could not bear to have on him clothing or linen even of the very lightest description; or

[1] *Libya:* the ancient name for North Africa, excluding Egypt

[2] *Piræus:* the seaport of Athens

[3] *Peloponnesians:* people inhabiting the southern peninsula of Greece who were hostile to Athens

indeed to be otherwise than stark naked. What they would
have liked best would have been to throw themselves into
cold water; as indeed was done by some of the neglected sick,
who plunged into the rain-tanks in their agonies of unquench-
able thirst; though it made no difference whether they drank
little or much. Besides this, the miserable feeling of not being able to rest or sleep never ceased to torment them. The
body meanwhile did not waste away so long as the distemper
was at its height, but held out to a marvel against its ravages;
so that when they succumbed, as in most cases, on the seventh
or eighth day to the internal inflammation, they had still
some strength in them. But if they passed this stage, and the
disease descended further into the bowels, inducing a violent ulceration there accompanied by severe diarrhœa, this
brought on a weakness which was generally fatal. For the
disorder first settled in the head, ran its course from thence
through the whole of the body, and even where it did not
prove mortal, it still left its mark on the extremities; for it
settled in the privy parts, the fingers and the toes, and many
escaped with the loss of these, some too with that of their
eyes. Others again were seized with an entire loss of memory
on their first recovery, and did not know either themselves
or their friends.

But while the nature of the distemper was such as to baf-
fle all description, and its attacks almost too grievous for human nature to endure, it was still in the following circum-
stance that its difference from all ordinary disorders was
most clearly shown. All the birds and beasts that prey upon
human bodies, either abstained from touching them (though
there were many lying unburied), or died after tasting them.
In proof of this, it was noticed that birds of this kind actually
disappeared; they were not about the bodies, or indeed to
be seen at all. But of course the effects which I have mentioned could best be studied in a domestic animal like the
dog.

Such then, if we pass over the varieties of particular cases, which were many and peculiar, were the general features of the distemper. Meanwhile the town enjoyed an immunity from all the ordinary disorders; or if any case occurred, it ended in this. Some died in neglect, others in the midst of every attention. No remedy was found that could be used as a specific; for what did good in one case, did harm in another. Strong and weak constitutions proved equally incapable of resistance, all alike being swept away, although dieted with the utmost precaution. By far the most terrible feature in the malady was the dejection which ensued when any one felt himself sickening, for the despair into which they instantly fell took away their power of resistance, and left them a much easier prey to the disorder; besides which, there was the awful spectacle of men dying like sheep, through having caught the infection in nursing each other. This caused the greatest mortality. On the one hand, if they were afraid to visit each other, they perished from neglect; indeed many houses were emptied of their inmates for want of a nurse: on the other, if they ventured to do so, death was the consequence. This was especially the case with such as made any pretensions to goodness: honour made them unsparing of themselves in their attendance in their friends' houses, where even the members of the family were at last worn out by the moans of the dying, and succumbed to the force of the disaster. Yet it was with those who had recovered from the disease that the sick and the dying found most compassion. These knew what it was from experience, and had now no fear for themselves; for the same man was never attacked twice—never at least fatally. And such persons not only received the congratulations of others, but themselves also, in the elation of the moment, half entertained the vain hope that they were for the future safe from any disease whatsoever.

An aggravation of the existing calamity was the influx from the country into the city, and this was especially felt by the new arrivals. As there were no houses to receive them, they had to be lodged at the hot season of the year in stifling cabins, where the mortality raged without restraint. The bodies of dying men lay one upon another, and half-dead creatures reeled about the streets and gathered round all the fountains in their longing for water. The sacred places also in which they had quartered themselves were full of corpses of persons that had died there, just as they were; for as the disaster passed all bounds, men, not knowing what was to become of them, became utterly careless of everything, whether sacred or profane. All the burial rites before in use were entirely upset, and they buried the bodies as best they could. Many from want of the proper appliances, through so many of their friends having died already, had recourse to the most shameless sepultures: sometimes getting the start of those who had raised a pile, they threw their own dead body upon the stranger's pyre and ignited it; sometimes they tossed the corpse which they were carrying on the top of another that was burning, and so went off.

Nor was this the only form of lawless extravagance which owed its origin to the plague. Men now coolly ventured on what they had formerly done in a corner, and not just as they pleased, seeing the rapid transitions produced by persons in prosperity suddenly dying and those who before had nothing succeeding to their property. So they resolved to spend quickly and enjoy themselves, regarding their lives and riches as alike things of a day. Perseverance in what men called honour was popular with none, it was so uncertain whether they would be spared to attain the object; but it was settled that present enjoyment, and all that contributed to it, was both honourable and useful. Fear of gods or law of man there was none to restrain them. As for the first, they judged it to be just the same whether they worshipped them or not, as they saw all alike perishing; and for the last, no one expected to live to be brought to trial for his offences, but each felt that a far severer sentence had been already passed upon them all and hung ever over their heads, and before this fell it was only reasonable to enjoy life a little.

Such was the nature of the calamity, and heavily did it weigh on the Athenians; death raging within the city and devastation without. Among other things which they remembered in their distress was, very naturally, the following verse which the old men said had long ago been uttered:

'A Dorian[1] war shall come and with it death.'

So a dispute arose as to whether dearth and not death had not been the word in the verse; but at the present juncture, it was of course decided in favour of the latter; for the people made their recollecton fit in with their sufferings. I fancy, however, that if another Dorian war should ever afterwards come upon us, and a dearth should happen to accompany it, the verse will probably be read accordingly. The oracle also which had been given to the Lacedæmonians was now remembered by those who knew of it. When the God was asked whether they should go to war, he answered that if they put their might into it, victory would be theirs, and that he would himself be with them. With this oracle events were supposed to tally. For the plague broke out so soon as the Peloponnesians invaded Attica, and never entering Peloponnese (not at least to an extent worth noticing), committed its worst ravages at Athens, and next to Athens, at the most populous of the other towns. Such was the history of the plague.

Questions and Comments

1. Why does the author say that the physicians were of no help when the plague first broke out?

2. Where, according to the author, did the plague first start?

[1] *Dorian:* Doris was a region in central Greece that included the cities of Sparta and Corinth.

3. At first, who did the Athenians believe were responsible for the plague? What is the author's opinion of this theory? As a historian, what does he consider his task to be?

4. What happened to birds or animals that preyed on the bodies of those who had died from the plague?

5. What does the author say is the most terrible feature of this malady?

6. What group of people were able to be most helpful to those afflicted with the plague? Why?

7. What situation in Athens served to aggravate the existing condition?

8. What does the author mean when he says that men became "utterly careless of everything, whether sacred or profane"? What examples does he cite to support this belief?

9. What changes in the attitude and morals of the Greeks took place during the plague?

Word Study

1. In the first paragraph the author states that both *supplications* in the temple and *divinations* are equally futile. What do the italicized words mean?

2. In the third paragraph the author describes the stages of the disease. The meaning of these words is partially revealed by the context: *ostensible* in "no ostensible cause," *fetid* in "an unnatural and fetid breath," *succumbed* in "when they succumbed, as in most cases, on the seventh or eighth day." What do these words mean?

3. In the same paragraph are words that are not explained by the context but may be familiar to a reader with some knowledge of physiology. If you do not know the meaning of the following words, look them up in a dictionary: *bile, retching, pustules, ulcers, distemper, diarrhoea.*

4. What does the noun *specific* mean in "No remedy was found that could be used as a specific"? (page 195)

5. What is the meaning of *influx* in "An aggravation of the existing calamity was the influx from the country into the city"? (page 195)

6. The word *pyre* comes from the Greek word *pyr* meaning "fire." How does this derivation reveal what we mean by a "funeral pyre"?

Composition

1. The author states that during the plague of Athens the attitudes and morality of the Greeks underwent a drastic change. Discuss what changes you feel would take place in the normal behavior of Americans suddenly confronted with a major crisis.

2. Write a short story in which you portray the physical as well as moral effects of a terrible calamity on a small American town.

Daniel Defoe, author of *Robinson Crusoe,* was a noted journalist, distinguished for his dramatic and realistic style. Since Defoe was only four years old when the great Plague of 1665 took place, his account of it can scarcely be called firsthand. Its amazingly realistic detail is due to Defoe's superb journalistic ability and to his painstaking research.

from A JOURNAL OF THE PLAGUE YEAR

Daniel Defoe

ONE of the worst days we had in the whole time, as I thought, was in the beginning of September, when, indeed, good people began to think that God was resolved to make a full end of the people in this miserable city. This was at that time when the plague was fully come into the eastern parishes. The parish of Aldgate, if I may give my opinion, buried above a thousand a week for two weeks, though the bills did not say so many; but it surrounded me at so dismal a rate that there was not a house in twenty uninfected in the Minories,[1] in Houndsditch, and in those parts of Aldgate parish about the Butcher Row and the alleys over against me. I say, in those places death reigned in every corner. Whitechapel parish was in the same condition, and though much less than the parish I lived in, yet buried near six hundred a week by the bills, and in my opinion near twice as many. Whole families, and indeed whole streets of families, were

---

[1] *Minories:* a street in London, once famous for its gun-makers. Its name is derived from an old convent of Minoresses.

swept away together; insomuch that it was frequent for neighbours to call to the bellman[1] to go to such-and-such houses and fetch out the people, for that they were all dead.

And, indeed, the work of removing the dead bodies by carts was now grown so very odious and dangerous that it was complained of that the bearers did not take care to clear such houses where all the inhabitants were dead, but that sometimes the bodies lay several days unburied, till the neighbouring families were offended with the stench, and consequently infected; and this neglect of the officers was such that the churchwardens and constables were summoned to look after it, and even the justices of the Hamlets[2] were obliged to venture their lives among them to quicken and encourage them, for innumerable of the bearers died of the distemper, infected by the bodies they were obliged to come so near. And had it not been that the number of poor people who wanted employment and wanted bread (as I have said before) was so great that necessity drove them to undertake anything and venture anything, they would never have found people to be employed. And then the bodies of the dead would have lain above ground, and have perished and rotted in a dreadful manner.

But the magistrates cannot be enough commended in this, that they kept such good order for the burying of the dead, that as fast as any of those they employed to carry off and bury the dead fell sick or died, as was many times the case, they immediately supplied the places with others, which, by reason of the great number of poor that was left out of business, as above, was not hard to do. This occasioned that notwithstanding the infinite number of people which died and were sick, almost all together, yet they were always cleared away and carried off every night, so that it was never to be said of London that the living were not able to bury the dead.

---

[1] *bellman:* a town crier or a watchman
[2] *Hamlets:* small villages

As the desolation was greater during those terrible times, so the amazement of the people increased, and a thousand unaccountable things they would do in the violence of their fright, as others did the same in the agonies of their distemper, and this part was very affecting. Some went roaring and crying and wringing their hands along the street; some would go praying and lifting up their hands to heaven, calling upon God for mercy. I cannot say, indeed, whether this was not in their distraction, but, be it so, it was still an indication of a more serious mind, when they had the use of their senses, and was much better, even as it was, than the frightful yellings and cryings that every day, and especially in the evenings, were heard in some streets. I suppose the world has heard of the famous Solomon Eagle, an enthusiast. He, though not infected at all but in his head, went about denouncing of judgment upon the city in a frightful manner, sometimes quite naked, and with a pan of burning charcoal on his head. What he said, or pretended, indeed I could not learn.

I will not say whether that clergyman was distracted or not, or whether he did it in pure zeal for the poor people, who went every evening through the streets of Whitechapel, and, with his hands lifted up, repeated that part of the Liturgy[1] of the Church continually, "Spare us, good Lord; spare Thy people, whom Thou hast redeemed with Thy most precious blood." I say, I cannot speak positively of these things, because these were only the dismal objects which represented themselves to me as I looked through my chamber windows (for I seldom opened the casements), while I confined myself within doors during that most violent raging of the pestilence; when, indeed, as I have said, many began to think, and even to say, that there would none escape; and indeed I began to think so too, and therefore kept within doors for about a fortnight, and never stirred out. But

[1] *Liturgy:* the public rites and services of the Christian church; sometimes a Eucharistic rite

I could not hold it. Besides, there were some people who, notwithstanding the danger, did not omit publickly to attend the worship of God, even in the most dangerous times; and though it is true that a great many clergymen did shut up their churches, and fled, as other people did, for the safety of their lives, yet all did not do so. Some ventured to officiate and to keep up the assemblies of the people by constant prayers, and sometimes sermons or brief exhortations to repentance and reformation, and this as long as any would come to hear them. And Dissenters[1] did the like also, and even in the very churches where the parish ministers were either dead or fled; nor was there any room for making difference at such a time as this was.

It was indeed a lamentable thing to hear the miserable lamentations of poor dying creatures calling out for ministers to comfort them and pray with them, to counsel them and to direct them, calling out to God for pardon and mercy, and confessing aloud their past sins. It would make the stoutest heart bleed to hear how many warnings were then given by dying penitents to others not to put off and delay their repentance to the day of distress; that such a time of calamity as this was no time for repentance, was no time to call upon God. I wish I could repeat the very sound of those groans and of those exclamations that I heard from some poor dying creatures when in the height of their agonies and distress, and that I could make him that reads this hear, as I imagine I now hear them, for the sound seems still to ring in my ears.

If I could but tell this part in such moving accents as should alarm the very soul of the reader, I should rejoice that I recorded those things, however short and imperfect.

It pleased God that I was still spared, and very hearty and sound in health, but very impatient of being pent up within doors without air, as I had been for fourteen days or thereabouts, and I could not restrain myself, but I would go to

---

[1] *Dissenters:* those who rebelled against the Church of England; Protestants

carry a letter for my brother to the post-house.[1] Then it was
indeed that I observed a profound silence in the streets.
When I came to the post-house, as I went to put in my letter, I saw a man stand in one corner of the yard and talking
to another at a window, and a third had opened a door belonging to the office. In the middle of the yard lay a small
leather purse with two keys hanging at it, with money in it,
but nobody would meddle with it. I asked how long it had
lain there; the man at the window said it had lain almost an
hour, but that they had not meddled with it, because they
did not know but the person who dropped it might come
back to look for it. I had no such need of money, nor was the
sum so big that I had any inclination to meddle with it,
or to get the money at the hazard it might be attended with;
so I seemed to go away, when the man who had opened the
door said he would take it up, but so that if the right owner
came for it he should be sure to have it. So he went in and
fetched a pail of water, and set it down hard by the purse,
then went again and fetched some gunpowder, and cast a
good deal of powder upon the purse, and then made a train
from that which he had thrown loose upon the purse. The
train reached about two yards. After this he goes in a third
time and fetches out a pair of tongs red hot, and which he
had prepared, I suppose, on purpose, and first setting fire to
the train of powder, that singed the purse, and also smoked
the air sufficiently. But he was not content with that, but
he then takes up the purse with the tongs, holding it so long
till the tongs burnt through the purse, and then he shook the
money out into the pail of water, so he carried it in. The
money, as I remember, was about thirteen shillings and some
smooth groats and brass farthings.[2]

There might perhaps have been several poor people, as I
have observed above, that would have been hardy enough to

---

[1] *post-house:* a post office
[2] *shillings . . . groats . . . farthings:* British coins, the shilling being worth
20 pence; the groat, 4 pence; and the farthing, $\frac{1}{4}$ of a penny

have ventured for the sake of the money; but you may easily see by what I have observed that the few people who were spared were very careful of themselves at that time when the distress was so exceeding great.

Much about the same time I walked out into the fields towards Bow; for I had a great mind to see how things were managed in the river and among the ships; and as I had some concern in shipping, I had a notion that it had been one of the best ways of securing one's self from the infection to have retired into a ship; and musing how to satisfy my curiosity in that point, I turned away over the fields from Bow to Bromley, and down to Blackwall to the stairs, which are there for landing or taking water.

Here I saw a poor man walking on the bank, or seawall, as they call it, by himself. I walked a while also about, seeing the houses all shut up. At last I fell into some talk, at a distance, with this poor man; first I asked him how people did thereabouts. "Alas, sir!" says he, "almost desolate; all dead or sick. Here are very few families in this part, or in that village" (pointing at Poplar), "where half of them are not dead already, and the rest sick." Then pointing to one house, "There they are all dead," said he, "and the house stands open; nobody dares go into it. A poor thief," says he, "ventured in to steal something, but he paid dear for his theft, for he was carried to the churchyard too last night." Then he pointed to several other houses. "There," says he, "they are all dead, the man and his wife, and five children. There," says he, "they are shut up; you see a watchman at the door;" and so of other houses. "Why," says I, "what do you here all alone?" "Why," says he, "I am a poor, desolate man; it has pleased God I am not yet visited, though my family is, and one of my children dead." "How do you mean, then," said I, "that you are not visited?" "Why," says he, "that's my house" (pointing to a very little, low-boarded house), "and there my poor wife and two children live," said he, "if they may be said to live, for my wife and one of the children are visited, but I do not come at them." And with that word I saw the tears run very plentifully down his face; and so they did down mine too, I assure you.

"But," said I, "why do you not come at them? How can you abandon your own flesh and blood?" "Oh, sir," says he, "the Lord forbid! I do not abandon them; I work for them as much as I am able; and, blessed be the Lord, I keep them from want;" and with that I observed he lifted up his eyes to heaven, with a countenance that presently told me I had happened on a man that was no hypocrite, but a serious, religious, good man, and his ejaculation was an expression of thankfulness that, in such a condition as he was in, he should be able to say his family did not want. "Well," says I, "honest man, that is a great mercy as things go now with the poor. But how do you live, then, and how are you kept from the dreadful calamity that is now upon us all?" "Why, sir," says he, "I am a waterman, and there's my boat," says he, "and the boat serves me for a house. I work in it in the day, and I sleep in it in the night; and what I get I lay down upon that stone," says he, shewing me a broad stone on the other side of the street, a good way from his house; "and then," says he, "I halloo, and call to them till I make them hear; and they come and fetch it."

"Well, friend," says I, "but how can you get any money as a waterman?[1] Does anybody go by water these times?" "Yes, sir," says he, "in the way I am employed there does. Do you see there," says he, "five ships lie at anchor" (pointing down the river a good way below the town), "and do you see," says he, "eight or ten ships lie at the chain there, and at anchor yonder?" (pointing above the town). "All those ships have families on board, of their merchants and owners, and such-like, who have locked themselves up and live on board, close shut in, for fear of the infection; and I tend on them to fetch things for them, carry letters, and do what is absolutely necessary, that they may not be obliged to come on shore;

[1] *waterman:* a man who plies the services of himself and his boat

and every night I fasten my boat on board one of the ship's boats, and there I sleep by myself, and, blessed be God, I am preserved hitherto."

"Well," said I, "friend, but will they let you come on board after you have been on shore here, when this is such a terrible place, and so infected as it is?"

"Why, as to that," said he, "I very seldom go up the ship-side, but deliver what I bring to their boat, or lie by the side, and they hoist it on board. If I did, I think they are in no danger from me, for I never go into any house on shore, or touch anybody, no, not of my own family; but I fetch provisions for them."

"Nay," says I, "but that may be worse, for you must have those provisions of somebody or other; and since all this part of the town is so infected, it is dangerous so much as to speak with anybody; for the village," said I, "is, as it were, the beginning of London, though it be at some distance from it."

"That is true," added he; "but you do not understand me right; I do not buy provisions for them here. I row up to Greenwich and buy fresh meat there, and sometimes I row down the river to Woolwich and buy there; then I go to single farm-houses on the Kentish side, where I am known, and buy fowls and eggs and butter, and bring to the ships, as they direct me, sometimes one, sometimes the other. I seldom come on shore here, and I came now only to call to my wife and hear how my little family do, and give them a little money, which I received last night."

"Poor man!" said I; "and how much hast thou gotten for them?"

"I have gotten four shillings," said he, "which is a great sum, as things go now with poor men; but they have given me a bag of bread too, and a salt fish, and some flesh; so all helps out."

"Well," said I, "and have you given it them yet?"

"No," said he; "but I have called, and my wife has answered that she cannot come out yet, but in half an hour

she hopes to come, and I am waiting for her. Poor woman!"
says he, "she is brought sadly down. She has a swelling, and
it is broke, and I hope she will recover; but I fear the child
will die, but it is the Lord—"

Here he stopped, and wept very much.

"Well, honest friend," said I, "thou hast a sure Comforter,
if thou hast brought thyself to be resigned to the will of God;
He is dealing with us all in judgment."

"Oh, sir!" says he, "it is infinite mercy if any of us are
spared, and who am I to repine!"

"Sayest thou so?" said I, "and how much less is my faith
than thine?" And here my heart smote me, suggesting how
much better this poor man's foundation was on which he
stayed in the danger than mine; that he had nowhere to fly;
that he had a family to bind him to attendance, which I had
not; and mine was meer presumption, his a true dependence,
and a courage resting on God; and yet that he used all possible caution for his safety.

I turned a little way from the man while these thoughts
engaged me, for, indeed, I could no more refrain from tears
than he.

At length, after some further talk, the poor woman opened
the door and called, "Robert, Robert." He answered, and
bid her stay a few moments and he would come; so he ran
down the common stairs to his boat and fetched up a sack, in
which was the provisions he had brought from the ships; and
when he returned he hallooed again. Then he went to the
great stone which he shewed me and emptied the sack, and
laid all out, everything by themselves, and then retired; and
his wife came with a little boy to fetch them away, and he
called and said such a captain had sent such a thing, and such
a captain such a thing, and at the end adds, "God has sent it
all; give thanks to Him." When the poor woman had taken
up all, she was so weak she could not carry it at once in,
though the weight was not much neither; so she left the
biscuit, which was in a little bag, and left a little boy to watch
it till she came again.

"Well, but," says I to him, "did you leave her the four shillings too, which you said was your week's pay?"

"Yes, yes," says he; "you shall hear her own it." So he calls again, "Rachel, Rachel," which, it seems, was her name, "did you take up the money?" "Yes," said she. "How much was it?" said he. "Four shillings and a groat," said she. "Well, well," says he, "the Lord keep you all;" and so he turned to go away.

As I could not refrain contributing tears to this man's story, so neither could I refrain my charity for his assistance. So I called him, "Hark thee, friend," said I, "come hither, for I believe thou art in health, that I may venture thee;" so I pulled out my hand, which was in my pocket before, "Here," says I, "go and call thy Rachel once more, and give her a little more comfort from me. God will never forsake a family that trust in Him as thou dost." So I gave him four other shillings, and bid him go lay them on the stone and call his wife.

I have not words to express the poor man's thankfulness, neither could he express it himself but by tears running down his face. He called his wife, and told her God had moved the heart of a stranger, upon hearing their condition, to give them all that money, and a great deal more such as that he said to her. The woman, too, made signs of the like thankfulness, as well to Heaven as to me, and joyfully picked it up; and I parted with no money all that year that I thought better bestowed.

I then asked the poor man if the distemper had not reached to Greenwich. He said it had not till about a fortnight before; but that then he feared it had, but that it was only at that end of the town which lay south towards Deptford Bridge; that he went only to a butcher's shop and a grocer's, where he generally bought such things as they sent him for, but was very careful.

I asked him then how it came to pass that those people who had so shut themselves up in the ships had not laid in sufficient stores of all things necessary. He said some of them had, but, on the other hand, some did not come on board till they were frighted into it, and till it was too dangerous for them to go to the proper people to lay in quantities of things, and that he waited on two ships, which he shewed me, that had laid in little or nothing but biscuit bread and ship beer, and that he had bought everything else almost for them. I asked him if there was any more ships that had separated themelves as those had done. He told me yes, all the way up from the point, right against Greenwich, to within the shore of Limehouse and Redriff, all the ships could have room rid two and two[1] in the middle of the stream, and that some of them had several families on board. I asked him if the distemper had not reached them. He said he believed it had not, except two or three ships, whose people had not been so watchful to keep the seamen from going on shore, as others had been, and he said it was a very fine sight to see how the ships lay up the Pool.*

When he said he was going over to Greenwich as soon as the tide began to come in, I asked if he would let me go with him, and bring me back, for that I had a great mind to see how the ships were ranged, as he had told me. He told me, if I would assure him on the word of a Christian and of an honest man that I had not the distemper, he would. I assured him that I had not; that it had pleased God to preserve me; that I lived in Whitechapel, but was too impatient of being so long within doors, and that I had ventured out so far for the refreshment of a little air, but that none in my house had so much as been touched with it.

"Well, sir," says he, "as your charity has been moved to pity me and my poor family, sure you cannot have so little pity left as to put yourself into my boat if you were not sound in health, which would be nothing less than killing me, and ruining my whole family." The poor man troubled me so much when he spoke of his family with such a sensible con-

---

[1] *rid two and two:* lined up in two rows

* *author's note:* That part of the river where the ships lie up when they come home is called the Pool, and takes in all the river on both sides of the water, from the Tower to Cuckold's Point and the Limehouse.

cern, and in such an affectionate manner, that I could not satisfy myself at first to go at all. I told him I would lay aside my curiosity rather than make him uneasy, though I was sure, and very thankful for it, that I had no more distemper upon me than the freshest man in the world. Well, he would not have me put it off neither, but, to let me see how confident he was that I was just to him, now importuned me to go; so when the tide came up to his boat I went in, and he carried me to Greenwich. While he bought the things which he had in his charge to buy, I walked up to the top of the hill under which the town stands, and on the east side of the town, to get a prospect of the river. But it was a surprizing sight to see the number of ships which lay in rows, two and two, and some places two or three such lines in the breadth of the river, and this not only up quite to the town, between the houses which we call Ratcliff and Redriff, which they name the Pool, but even down the whole river, as far as the head of Long Reach, which is as far as the hills give us leave to see it.

I cannot guess at the number of ships, but I think there must be several hundreds of sail; and I could not but applaud the contrivance, for ten thousand people, and more, who attended ship affairs were certainly sheltered here from the violence of the contagion, and lived very safe and very easy.

I returned to my own dwelling very well satisfied with my day's journey, and particularly with the poor man; also, I rejoiced to see that such little sanctuaries were provided for so many families in a time of such desolation. I observed also, that as the violence of the plague had increased, so the ships which had families on board removed and went farther off, till, as I was told, some went quite away to sea, and put into such harbours and safe roads on the north coast as they could best come at.

But it was also true that all the people who thus left the land and lived on board the ships were not entirely safe from the infection, for many died and were thrown overboard into the river, some in coffins, and some, as I heard, without coffins, whose bodies were seen sometimes to drive up and down with the tide in the river.

But I believe I may venture to say that in those ships which were thus infected it either happened where the people had recourse to them too late, and did not fly to the ship till they had stayed too long on shore and had the distemper upon them, though perhaps they might not perceive it, and so the distemper did not come to them on board the ships, but they really carried it with them; or it was in these ships where the poor waterman said they had not had time to furnish themselves with provisions, but were obliged to send often on shore to buy what they had occasion for, or suffered boats to come to them from the shore. And so the distemper was brought insensibly among them.

Questions and Comments

1. What facts concerning the size and the extent of the plague does the author give you in the first paragraph?

2. Why is it so great a problem to dispose of the bodies of people who died in the plague? How do the magistrates finally solve the problem?

3. What cries from the street does the author hear from his windows? What comments does he make about human behavior at a time of calamity?

4. What facts do you know about the narrator? What is his physical condition at the height of the plague? How does he account for it?

5. What point does the author wish to make by relating the incident of the leather purse?

6. What does the waterman mean when he says ". . . but I do not come at them"? What method does he use to provide his family with food and money?

7. Why does the author say that the waterman is better equipped to cope with disaster than he himself is? What effect does the waterman have on the author? Cite evidence from the selection to support your answer.

8. Why does the author want to go to Greenwich with the waterman? Why is the waterman afraid to take him?

9. What does the author see in the river at Greenwich? What does he tell us about the survival rate of people who left the land to live on boats?

10. What do you think the author's attitude is toward all the suffering and hardship caused by the plague? Does he feel pity toward those who were afflicted, or does he feel indifference? Cite evidence from the selection to support your answer.

Word Study

1. Refer to the selection for clues that may help to reveal the meaning of the italicized words. If you are not sure of the meaning of a word, use a dictionary to check your guess.

   "And indeed, the work of removing the dead bodies by carts was now grown so very *odious* and dangerous. . . ." (page 201)

   "Some ventured . . . to keep up the assemblies of the people by . . . sermons or brief *exhortations* to repentance. . . ." (page 203)

   "It would make the stoutest heart bleed to hear how many warnings were then given by dying *penitents* not to put off and delay their repentance. . . ." (page 203)

   "I rejoiced to see that such little *sanctuaries* were provided for so many families. . . ." (page 211)

2. You may have thought the words *publickly, shewing,* and *meer* in the selection were all misspelled. Actually, they are obsolete spellings of words that we spell differently today. What are the modern spellings of the words?

3. Use the word *importuned* in a sentence that clearly shows that you know what it means.

Composition

1. Compare the literary style of "The Plague of Athens" with the selection from *A Journal of the Plague Year*. Comment on such factors as vividness and completeness of descriptive detail, organization of ideas, and reader interest.

2. Pretend that you are a reporter. Write a newspaper account of some present-day disaster that you have actually observed. Fire, tornado, flood, or riot are a few good examples of disasters. Describe clearly and dramatically your experience, always remembering that a good reporter tries to be absolutely objective and never permits his feelings to mar the accuracy of his writing.

3. Give your opinion of the following statement: "Terrible disasters tend to bring out the worst in people."

The little English village in which Laurie Lee was brought up was a town largely untouched by the progress wrought by the industrial revolution. In this chapter from his autobiography Laurie Lee has poetically captured for us the quaintness and the poignancy of his experiences as a child.

FIRST LIGHT

Laurie Lee

I WAS set down from the carrier's cart at the age of three; and there with a sense of bewilderment and terror my life in the village began.

The June grass, amongst which I stood, was taller than I was, and I wept. I had never been so close to grass before. It towered above me and all around me, each blade tattooed with tiger skins of sunlight. It was knife-edged, dark and a wicked green, thick as a forest and alive with grasshoppers that chirped and chattered and leapt through the air like monkeys.

I was lost and didn't know where to move. A tropic heat oozed up from the ground, rank with sharp odours of roots and nettles. Snow clouds of elderblossom banked in the sky, showering upon me the fumes and flakes of their sweet and giddy suffocation. High overhead ran frenzied larks, screaming, as though the sky were tearing apart.

For the first time in my life I was out of the sight of humans. For the first time in my life I was alone in a world whose behaviour I could neither predict nor fathom: a world of birds that squealed, of plants that stank, of insects that sprang about without warning. I was lost and I did not expect to be found again. I put back my head and howled, and the sun hit me smartly on the face, like a bully.

From this daylight nightmare I was wakened, as from many another, by the appearance of my sisters. They came scrambling and calling up the steep rough bank and, parting the long grass, found me. Faces of rose, familiar, living; huge shining faces hung up like shields between me and the sky; faces with grins and white teeth (some broken) to be conjured up like genii with a howl, brushing off terror with their broad scoldings and affection. They leaned over me—one, two, three—their mouths smeared with red currants and their hands dripping with juice.

"There, there, it's all right, don't you wail anymore. Come down 'ome and we'll stuff you with currants."

And Marjorie, the eldest, lifted me into her long brown hair, and ran me jogging down the path and through the steep rose-filled garden, and set me down on the cottage doorstep, which was our home, though I couldn't believe it.

That was the day we came to the village, in the summer of the last year of the First World War. To a cottage that stood in a half-acre of garden on a steep bank above a lake; a cottage with three floors and a cellar and a treasure in the walls, with a pump and apple trees, syringa and strawberries, rooks in the chimneys, frogs in the cellar, mushrooms on the ceiling, and all for three and sixpence a week.

I don't know where I lived before then. My life began on the carrier's cart which brought me up the long slow hills to the village, and dumped me in the high grass, and lost me. I had ridden wrapped up in a Union Jack[1] to protect me from the sun, and when I rolled out of it, and stood piping loud among the buzzing jungle of that summer bank, then, I feel, was I born. And to all the rest of us, the whole family of eight, it was the beginning of a life.

[1] *Union Jack:* the national flag of Great Britain

But on that first day we were all lost. Chaos was come in cartloads of furniture, and I crawled the kitchen floor through forests of upturned chairlegs and crystal fields of glass. We were washed up in a new land, and began to spread out, searching its springs and treasures. The sisters spent the light of that first day stripping the fruit bushes in the garden. The currants were at their prime, clusters of red, black and yellow berries all tangled up with wild roses. Here was bounty the girls had never known before, and they darted squawking from bush to bush, clawing the fruit like sparrows.

Our Mother too was distracted from duty, seduced by the rich wilderness of the garden so long abandoned. All day she trotted to and fro, flushed and garrulous, pouring flowers into every pot and jug she could find on the kitchen floor. Flowers from the garden, daisies from the bank, cow parsley, grasses, ferns and leaves—they flowed in armfuls through the cottage door until its dim interior seemed entirely possessed by the world outside—a still green pool flooding with honeyed tides of summer.

I sat on the floor on a raft of muddles and gazed through the green window which was full of the rising garden. I saw the long black stockings of the girls, gaping with white flesh, kicking among the currant bushes. Every so often one of them would dart into the kitchen, cram my great mouth with handfuls of squashed berries, and run out again. And the more I got the more I called for more. It was like feeding a fat young cuckoo.

The long day crowed and chirped and rang. Nobody did any work, and there was nothing to eat save berries and bread. I crawled about among the ornaments on the unfamiliar floor—the glass fishes, china dogs, shepherds and shepherdesses, bronze horsemen, stopped clocks, barometers, and photographs of bearded men. I called on them each in turn, for they were the shrines and faces of a half-remembered landscape. But as I watched the sun move around the walls, drawing rainbows from the cut-glass jars in the corner, I longed for a return of order.

Then, suddenly, the day was at an end, and the house was furnished. Each stick and cup and picture was nailed immovably in place; the beds were sheeted, the windows curtained, the straw mats laid, and the house was home. I don't remember seeing it happen, but suddenly the inexorable tradition of the house, with its smell, chaos and complete logic, occurred as though it had never been otherwise. The furnishing and founding of the house came like the nightfall of that first day. From that uneasy loneliness of objects strewn on the kitchen floor, everything flew to its place and was never again questioned.

And from that day we grew up. The domestic arrangement of the house was shaken many times, like a snowstorm toy, so that beds and chairs and ornaments swirled from room to room, pursued by the gusty energies of Mother and the girls. But always these things resettled within the pattern of the walls, nothing escaped or changed, and so it remained for twenty years.

Now I measured that first growing year by the widening fields that became visible to me, the new tricks of dressing and getting about with which I became gradually endowed. I could open the kitchen door by screwing myself into a ball and leaping and banging the latch with my fist. I could climb into the high bed by using the ironwork as a ladder. I could whistle, but I couldn't lace my shoes. Life became a series of experiments which brought grief or the rewards of accomplishment: a pondering of patterns and mysteries in the house, while time hung golden and suspended, and one's body, from leaping and climbing, took on the rigid insanity of an insect, petrified, as it were, for hours together, breathing and watching. Watching the grains of dust fall in my sunny room, following an ant from its cradle to the grave, going over the knots in the bedroom ceiling—knots that seemed to dilate and run in the half-light of dawn and form the fluid shapes of monsters, or moved stealthily from board to board; but which settled again in the wax light of day no more monstrous than fossils in coal.

These knots on the bedroom ceiling were the whole range of a world, and over them my eyes went endlessly voyaging in that long primeval light of waking to which a child is condemned. They were archipelagoes in a sea of blood-coloured varnish, they were armies grouped and united against me, they were the alphabet of a macabre tongue, the first book I ever learned to read.

Radiating from that house, with its crumbling walls, its thumps and shadows, its fancied foxes under the floor, I moved along paths that lengthened inch by inch with my mounting strength of days. From stone to stone in the trackless yard I sent forth my acorn shell of senses, moving through unfathomable oceans like a South Sea savage island-hopping across the Pacific. Antennae of eyes and nose and grubbing fingers captured a new tuft of grass, a fern, a slug, the skull of a bird, a grotto of bright snails. Through the long summer ages of those first few days I enlarged my world and mapped it in my mind: its secure havens, its dust-deserts and puddles, its peaks of dirt and flag-flying bushes. Returning too, dry-throated, over and over again, to its several well-prodded horrors: the bird's gaping bones in its cage of old sticks; the black flies in the corner, slimy dead; dry rags of snakes; and the crowded, rotting, silent-roaring city of a cat's grub-captured carcass.

Once seen, these relics passed within the frontiers of the known lands, to be remembered with a buzzing in the ears, to be revisited when the stomach was strong. They were the first tangible victims of that destroying force whose job I knew went on both night and day, though I could never catch him at it. Nevertheless I was grateful for them. Though they haunted my eyes and stuck in my dreams, they reduced for me the first infinite possibilities of horror. They chastened the imagination with the proof of a limited frightfulness.

From the harbour mouth of the scullery door I learned the rocks and reefs and the channels where safety lay. I discovered the physical pyramid of the cottage, its stores and labyrinths, its centres of magic, and of the green, sprouting island-garden upon which it stood. My Mother and sisters sailed past me like galleons in their busy dresses, and I learned the smells and sounds which followed in their wakes, the surge of breath, air of carbolic, song and grumble, and smashing of crockery.

How magnificent they appeared, full-rigged, those towering girls, with their flying hair and billowing blouses, their white-mast arms stripped for work or washing. At any moment one was boarded by them, bussed and buttoned, or swung up high like a wriggling fish to be hooked and held in their lacy linen.

The scullery was a mine of all the minerals of living. Here I discovered water—a very different element from the green crawling scum that stank in the garden tub. You could pump it in pure blue gulps out of the ground; you could swing on the pump handle and it came out sparkling like liquid sky. And it broke and ran and shone on the tiled floor, or quivered in a jug, or weighted your clothes with cold. You could drink it, draw with it, froth it with soap, swim beetles across it, or fly it in bubbles in the air. You could put your head in it, and open your eyes, and see the sides of the bucket buckle, and hear your caught breath roar, and work your mouth like a fish, and smell the lime from the ground. Substance of magic—which you could tear or wear, confine or scatter, or send down holes, but never burn or break or destroy.

The scullery was water, where the old pump stood. And it had everything else that was related to water: thick steam of Mondays, edgy with starch; soapsuds boiling, bellying and popping, creaking and whispering, rainbowed with light and winking with a million windows. Bubble, bubble, toil and grumble, rinsing and slapping of sheets and shirts, and panting Mother rowing her red arms like oars in the steaming waves. Then the linen came up on a stick out of the pot, like pastry, or woven suds, or sheets of moulded snow.

Here, too, was the scrubbing of floors and boots, of arms and necks, of red and white vegetables. Walk into the morning disorder of this room and all the garden was laid out dripping on the table. Chopped carrots like copper pennies, radishes and chives, potatoes dipped and stripped clean from their coats of mud, the snapping of tight pea-pods, long shells of green pearls, and the tearing of glutinous beans from their nests of wool.

Grown stealthy, marauding among these preparations, one nibbled one's way like a rat through roots and leaves. Peas rolled under the tongue, fresh cold, like solid water; teeth chewed green peel of apples, acid sharp, and the sweet white starch of swedes.[1] Beaten away by wet hands gloved with flour, one returned in a morose and speechless lust. Slivers of raw pastry, moulded, warm, went down in the shapes of men and women—heads and arms of unsalted flesh seasoned with nothing but a dream of cannibalism.

Large meals were prepared in this room, cauldrons of stew for the insatiate hunger of eight. Stews of all that grew on these rich banks, flavoured with sage, coloured with Oxo[2] and laced with a few bones of lamb. There was, it is true, little meat at those times; sometimes a pound of bare ribs for boiling, or an occasional rabbit dumped at the door by a neighbour. But there was green food of great weight in season, and lentils and bread for ballast. Eight to ten loaves came to the house every day, and they never grew dry. We tore them to pieces with their crusts still warm, and their monotony was brightened by the objects we found in them —string, nails, paper, and once a mouse; for those were days of happy-go-lucky baking. The lentils were cooked in a great pot which also heated the water for the Saturday-night baths.

[1] *swedes:* rutabagas, a variety of turnip
[2] *Oxo:* bouillon

Our small wood fire could heat sufficient water to fill one bath only, and this we shared in turn. Being the youngest but one, my water was always the dirtiest but one, and the implications of this privilege remain with me to this day.

Waking one morning in the white-washed bedroom, I opened my eyes and found them blind. Though I stretched them and stared where the room should be, nothing was visible but a glare of gold, flat on my throbbing eyelids. I groped for my body and found it there. I heard the singing of birds. Yet there was nothing at all to be seen of the world save this quivering yellow light. Was I dead? I wondered. Was I in heaven? Whatever it was, I hated it. I had wakened too soon from a dream of crocodiles and I was not ready for this further outrage. Then I heard the girls' steps on the stairs.

"Our Marge!" I shouted, "I can't see nothing!" And I began to give out my howl.

A slap of bare feet slithered across the floor, and I heard sister Marjorie's giggle.

"Just look at him," she said. "Pop and fetch a flannel, Doth—'is eyes've got stuck down again."

The cold edge of the flannel passed over my face, showered me with water, and I was back in the world. Bed and beams, and the sun-square window, and the girls bending over me grinning.

" 'Oo did it?" I yelled.

"Nobody, silly. Your eyes got bunged up, that's all."

The sweet glue of sleep; it had happened before but somehow I always forgot. So I threatened the girls I'd bung theirs up too; I was awake, I could see, I was happy. I lay looking out of the small green window. The world outside was crimson and on fire. I had never seen it looking like that before.

"Doth?" I said, "what's happening to them trees?"

Dorothy was dressing. She leaned out of the window, slow and sleepy, and the light came through her nightdress like sand through a sieve.

"Nothing's happening," she said.

"Yes it is then," I said. "They're falling to bits."

Dorothy scratched her dark head, yawning wide, and white feathers floated out of her hair.

"It's only the leaves droppin'. We're in autumn now. The leaves always drop in autumn."

Autumn? In autumn. Was that were we were? Where the leaves always dropped and there was always this smell. I imagined it continuing, with no change, for ever, these wet flames of woods burning on and on like the bush of Moses,[1] as natural a part of this newfound land as the eternal snows of the poles. Why had we come to such a place?

Marjorie, who had gone down to help with the breakfast, suddenly came tumbling back up the stairs.

"Doth," she whispered; she seemed excited and frightened; "Doth . . . 'e's turned up again. 'Elp on Loll with 'is clothes and come on down, quick."

We went down and found him sitting by the fireside, smiling, wet and cold. I climbed up to the breakfast table and stared at him, the stranger. To me he did not so much appear to be a man as a conglomeration of woody things. His face was red and crinkled, brilliant like fungus. There were leaves in his mud-matted hair, and leaves and twigs on his crumbling clothes, and all over him. His boots were like the black pulp you find when you dig under a tree. Mother gave him porridge and bread and he smiled palely at us all.

"It must have been cruel in the wood," said our Mother.

"I've got some sacks, ma'am," he said, spooning his porridge. "They keep out the wet."

They wouldn't; they'd suck it up like a wick and wrap him in it.

"You oughtn't to live like that," said Mother. "You ought to get back to your home."

"No," smiled the man. "That wouldn't do. They'd jump on me before you could say 'knife.' "

[1] *bush of Moses:* the bush that burned but was not consumed

Mother shook her head sadly, and sighed, and gave him more porridge. We boys adored the look of the man; the girls, fastidious, were more uncertain of him. But he was no tramp or he wouldn't be in the kitchen. He had four bright medals in his pocket, which he would produce and polish and lay on the table like money. He spoke like nobody else we knew, in fact we couldn't understand many of his words. But Mother seemed to understand him, and would ask him questions, and look at the photographs he carried in his shirt and sigh and shake her head. He talked something of battles and of flying in the air, and it was all wonderful to us.

He was no man from these parts. He had appeared on the doorstep one early morning, asking for a cup of tea. Our Mother had brought him in and given him a whole breakfast. There had been blood on his face and he had seemed very weak. Now he was in a kitchen with a woman and a lot of children, and his eyes shone brightly, and his whiskers smiled. He told us he was sleeping in the wood, which seemed to me a good idea. And he was a soldier, because Mother had said so.

I knew about war; all my uncles were in it; my ears from birth had been full of the talk of it. Sometimes I used to climb into the basket chair by the fire and close my eyes and see brown men moving over a field in battle. I was three, but I saw them grope and die and felt myself older than they.

This man did not look like a soldier. He had a beard and his khaki was torn. But the girls insisted he was a soldier, and said it in whispers, like a secret. And when he came down to our house for breakfast, and sat hunched by the fire, steaming with damp and coated with leaves and dirt, I thought of him sleeping up there in the wood. I imagined him sleeping, then having a go at the battle, then coming down to us for a cup of tea. He was the war, and the war was up there; I wanted to ask, "How's the war in that wood?"

But he never told us. He sat drinking his tea, gulping and gasping, the fire drawing the damp out of his clothes as if ghosts were rising from him. When he caught our eyes he smiled from his beard. And when brother Jack shot at him with a spoon, saying, "I'm a sodger," he replied softly, "Aye, and you'd make a better one than me, son, any day."

When he said that, I wondered what had happened to the war. Was he in those rags because he was such a bad soldier? Had he lost the war in the wood?

When he didn't come any more, I knew he had. The girls said some policemen had taken him away in a cart. And Mother sighed and was sad over the poor man.

In weather that was new to me, and cold, and loud with bullying winds, my Mother disappeared to visit my father. This was a long way off, out of sight, and I don't remember her going. But suddenly there were only the girls in the house, tumbling about with brooms and dishcloths, arguing, quarreling, and putting us to bed at random. House and food had a new smell, and meals appeared like dismal conjuring tricks: cold, raw, or black with too much fire. Marjorie was breathless and everywhere; she was fourteen, with all the family in her care. My socks slipped down, and stayed down. I went unwashed for long periods of time. Black leaves swept into the house and piled up in the corners; it rained, and the floors sweated, and washing filled all the lines in the kitchen and dripped sadly on one and all.

But we ate; and the girls moved about in a giggling flurry, exhausted at their losing game. As the days went by, such a tide of muddles mounted in the house that I didn't know which room was which. I lived free, grubbing outside in the mud till I was black as a badger. And my nose ran free, as unchecked as my feet. I sailed my boots down the drain, I cut up sheets for puttees[1] and marched like a soldier through the swamps of leaves. Sensing my chance I wandered far, eating all manner of raw objects: coloured berries, twigs and grubs; sick every day, but with a sickness of which I was proud.

[1] *puttees:* a kind of legging wrapped around the lower leg

All this time the sisters went through the house, darting upstairs and down, beset on all sides by the rain coming in, boys growing filthier, sheets scorching, saucepans burning, and kettles boiling over. The doll's house became a mad-house, and the girls frail birds flying in a wind of chaos. Doth giggled helplessly, Phyl wept among the vegetables, and Marjorie would say, when the day was over: "I'd lie down and die, if there was a place to lie down in."

I was not at all surprised when I heard of the end of the world. Everything pointed to it. The sky was low and whirl-ing with black clouds; the woods roared night and day, stir-ring great seas of sound. One night we sat round the kitchen table, cracking walnuts with the best brass candlestick, when Marjorie came in from the town. She was shining with rain and loaded with bread and buns. She was also very white.

"The war's over," she said. "It's ended."

"Never," said Dorothy.

"They told me at the Stores," said Marjorie. "And they were giving away prunes." She gave us a bagful, and we ate them raw.

The girls got tea and talked about it. And I was sure it was the end of the world. All my life was the war, and the war was the world. Now the war was over. So the end of the world was come. It made no other sense to me.

"Let's go out and see what's happening," said Doth.

"You know we can't leave the kids," Marge said.

So we went too. It was dark, and the gleaming roofs of the village echoed with the buzz of singing. We went hand in hand through the rain, up the bank and down the street. A bonfire crackled in one of the gardens, and a woman jumped up and down in the light of it, red as a devil, a jug in her hand, uttering cries that were not singing. All down the other gardens there were other bonfires too. And a man came up and kissed the girls and hopped in the road and twisted on one toe. Then he fell down in the mud and lay there, work-ing his legs like a frog and croaking a loud song.

I wanted to stop. I had never seen a man like this, in such a wild good humour. But we hurried on. We got to the pub and stared through the windows. The bar seemed on fire with its many lamps. Rose-coloured men, through the rain-wet windows, seemed to bulge and break into flame. They breathed out smoke, drank fire from golden jars, and I heard their great din with awe. Now anything might happen. And it did. A man rose up and crushed a glass like a nut between his hands, then held them out laughing for all to see his wounds. But the blood was lost in the general light of blood. Two other men came waltzing out of the door, locked in each other's arms. Fighting and cursing, they fell over the wall and rolled down the bank in the dark.

There was a screaming woman we could not see. "Jimmy! Jimmy!" she wailed. "Oh, Jimmy! Thee s'll kill 'im! I'll fetch the vicar, I will! Oh, Jimmy!"

"Just 'ark at 'em," said Dorothy, shocked and delighted.

"The kids ought to be in bed," said Marjorie.

"Stop a minute longer. Only a minute. It wouldn't do no 'arm."

Then the schoolhouse chimney caught fire. A fountain of sparks shot high into the night, writhing and sweeping on the wind, falling and dancing along the road. The chimney hissed like a firework, great rockets of flame came gushing forth, emptying the tiny house, so that I expected to see chairs and tables, knives and forks, radiant and burning, follow. The moss-tiles smouldered with sulphurous soot, yellow jets of smoke belched from cracks in the chimney. We stood in the rain and watched it, entranced, as if the sight had been saved for this day. As if the house had been saved, together with the year's bad litter, to be sent up in flames and rejoicing.

How everyone bellowed and scuffled and sang, drunk with their beer and the sight of the fire. But what would happen now that the war was over? What would happen to my uncles who lived in it?—those huge remote men who appeared suddenly at our house, reeking of leather and horses. What would happen to our father, who was khakied like every other man, yet special, not like other men? His picture hung over the piano, trim, haughty, with a badged cap and a spiked moustache. I confused him with the Kaiser.[1] Would he die now the war was over?

As we gazed at the flaming schoolhouse chimney, and smelt the burning throughout the valley, I knew something momentous was occurring. At any moment I looked for a spectacular end to my already long life. Oh, the end of the war and the world! There was rain in my shoes, and Mother had disappeared. I never expected to see another day.

Questions and Comments

Laurie Lee is known chiefly as a poet, and this no doubt accounts for the many startlingly beautiful phrases and rich imagery that flood his prose. "First Light" comes from a biography of his boyhood, *The Edge of Day*. In addition to several books of poems, Mr. Lee has also written a travel book on Spain entitled *A Rose for Winter: Travels in Andalusia*.

1. What major event was taking place in the world at the time of which the author writes?

2. Early in the selection the author says, "I was lost and I did not expect to be found again." What was the cause of this feeling in him?

3. By what means of transportation did the author and his family arrive at their new home? At what point in the selection does the author say he "was born"? What does he mean by this?

4. What visible proof did the author have as a three-year-old child that he was growing bigger and stronger?

[1] *the Kaiser:* Wilhelm II, ruler of Germany during World War I

5. To what does the author compare the knots in the bedroom ceiling? Why does he call them the first book he ever learned to read?

6. What does the author mean by his "acorn shell of senses"?

7. What is the "destroying force" that the author speaks of? What objects that he saw first made him aware of this force? Why does he say he is grateful to these objects?

8. At one point the author compares his mother and sisters to galleons, or sailing ships. Point out some of the nouns and adjectives he uses to carry out the comparison.

9. How did the author discover water? What are some of the things he learned could be done with water?

10. What indications are there in the selection that the author's family was poor? What is the author's attitude toward this situation?

11. Who was the man who came to the kitchen? What facts about his life are you able to infer from the author's deliberately childish description of him?

12. Why did the author think of the end of the war as the end of the world?

Word Study

1. Refer to the selection and give the meaning of the italicized words as revealed by the context. Use a dictionary to check your guesses.

   "They *chastened* the imagination with the proof of a limited frightfulness." (page 220)

   "Grown stealthy, *marauding* among these preparations, one nibbled one's way like a rat. . . ." (page 221)

   "Large meals were prepared in this room, *cauldrons* of stew for the *insatiate* hunger of eight." (page 221)

   "To me he did not so much appear to be a man as a *conglomeration* of woody things." (page 223)

2. A slug may be a counterfeit coin, and a sage may be a wise man. What does *slug* mean as used in "a fern, a slug, the skull of a bird, a grotto of bright snails"? What does *sage* mean as used in "flavoured with sage"?

3. Can you guess the meaning of the italicized words from their origins? Use a dictionary to check your guesses.

"All day she trotted to and fro, flushed and *garrulous*. . . ." (The Latin verb *garrire* means "to chatter.")

". . . my eyes went endlessly voyaging into that long *primeval* light of waking. . . ." (In Latin, *primus* means "first" and *aevum* means "age.")

"They were *archipelagoes* in a sea of blood-colored varnish. . . ." (In Greek, *archi* means "first" and *pelagos* means "sea.")

Composition

1. Because of the richness of their imagination and their extraordinary skill with words, poets are able to help us to discover the beautiful in the commonplace, often through the use of vivid and interesting comparisons. Some of those used by the author in this selection are "snow clouds of elderblossoms," "wet flames of woods," and "burning . . . like the bush of Moses." Find a number of such comparisons in the selection and give your opinion of their effectiveness.

2. The author describes the world about him from a child's point of view. Show how this point of view is maintained throughout the selection.

3. In one of the most delightful passages of the selection, the author discovers an endless source of enjoyment in something as seemingly commonplace as water. You may have made a similar discovery with something other than water. Tell about your discovery.

4. Describe your own earliest memories.

Anne Frank's family were forced to flee their native Germany in the wake of Nazi persecution of the Jews. They found refuge in Holland. But when the Germans swept into Holland, the Franks were forced to hide in the "Secret Annexe"—an abandoned section of an old office building in Amsterdam. After two years of successfully eluding the Germans, they were discovered. Seven months later Anne died in a concentration camp at Bergen-Belsen. She left a diary which was later discovered and then published. It is written to "Kitty," an imaginary friend.

Those in hiding with Anne were her parents, her older sister, Margot, a dentist by the name of Mr. Dussel, and Mr. and Mrs. Van Daan and their teen-age son, Peter. The names of other persons who were associated with the Franks are mentioned in the following selection.

from THE DIARY OF A YOUNG GIRL

Anne Frank

Thursday, 25 March, 1943

Dear Kitty,

Yesterday Mummy, Daddy, Margot, and I were sitting pleasantly together when suddenly Peter came in and whispered something in Daddy's ear. I heard something about "a barrel fallen over in the warehouse" and "someone fumbling about at the door." Margot had heard it too; but when Daddy and Peter went off immediately, she tried to calm me down a bit, because I was naturally as white as a sheet and very jittery.

The three of us waited in suspense. A minute or two later Mrs. Van Daan came upstairs; she'd been listening to the wireless in the private office. She told us that Pim[1] had asked her to turn off the wireless and go softly upstairs. But you know what that's like, if you want to be extra quiet, then each step of the old stairs creaks twice as loudly. Five minutes later Pim and Peter appeared again, white to the roots of their hair, and told us their experiences.

They had hidden themselves under the stairs and waited, with no result at first. But suddenly, yes, I must tell you, they heard two loud bumps, just as if two doors were banged here in the house. Pim was upstairs in one leap. Peter warned Dussel first, who finally landed upstairs with a lot of fuss and noise. Then we all went up in stockinged feet to the Van Daans on the next floor. Mr. Van Daan had a bad cold and had already gone to bed, so we all drew up closely around his bed and whispered our suspicions to him.

Each time Mr. Van Daan coughed loudly, Mrs. Van Daan and I were so scared that we thought we were going to have a fit. That went on until one of us got the bright idea of giving him some codeine, which soothed the cough at once. Again we waited and waited, but we heard no more and finally we all came to the conclusion that the thieves had taken to their heels when they heard footsteps in the house, which was otherwise so silent.

Now it was unfortunate that the wireless downstairs was still turned to England, and that the chairs were neatly arranged round it. If the door had been forced, and the air-raid wardens had noticed and warned the police, then the results might have been very unpleasant. So Mr. Van Daan got up and put on his coat and hat and followed Daddy cautiously downstairs, Peter took up the rear, armed with a large hammer in case of emergencies. The ladies upstairs (including Margot and me) waited in suspense, until the gentlemen

[1] *Pim:* Anne's nickname for her father

reappeared five minutes later and told us that all was quiet in the house.

We arranged that we would not draw any water or pull the plug in the lavatory. But as the excitement had affected most of our tummies, you can imagine what the atmosphere was like when we had each paid a visit in succession.

When something like that happens, heaps of other things seem to come at the same time, as now. Number One was that the clock at the Westertoren, which I always find so reassuring, did not strike. Number Two was that, Mr. Vossen having left earlier than usual the previous evening, we didn't know definitely whether Elli had been able to get hold of the key, and had perhaps forgotten to shut the door. It was still evening and we were still in a state of uncertainty, although we certainly did feel a bit reassured by the fact that from about eight o'clock, when the burglar had alarmed the house, until half past ten we had not heard a sound. On further reflection it also seemed very unlikely to us that a thief would have forced open a door so early in the evening, while there were still people about in the street. Moreover, one of us got the idea that it was possible that the caretaker of the warehouse next door was still at work since, in the excitement, and with the thin walls, one can easily make a mistake, and what's more, one's imagination can play a big part at such critical moments.

So we all went to bed; but none of us could get to sleep. Daddy as well as Mummy and Mr. Dussel were awake, and without much exaggeration I can say that I hardly slept a wink. This morning the men went downstairs to see whether the outside door was still shut, and everything turned out to be quite safe. We gave everyone a detailed description of the nerve-racking event. They all made fun of it, but it is easy to laugh at such things afterwards. Elli was the only one who took us seriously.

Yours, Anne

Wednesday, 4 August, 1943

Dear Kitty,

Now that we have been in the "Secret Annexe" for over a year, you know something of our lives, but some of it is quite indescribable. There is so much to tell, everything is so different from ordinary times and from ordinary people's lives. But still, to give you a closer look into our lives, now and again I intend to give you a description of an ordinary day. Today I'm beginning with the evening and night.

Nine o'clock in the evening. The bustle of going to bed in the "Secret Annexe" begins and it is always really quite a business. Chairs are shoved about, beds are pulled down, blankets unfolded, nothing remains where it is during the day. I sleep on the little divan, which is not more than one and a half meters long. So chairs have to be used to lengthen it. A feather duster, sheets, pillows, blankets, are all fetched from Dussel's bed where they remain during the day. One hears terrible creaking in the next room: Margot's concertina-bed being pulled out. Again, divan, blankets, and pillows, everything is done to make the wooden slats a bit more comfortable. It sounds like thunder above, but it is only Mrs. Van Daan's bed. This is shifted to the window, you see, in order to give Her Majesty in the pink bed jacket fresh air to tickle her dainty nostrils!

After Peter's finished, I step into the washing cubicle, where I give myself a thorough wash and general toilet; it occasionally happens (only in the hot weeks or months) that there is a tiny flea floating in the water. Then teeth cleaning, hair curling, manicure, and my cotton-wool pads with hydrogen peroxide (to bleach black mustache hairs)—all this in under half an hour.

Half past nine. Quickly into dressing gown, soap in one hand, pottie, hairpins, pants, curlers, and cotton wool in the other, I hurry out of the bathroom; but usually I'm called back once for the various hairs which decorate the washbasin in graceful curves, but which are not approved of by the next person.

Ten o'clock. Put up the blackout. Good night! For at least a quarter of an hour there is creaking of beds and a sighing of broken springs, then all is quiet, at least that is if our neighbors upstairs don't quarrel in bed.

Half past eleven. The bathroom door creaks. A narrow strip of light falls into the room. A squeak of shoes, a large coat, even larger than the man inside it—Dussel returns from his night work in Kraler's office. Shuffling on the floor for ten minutes, crackle of paper (that is the food which has to be stowed away), and a bed is made. Then the form disappears again and one only hears suspicious noises from the lavatory from time to time.

Three o'clock. I have to get up for a little job in the metal pot under my bed, which is on a rubber mat for safety's sake in case of leakage. When this has to take place, I always hold my breath, as it clatters into the tin like a brook from a mountain. Then the pot is returned to its place and the figure in the white nightgown, which evokes the same cry from Margot every evening: "Oh, that indecent nightdress!" steps back into bed.

Then a certain person lies awake for about a quarter of an hour, listening to the sounds of the night. Firstly, to whether there might not be a burglar downstairs, then to the various beds, above, next door, and in my room, from which one is usually able to make out how the various members of the household are sleeping, or how they pass the night in wakefulness.

The latter is certainly not pleasant, especially when it concerns a member of the family by the name of Dussel. First, I hear a sound like a fish gasping for breath, this is repeated nine or ten times, then with much ado and interchanged with little smacking sounds, the lips are moistened, followed by a lengthy twisting and turning in bed and rearranging of pillows. Five minutes' perfect peace and then

the same sequence of events unfolds itself at least three
times more, after the doctor has soothed himself to sleep
again for a little while. It can also happen that we get a bit
of shooting in the night, varying between one o'clock and
four. I never really realize it, until from habit I am already
standing at my bedside. Sometimes I'm so busy dreaming
that I'm thinking about French irregular verbs or a quarrel
upstairs. It is some time before I begin to realize that guns
are firing and that I am still in the room. But it usually
happens as described above. I quickly grab a pillow and
handkerchief, put on my dressing gown and slippers, and
scamper to Daddy, like Margot wrote in this birthday poem:

> *The first shot sounds at dead of night.*
> *Hush, look! A door creaks open wide,*
> *A little girl glides into sight,*
> *Clasping a pillow to her side.*

Once landed in the big bed, the worst is over, except if
the firing gets very bad.

Quarter to seven. Trrrrr—the alarm clock that raises its
voice at any hour of the day (if one asks for it and sometimes when one doesn't). Crack—ping—Mrs. Van Daan has
turned it off. Creak—Mr. Van Daan gets up. Puts on water
and then full speed to the bathroom.

Quarter past seven. The door creaks again. Dussel can go
to the bathroom. Once alone, I take down the blackout—
and a new day in the "Secret Annexe" has begun.

Yours, Anne

Tuesday, 14 March, 1944

Dear Kitty,

Perhaps it would be entertaining for you—though not in
the least for me—to hear what we are going to eat today. As
the charwoman is at work downstairs, I'm sitting on the
Van Daans' table at the moment. I have a handkerchief
soaked in some good scent (bought before we came here)

over my mouth and held against my nose. You won't gather much from this, so let's "begin at the beginning."

The people from whom we obtained food coupons have been caught, so we just have our five ration cards and no extra coupons, and no fats. As both Miep and Koophuis are ill, Elli hasn't time to do any shopping, so the atmosphere is dreary and dejected, and so is the food. From tomorrow we shall not have a scrap of fat, butter, or margarine left. We can't have fried potatoes (to save bread) for breakfast any longer, so we have porridge instead, and as Mrs. Van Daan thinks we're starving, we have bought some full cream milk "under the counter." Our supper today consists of a hash made from kale which has been preserved in a barrel. Hence the precautionary measure with the handkerchief! It's incredible how kale can stink when it's a year old! The smell in the room is a mixture of bad plums, strong preservatives, and rotten eggs. Ugh! the mere thought of eating that muck makes me feel sick.

Added to this, our potatoes are suffering from such peculiar diseases that out of two buckets of *pommes de terre*,[1] one whole one ends up on the stove. We amuse ourselves by searching for all the different kinds of diseases, and have come to the conclusion that they range from cancer and smallpox to measles! Oh, no, it's no joke to be in hiding during the fourth year of the war. If only the whole rotten business was over!

Quite honestly, I wouldn't care so much about the food, if only it were more pleasant here in other ways. There's the rub: this tedious existence is beginning to make us all touchy.

The following are the views of the five grownups on the present situation:

Mrs. Van Daan: "The job as queen of the kitchen lost its attraction a long time ago. It's dull to sit and do nothing, so I go back to my cooking again. Still, I have to complain that it's impossible to cook without any fats, and all these

---

[1] *pommes de terre:* French for *potatoes*

nasty smells make me feel sick. Nothing but ingratitude and rude remarks do I get in return for my services. I am always the black sheep, always the guilty one. Moreover, according to me, very little progress is being made in the war; in the end the Germans will still win. I'm afraid we're going to starve, and if I'm in a bad mood I scold everyone."

Mr. Van Daan: "I must smoke and smoke and smoke, and then the food, the political situation, and Kerli's[1] moods don't seem so bad. Kerli is a darling wife."

But if he hasn't anything to smoke, then nothing is right, and this is what one hears: "I'm getting ill, we don't live well enough, I must have meat. Frightfully stupid person, my Kerli!" After this a terrific quarrel is sure to follow.

Mrs. Frank: "Food is not very important, but I would love a slice of rye bread now, I feel so terribly hungry. If I were Mrs. Van Daan I would have put a stop to Mr. Van Daan's everlasting smoking a long time ago. But now I must definitely have a cigarette, because my nerves are getting the better of me. The English make a lot of mistakes, but still the war is progressing. I must have a chat and be thankful I'm not in Poland."

Mr. Frank: "Everything's all right, I don't require anything. Take it easy, we've ample time. Give me my potatoes and then I will keep my mouth shut. Put some of my rations on one side for Elli. The political situation is very promising, I'm extremely optimistic!"

Mr. Dussel: "I must get my task for today, everything must be finished on time. Political situation 'outschtänding' and it is 'eempossible' that we'll be caught.

"I, I, I . . . !"

Yours, Anne

Sunday, 19 March, 1944

Dear Kitty,

Yesterday was a great day for me. I had decided to talk things out with Peter. Just as we were going to sit down to

[1] *Kerli:* Mr. Van Daan's nickname for his wife

supper I whispered to him, "Are you going to do shorthand this evening, Peter?" "No," was his reply. "Then I'd just like to talk to you later!" He agreed. After the dishes were done, I stood by the window in his parents' room awhile for the look of things, but it wasn't long before I went to Peter. He was standing on the left side of the open window, I went and stood on the right side, and we talked. It was much easier to talk beside the open window in semidarkness than in bright light, and I believe Peter felt the same.

We told each other so much, so very very much, that I can't repeat it all, but it was lovely; the most wonderful evening I have ever had in the "Secret Annexe." I will just tell you briefly the various things we talked about. First we talked about the quarrels and how I regard them quite differently now, and then about the estrangement between us and our parents.

I told Peter about Mummy and Daddy, and Margot, and about myself.

At one moment he asked, "I suppose you always give each other a good night kiss, don't you?"

"*One,* dozens, why, don't you?"

"No, I have hardly ever kissed anyone."

"Not even on your birthday?"

"Yes, I have then."

We talked about how we neither of us confide in our parents, and how his parents would have loved to have his confidence, but that he didn't wish it. How I cry my heart out in bed, and he goes up into the loft and swears. How Margot and I really only know each other well for a little while, but that, even so, we don't tell each other everything, because we are always together. Over every imaginable thing —oh, he was just as I thought!

Then we talked about 1942, how different we were then. We just don't recognize ourselves as the same people any more. How we simply couldn't bear each other in the beginning. He thought I was much too talkative and unruly, and I soon came to the conclusion that I'd no time for him. I couldn't understand why he didn't flirt with me, but now I'm glad. He also mentioned how much he isolated himself from us all. I said that there was not much difference between my noise and his silence. That I love peace and quiet too, and have nothing for myself alone, except my diary. How glad he is that my parents have children here, and that I'm glad he is here. That I understand his reserve now and his relationship with his parents, and how I would love to be able to help him.

"You always do help me," he said. "How?" I asked, very surprised. "By your cheerfulness." That was certainly the loveliest thing he said. It was wonderful, he must have grown to love me as a friend, and that is enough for the time being. I am so grateful and happy, I just can't find the words. I must apologize, Kitty, that my style is not up to standard today.

I have just written down what came into my head. I have the feeling now that Peter and I share a secret. If he looks at me with those eyes that laugh and wink, then it's just as if a little light goes on inside me. I hope it will remain like this and that we may have many, many more glorious times together!

Your grateful, happy Anne

Questions and Comments

1. In her letter of March 25, 1943, Anne speaks of a "nerve-racking event." What is it?

2. What interruptions in the normal routine occurred that night to add to Anne's anxiety?

3. What is Mrs. Van Daan's opinion of the progress of the war? How does her opinion differ from Mr. Frank's?

4. In the letter of March 19, 1944, Anne and Peter have a heart-to-heart talk. What do they discuss? What do they discover about themselves?

5. At one point Peter says that Anne helps him by her cheerfulness. What does he mean?

6. Anne and Peter confess that they do not recognize themselves as the same people any more. What do they mean?

Word Study

1. In the March 25, 1943, letter Anne mentions that Mr. Van Daan was given *codeine* for his cough. What is codeine?

2. In the August 4, 1943, letter Anne mentions the *divan* on which she sleeps, Margot's *concertina-bed,* and the washing *cubicle*. Give a definition of the italicized terms.

3. Anne's nightgown evokes the same cry from Margot every evening. The work *evoke* comes from the Latin verb *vocare* meaning "to call." What does *evoke* mean? What other words derived from *vocare* can you give?

4. In the March 14, 1944, letter Anne mentions the *charwoman,* says they have bought milk *"under the counter,"* and tells of their supper of a hash made from *kale*. Look up *charwoman* in a dictionary and give its meaning (Hint: compare *char* and *chore*). What does *under the counter* mean? What is *kale*?

5. In the March 19, 1944, letter Anne uses the words *estrangement* (the estrangement between the children and the parents) and *unruly* (Peter at first thought Anne too talkative and unruly). What do these words mean?

Composition

1. Discuss your opinion of a diary as a method of reporting and re-creating events. State the advantages and disadvantages of such a method.

2. In her letter of March 25, 1943, Anne says ". . . one's imagination can play a big part at such critical moments." Explain what she means and show how this is true by describing an actual experience in which your own imagination played strange tricks on you.

3. Describe the impression you get of Anne from her daily routine, her fears, her hopes, and her attitude toward herself and others.

A courageous leader can inspire courage in other men, and that is exactly what Lt. John F. Kennedy, skipper of PT-109, did for the members of his crew who survived the sinking of their ship in the Solomon Islands. The following is an account of that fateful night in August of 1943 and the struggle to survive in the difficult days that followed.

TEN LIVES FOR KENNEDY

Edward Oxford

PT-109 had seen much of the best and the worst of it on long raiding sweeps off the Solomons during that wearying spring of 1943. On difficult dusk-to-dawn patrols all along the Slot,[1] the old seventy-seven-footer had whacked the enemy's transports, strafed his barges and mauled his shore installations. By August, it had become part of the great counter-thrust gathering against the Japanese around New Georgia. To the eleven enlisted men and two officers, who more than a few times had watched its young skipper edge their luck to the brim point, PT-109 seemed, perhaps reasonably enough, indestructible. . . .

Radioman John Maguire: I looked for a long time out across the bow of PT-109 into the night and squinched hard ahead, trying my best to glimpse some shape or movement on the seas, or maybe even the light of a star. It was the black heart of a squally night, the kind of 2 A.M. the Solomon Islands know in August. No moon, no sound at all, and not an awful lot to really get smiling about.

[1] *Slot:* a narrow passage between islands

Somewhere ahead were elements of the Japanese Imperial Fleet hard about their business of evacuating men northward from the islands; we'd been hunting them all afternoon and night, and now we were going home empty-handed. Somewhere above were Jap float planes, the kind that liked to follow the wakes of our PTs in moonlight and splatter the plywood decks to splinters. And somewhere around us were volcanic and jungle islands, filled to standing room only with some of the unkindest soldiers it has never, thank heaven, been my misfortune to meet.

The skipper was at the wheel, a gangling kid who said he was twenty-six—but I always thought that was kind of high. One of the officers had tagged him with the nickname "Shafty"—partly, I guess, because he was so skinny-looking and had maybe just a few muscles, and also because it sounded like New England, which was where he was from.

He was Jack Kennedy, a lieutenant, jg. I'd been with him on earlier missions and I knew just three things about him. The kid himself was a millionaire. His father was an ambassador. And once, when a ship's carpenter bawled hell out of him for accidentally splashing some water on him, the lieutenant just stood there in his skinny green shorts and said, "Excuse me," and let it go at that. That carpenter did a lot of gulping later when he found out the kid was PT-109's skipper.

Kennedy was at my left in the cockpit, the little open bridge up in the bow. I had a voice mike plugged in there, but we didn't have anything to say to anyone, and nobody seemed to want to talk to us. At my right elbow, jammed into the starboard gun turret, was our 20-mm man, Marney. To keep our movements silent, we held the middle engine low, and throttled the starboard and port engines down to neutral. Aft, the rest of the crew were having just as bad luck as we, trying to find something for the thin one to shoot at.

The sea was silent. Other nights, we had feasted our guns on Jap barges and supply craft, but this haul seemed a sure blank.

Then Marney yelled at the top of his voice, "Ship at two o'clock!"[1]

Kennedy and I suddenly saw something fast and tough bearing down on us. It was a Jap destroyer, moving like lightning.

"Hey," Kennedy yelled, "look at this!" He hit me on the arm and shouted, "Sound general quarters!"

I ran aft about six steps, yelled general quarters, and stumbled back to the cockpit.

The skipper sounded the engine-room buzzer, signalling MacMahon, the engineer, to throttle starboard and port engines full ahead. MacMahon never had a chance to move. Up on the bow, Ensign George Ross was trying to fire the old World War I 37-mm field piece we had mounted there on a log. He had gotten his projectile in, but had no time to ram it home.

The destroyer hit us like the *Queen Mary*. Its bow crushed into our side about three feet in front of Marney's turret, sweeping him down into the sea and under the Jap's propellers. He didn't even have a chance to scream.

Kennedy went slamming down smack on his back, and I went down with him. I could hear him gasping on the deck when he hit. I didn't go out, but I felt dizzy and I could hear the planks and decking crack apart.

The destroyer didn't even slow down. Its bow carried along our starboard side, shearing away the middle two-thirds of PT-109. Our boat snapped in two, and we never saw the after half again. Kirksey, our after gunner, went with it.

I was trying to stand, and I was praying harder than ever I'd done before in my entire life.

---

[1] *two o'clock:* direction indicated by the hour hand of the clock

Kennedy kept trying to get up. He said, "Are you all right, Mac?"

On the bridge of the Japanese destroyer *Amagiri*, Commander Kahii Hanami scarcely bothered to look back. He had spotted the slow-cruising PT-109 from a half-mile, ordered his helmsmen to cut starboard ten degrees, and before the Americans knew what hit them, proceeded to cut her neatly in half with the full brunt of a thirty-five-knot prow. The PT boat's fuel tanks exploded at once, lighting the sky with the blaze of its Packard engines' high-octane, aviation gasoline. Hanami contented himself with a few rounds from his stern guns into the flames, then hurried toward home. There'd be, he was sure, no survivors. . . .

Gunner's Mate Charles Harris: I heard general quarters[1] and I jumped up and saw the destroyer right on top of us. I dove over the torpedo tube and went under. Next thing I knew, I was sitting 'way out in water and flames were exploding all around me.

I didn't even know I had my life jacket on. I thought I had left it aboard. Somewhere, I could hear MacMahon yelling for help; then, suddenly, there he was; he had come up smack in the flames of our own high-octane gasoline. I tried to get close to him. He was burned bad, his face and hands and arms. He must have been dragged under by the destroyer, because the helmet was jammed down over his face and he hardly knew what was happening. I tried to move him toward the 109 wreckage, but a steady breeze kept moving it away from us. My left leg wouldn't move; I had hit it against the torpedo tube, diving in.

I yelled for Kennedy. "Skipper! Skipper!" I kept yelling. "MacMahon's burned bad. Can you give him a hand!"

In a couple of minutes, he reached us. He grabbed Mac-Mahon and started towing him. I could see Kennedy trying

[1] *general quarters:* alert that a warship be at maximum readiness for action with all hands at battle stations

to dig fast for it, because 109 kept edging away. He half lifted MacMahon out of the water so the others could get him aboard, then started back for us.

He held me up in the water while I took off sweater and shoes and my heavy undergear and then he put my life jacket back on me. I tried to swim, but I couldn't kick with my left leg.

I said, "Skipper, I can't swim!"

"Try," he said.

"But I can't make it!"

He looked right at me and gave me hell. "For a man from Boston, you're really putting on some exhibition out here, Harris."

I guess I must have muttered at him, but by now he had me in tow and was swimming steadily back to the boat. I tried to kick a bit with my other leg, but he was plenty strong enough for both of us. It took us an hour to make the boat; it kept drifting from us.

The watertight compartments forward kept half of PT-109 afloat. We sprawled there in the dark, dazed. Kennedy took a head count, and one by one, the men answered. Maguire, Mauer, Albert, Thom, Zinser, Starkey and Ross were all alive. MacMahon, lying in a coma, was burned black. Johnston, an engineer, had been battered black and blue and was half dead from swallowing gasoline. We called out for Kirksey and Marney for an hour, but no answer came.

That night a naval action lighted the skies to the north, and the eleven survivors of PT-109 lay close to their wreckage, gasping in the fumes of their own gasoline. The skipper had salvaged a ship's lantern, a pistol and a waterlogged box of candy. The crew had among them a Thompson submachine gun, a .38 revolver, three .45s and nine clips. They had no food, no water, no medical supplies. Worst of all, they were adrift in enemy waters and already had been written off as lost by the squadron back in New Georgia.

Engineer Pat MacMahon: We were in the drift toward a big island; it was maybe a mile away. I was burned and banged-up bad, but I was conscious, and looked up at the morning sun. My left shoulder and arm ached, like they had been battered on a scrub board. But it was my right side and arm that had gotten the flames. And my face was burned all over. My whole body hurt a lot and I knew now I could hardly move. I was sprawled out on the deck, and I kept looking up at the sky. It kept bobbing.

I could hear the skipper and the men talking. Kennedy decided we'd stay with the current a while, and save our strength. He got the men into the water to make more room on the bow for me and Johnston, who had swallowed a load of gasoline. We all kept hoping the Japs wouldn't spot us from the islands and come out after us. On one island, just about a mile to the south, we could see a Jap camp, with trucks and men. But then we realized that we were gradually edging closer to it. Nobody wanted to be taken alive.

Then the bow of the PT-109 began to founder. Kennedy gave us the word:

"We're going to that small one," he said, pointing to a tiny island about three miles away. "We'll have to swim for it. Everyone on the log. I'll take MacMahon."

He was very matter-of-fact about it, like he was talking about the weather. He took the two long straps of my kapok which I had on over the Mae West, tied them together and eased me into the water. Then he put the damn straps in his mouth, holding them with his clenched teeth, and started swimming. I was on my back, my head toward him, trying to push my feet to help him. I wasn't much good to him. I couldn't believe the skinny kid would get very far with me, but I tried to help him.

The others clambered onto the big-deck timber we had used for our 37-mm mounting. Kennedy towed me ahead and they followed, hanging onto the big plank.

An hour went by. The skipper would tug and pull me and then rest a while and get his breath and I could hear him coughing. Then we'd start again, yard by yard, him tugging and stroking ahead, me doing what little I could to kick my feet. Both of us kept swallowing water. I knew he was in no great shape himself; he had been bounced down bad by the ramming. And he never looked more than one hundred forty pounds to me, even on a good day, and today, was no good day. But he was swimming for both of us now and not counting the cost. He'd pull and rest, pull and rest, and say, "How are you, Mac?" to keep my spirits up.

The sky kept moving above me a little at a time as the sun left us. We went on for a long, long time like that. Then it was near night, and the skipper had been pulling me for more than four hours, dragging me by his teeth, towing me by the vest, thrashing his way ahead.

Sometime about the fifth hour, the skipper said, "Pappy, we're going in," and I thought I never heard such happy words in all my life. Then Kennedy half towed and half carried me ashore. I tried to help myself and walk in but coral cut both of us bad and when we got on the sand, Kennedy and I collapsed.

He had been in the water, counting night and morning, for about ten hours.

The survivors of PT-109 crawled onto the atoll and rested among its wind-bare palm trees. But the skipper didn't stay more than a brief time. He told his incredulous crew that he was going back into the sea, this time to swim out into Ferguson Passage, a few miles beyond the next island. PTs of their own squadron had been going through the passage on night patrols; he'd go out into the middle, he explained, tread water, and try to signal them for help.

Quartermaster Ed Mauer: So, without saying very much more about it, Kennedy hitched up his shorts, put on a vest, tied a .38 around his neck, picked up the ship's lantern and gave us a quick wave of the hand.

The he walked out into the sea and started swimming, slowly, toward Ferguson Passage.

The men were glum, and I'm sure some had given up hope of ever seeing Kennedy again. Bringing in MacMahon had exhausted him. His back was in bad shape. Then there were those currents. Who knew where they were pulling? And I had heard enough stories about the barracuda in these waters not to want to think about what kind of wild life might be swimming the passage with Kennedy.

But the funny thing was that I had no doubt about it. The skipper was part of the outfit; he had to come back. Back at base or on patrols, whenever he said he'd get us something, he'd never stop until he did. He used to come up with bread and candy out of the jungle for us. We made it a habit to count on his word. If he said he'd go get help, I knew he'd just go ahead and do it.

But this time the skipper just about died in the doing of it. He moved out east toward the next island, and we took turns on watch for him. If he found a boat, he would flash the lantern twice. The password would be "Roger," and our answer would be "Wilco."

It took him close to an hour to get past the reef into the passage, and then he just hung out there, hoping and holding his lantern through the night. We waited.

He hung out there for hours, but none of our boats were moving through that night, so he decided to swim back to us. Something went wrong and he started drifting away in the current right past us. He flashed the ship's lantern once and yelled, "Roger!"; and we went out onto the coral reef to try to reach him. But he was gone.

Kennedy, as I found out later, was pretty helpless and was being dragged away by the current. It pushed him in long, sweeping circles all through the night, moving him like driftwood around and among the Jap islands to the north and east. He felt sure he would die out there and kept lapsing into unconsciousness. We kept looking for him, but never saw a sign of him again that night.

Thinking about the skipper lost out there, I started to remember about the PT-109. PT-109 wasn't even supposed to have gone out on the mission in the first place. A Jap air attack on the base the afternoon we left knocked off some other boats in our squadron, so instead of having a day off, we were all of a sudden a replacement. Kirksey had sat with me in the base chart room, and he said he thought the PT-109 wouldn't come back this time, and I had tried to calm him down. But Kirksey was right and I was wrong.

Then, in the morning, I saw a ghost. There was the skipper, crawling out of the sea on his hands and knees. We ran to him and carried him. He was throwing up and he could barely move. He had been in the water for twelve hours that night and he was feverish. We carried him up the beach, where he passed out.

"Somehow, I knew he'd come back," somebody said.

That night Kennedy, cold and sick, lay on the beach. Ensign Ross swam out into the passage in his place, but had no better luck than his chief. Since the island offered neither food nor water, Kennedy insisted that the men move on to an island closer to the passage. They gathered again about the big log, pushed it into the sea, and again began to swim.

Torpedoman Ray Starkey: We began swimming to an island to the southeast, a little bigger and with more trees. It was the same gruelling swim as before. Kennedy took MacMahon ahead, pulling his life jacket strap with his teeth. But this time, Kennedy was much weaker, and MacMahon even more helpless than before. Kennedy moved painfully slowly, stroking ahead steadily, like a man caught in slow-motion film.

The rest of us hung onto our log and kept pushing. It took us three hours to cover the mile to that island.

MacMahon, somehow, was still alive. His burns were beginning to fester, but he didn't whimper. The skipper was looking terrible. His feet were blistered and swollen, and he threw up a lot from the salt water he swallowed while he was pulling MacMahon.

Some of the men found some coconuts and banged them open and gulped down the milk. Just about all of them turned inside out, they got so sick. We even tried to eat some live snails, but, believe me, they were punk.

That night, it rained a torrent and everyone went around licking water off the tree trunks and leaves.

The next morning, we found out why the water tasted so bitter. It was because the bushes were covered solid with bird dung. So we named the place Bird Island.

One fellow said to Maguire, "Mac, give that necklace a working over."

Maguire held onto his rosary beads and said, "Yes, don't worry. I'll take care of all you fellows."

Kennedy kept looking out at Nauru Island, the one right on the passage. There might be Japs on it, but we had no food and no water. He asked Ross if he'd go with him and Ross said yes.

"We're going to try it again," he told us. "Keep out of sight and watch for us."

The expected search patrols had not come. There were no American boats, and no American planes. Once a Japanese barge slowly circled the island, but did not spot them. Japanese planes frequently flew by, but moved too fast to notice the men on the atoll. The one hope now was to flag down a PT-boat in Ferguson Passage.

Ensign George "Barney" Ross: Kennedy and I were swimming side by side for Nauru. I guess you couldn't have found a sorrier sight than the two of us, just about inching ahead. My arms ached and my legs were numb, but I just kept going, staying with the skipper as he stroked. It took us more than an hour to make only a half-mile.

Beach coral cut us proper, and we half walked and half crawled across Nauru, expecting any minute to find Japs. We found instead a smashed landing barge with a cask of water and some old hardtack.[1] Delicious!

Both of us stayed up all night on the passage side of Nauru, hoping to hear the PTs go by. Not a one showed.

Next sunrise, Kennedy was prowling around and came on a one-man dugout canoe hidden under some palm trees. That night he was right out there again in the passage, searching tirelessly back and forth for PTs.

No luck. So he paddled back to the other island, and gave the men a keg of water and some hardtack biscuits. It was the first food they'd had since our boat had been rammed.

Coming back, Kennedy got into storm trouble. A tropic squall swept in on him in open water, sending his canoe under, and leaving him out there alone in the rain. Fortunately, a party of natives in a war canoe spotted him and dragged him to shore. I was supposed to be hidden, but these bushy-haired fellows with bones piercing their noses brought Kennedy right to me, there among the palm fronds. He looked like a goner.

For a long time, we tried to communicate with the natives in pidgin English. "Rendova, Rendova. American, American," we said, over and over.

Kennedy picked up a coconut and scratched a message on its shell with a jackknife: "ELEVEN ALIVE NATIVE KNOWS POST AND REEFS NAURU ISLAND KENNEDY."

Then he said to the bushy-hairs, "Rendova, Rendova"—the name of the base where our PTs were.

The natives finally got the idea. They showed us where there was a two-man canoe. Then, after a lot of chatter, they

---

[1] *hardtack:* a kind of biscuit

got back into their own war canoe and started toward Rendova. Kennedy and I were so exhausted we just passed out, and I thought he was finished.

But late that night, he turned to me and said in a tired voice, "Barney, we'll have to try again."

I could hardly walk, much less go out into the passage again.

"Skipper, I don't think we can make it."

"We're going to do it," he insisted.

As we paddled into the passage, we hit weather. The wind rose fast and, before we could do anything, we were in a howling storm. The waves swept in on us five feet high and swamped the canoe. Kennedy hung onto the bow and I held onto the stern, fighting a tide which was dragging us to open seas. We kicked and thrashed against the current, and for two gruelling hours, beat our way back toward the beach.

The wind got worse and the rain was so hard we could hardly see each other.

"Sorry I got you out here, Barney!" shouted Kennedy.

"This would be a great time to say I told you so," I shouted back, "but I won't."

Suddenly we heard the crash of surf and were in the reef tide. Kennedy went flying on the crest of a wave and disappeared. I was cart-wheeling under water, banging along on the coral. I could feel my right arm slam against the sharp edges and then I was kneeling in shoal water.

I could hear Kennedy yell: "Barney! Barney! Barney!"

He was crawling in the surf. Both of us were bleeding. We grabbed onto each other and stumbled ashore. I couldn't believe we were still alive. We went out as soon as we hit the sand.

I had been asleep a long time and then I heard a noise, and it was morning and four big natives were standing over us, looking at us. I shook Kennedy and he sat up, bolt-upright. They looked mean.

Then one stepped forward, and in a beautiful British accent said, "I have a letter for you, sir."

Kennedy ripped it open and read:

"On His Majesty's Service. To the Senior Officer, Nauru Island.

"I have just learned of your presence on Nauru Island. I am in command of a New Zealand infantry patrol operating on New Georgia. I strongly advise that you come with these natives to me. Meanwhile, I shall be in radio communication with your authorities at Rendova, and we can plan to collect balance of your party. Lieutenant Evans."

I jumped up and slapped the big boys on the back and we all laughed. It was the first time I had laughed in five days.

Back at Rendova, the PT squadron had listed 109 as destroyed in action. Accounts of the collision made it seem certain that the boat had exploded. Solemnly, men in the squadron had even toasted the lost men and had broken their glasses in remembrance. But now Kennedy's scrawled coconut message suddenly stirred hope for the lost men. . . .

Engineer Bill Johnston: The days were telling on us; so when people started squawking, I'd take it on myself to give them an ear-banging.

Somebody said that we would "rot out here forever." So I said, "Shut up, will you? You're too miserable to die." And once when one guy said he was going to do a lot of praying, I yelled, "You guys give me a pain. Ain't one of you said ten minutes of prayers in all your lives. And now, when you want something and start praying, who's going to listen to you?"

I figured by pepping up the men it would help them a little. It was the least I could do for the skipper. I was feeling like someone had rolled over me with a steamroller and my gut was still full of gasoline, but when I thought of Kennedy dragging himself in and out of the water on the swims and Ross out there with him, it gave me a terrific lift. I'd been with a lot of brave men in a lot of bad spots during my years in the boondocks, but this was one hell and half of a man, win, lose, or draw. I didn't pick him for my skipper, but I kept thanking God that the Navy'd picked him for me.

Then, like a miracle, these natives—now it was the sixth day for us—brought the skipper and Ensign Ross in their canoe to our beach and we almost bust out crying, we were so glad to see they were alive.

Kennedy shook our hands and grinned, and looked over MacMahon and me.

The natives built a lean-to for MacMahon to protect him from the sun. He was far gone now, but he kept fighting. The burns were bad. And they lay Ross down on the sand near where I was, and his arm had swollen three times its size from where the coral cut him. Everybody was haggard and weak.

The skipper stood up and said in that same matter-of-fact way, "I'm going to get the rescue boat now."

Then the natives stretched him out in the bottom of their canoe and covered him with old rags and palm leaves, in case Japanese planes started to buzz them, and they started on the long haul to New Georgia.

Kennedy made it. He waited that night in the canoe at a rendezvous point and heard four shots. He answered with four shots. A PT came alongside the canoe and the boys dragged him aboard.

"Where the hell you been?" Kennedy asked.

A few hours later, the PT reached us, and our ordeal was over. They carried MacMahon aboard and gave me a hand. We all looked like the leftovers from a bad dream.

There was a medic aboard and he gave us some brandy. Harris couldn't drink his, so I said to him, "Don't waste it," and drank it.

Then I had some more. Except for the Jap crackers, it was the first thing I had in my stomach for a week, and it was good.

I had some more brandy and then I went topside. A couple of the natives who had helped Kennedy were there and I put my arms around them and somehow we started singing a hymn a missionary taught them. I knew it as a kid. We sang for a long time.

Questions and Comments

1. What was PT-109's mission in the spring of 1943?

2. What impression did you get of Lt. Kennedy from Maguire's description of him? What quality of Lt. Kennedy did the incident with the carpenter reveal?

3. Why didn't the Commander of the Japanese destroyer bother to stop his ship after ramming PT-109?

4. What was the condition of PT-109's crew after the ramming? What equipment and supplies did they manage to salvage?

5. Why did Lt. Kennedy decide to swim to Ferguson Passage shortly after he and his crew reached the safety of the atoll?

6. Quartermaster Mauer was certain that Lt. Kennedy would get help. On what did he base his opinion?

7. Why did Lt. Kennedy insist that the crew move to an island closer to the passage?

8. How did Lt. Kennedy send a message to the American base at Rendova? What was the outcome of this message?

9. What was the final episode of the rescue?

Word Study

1. Tell the meaning of the italicized words: *squally* (the black heart of a squally night), *evacuating* (the business of evacuating men), *projectile* (he had gotten his projectile in), *shearing* (shearing away the middle two-thirds of the boat),

founder (the bow of the PT-109 began to founder), *kapok* (the two long straps of my kapok), *incredulous* (he told his incredulous crew), *atoll* (the men on the atoll).

2. Many new words were coined during World War II. Here are a few such words, italicized and given in context. Tell their meanings.

"He took two long straps of my kapok which I had over the *Mae West.* . . ." (page 248)

"The password would be '*Roger*,' and our answer would be '*Wilco.*'" (page 250)

"I'd been with a lot of brave men in a lot of bad spots during my years in the *boondocks.* . . ." (page 256)

Composition

1. This selection is unusual in that the action is reported through the eyes of not one man but seven. Discuss the value of this technique as a method of reporting. Point out the advantages and disadvantages of reading about an incident which is described from several different points of view.

2. Discuss the qualities demonstrated by Lt. Kennedy which were chiefly responsible for the rescue of the PT-109 crew. Which of these qualities were particularly important to him as a political leader in the years to come?

3. Write about someone you know or have heard about who demonstrated unusual courage in a time of crisis. Describe the crisis and explain what you feel was the source of this person's courage.

Theoretically, the office of the Presidency of the United States has always been open to any eligible and qualified American regardless of race or religion. Historically, however, an unwritten law of American politics declared that a candidate whose religious persuasions were those of any minority group could not seriously hope to capture the office of the Presidency.

In 1960, John F. Kennedy, a Catholic, became a candidate for the Presidency of the United States. Many of his opponents sought to block his election by introducing the so-called "religious issue" into the campaign.

In the following speech, delivered before the Greater Houston Ministerial Association on September 12, 1960, two months prior to the election, Mr. Kennedy answered his opponents.

REMARKS ON CHURCH AND STATE

John F. Kennedy

I AM grateful for your generous invitation to state my views. While the so-called religious issue is necessarily and properly the chief topic here tonight, I want to emphasize from the outset that I believe that we have far more critical issues in the 1960 election: the spread of Communist influence, until it now festers only ninety miles off the coast of Florida—the humiliating treatment of our President[1] and

[1] After President Eisenhower's admission of United States reconnaissance flights over Soviet territory, Premier Khrushchev broke up a May 1960 summit conference in Paris and withdrew his invitation for President Eisenhower to visit the U.S.S.R.

Vice President[1] by those who no longer respect our power—the hungry children I saw in West Virginia, the old people who cannot pay their doctor's bills, the families forced to give up their farms—an America with too many slums, with too few schools, and too late to the moon and outer space.

These are the real issues which should decide this campaign. And they are not religious issues—for war and hunger and ignorance and despair know no religious barrier.

But because I am a Catholic, and no Catholic has ever been elected President, the real issues in this campaign have been obscured—perhaps deliberately, in some quarters less responsible than this. So it is apparently necessary for me to state once again—not what kind of church I believe in, for that should be important only to me, but what kind of America I believe in.

I believe in an America where the separation of church and state is absolute—where no Catholic prelate would tell the President (should he be a Catholic) how to act and no Protestant minister would tell his parishioners for whom to vote—where no church or church school is granted any public funds or political preference—and where no man is denied public office merely because his religion differs from the President who might appoint him or the people who might elect him.

I believe in an America that is officially neither Catholic, Protestant nor Jewish—where no public official either requests or accepts instructions on public policy from the Pope, the National Council of Churches or any other ecclesiastical source—where no religious body seeks to impose its will directly or indirectly upon the general populace or the public acts of its officials—and where religious liberty is so indivisible that an act against one church is treated as an act against all.

For, while this year it may be a Catholic against whom the finger of suspicion is pointed, in other years it has been,

---

[1] Vice President Nixon faced mob violence while on a tour of Latin America in May 1958.

and may someday be again, a Jew—or a Quaker—or a Unitarian—or a Baptist. It was Virginia's harassment of Baptist preachers, for example, that led to Jefferson's statute of religious freedom.[1] Today, I may be the victim—but tomorrow it may be you—until the whole fabric of our harmonious society is ripped apart at a time of great national peril.

Finally, I believe in an America where religious intolerance will someday end—where all men and all churches are treated as equal—where every man has the same right to attend or not to attend the church of his choice—where there is no Catholic vote, no anti-Catholic vote, no bloc voting of any kind—and where Catholics, Protestants and Jews both the lay and the pastoral level, will refrain from those attitudes of disdain and division which have so often marred their works in the past, and promote instead the American ideal of brotherhood.

That is the kind of America in which I believe. And it represents the kind of Presidency in which I believe—a great office that must be neither humbled by making it the instrument of any religious group, nor tarnished by arbitrarily withholding it, its occupancy, from the members of any religious group. I believe in a President whose views on religion are his own private affair, neither imposed upon him by the nation or imposed by the nation upon him as a condition to holding that office.

I would not look with favor upon a President working to subvert the First Amendment's guarantees of religious liberty (nor would our system of checks and balances permit him to do so). And neither do I look with favor upon those who would work to subvert Article VI of the Constitution[2] by requiring a religious test—even by indirection—for if they disagree with that safeguard, they should be openly working to repeal it.

---

[1] Passed by the state assembly in 1786, the Virginia Statute of Religious Freedom guaranteed religious liberty in Virginia.

[2] A provision of Article VI is that "no religious test shall ever be required as a qualificaion to any office or public trust under the United States."

I want a chief executive whose public acts are responsible to all and obligated to none—who can attend any ceremony, service or dinner his office may appropriately require him to fulfill—and whose fulfillment of his Presidential office is not limited or conditioned by any religious oath, ritual or obligation.

This is the kind of America I believe in—and this is the kind of America I fought for in the South Pacific and the kind my brother died for in Europe.[1] No one suggested then that we might have a "divided loyalty," that we did "not believe in liberty" or that we belonged to a disloyal group that threatened "the freedoms for which our forefathers died."

And in fact this is the kind of America for which our forefathers did die when they fled here to escape religious test oaths, that denied office to members of less favored churches, when they fought for the Constitution, the Bill of Rights, the Virginia Statute of Religious Freedom—and when they fought at the shrine I visited today—the Alamo.[2] For side by side with Bowie and Crockett died Fuentes and McCafferty and Bailey and Bedillio and Carey—but no one knows whether they were Catholics or not. For there was no religious test there.

I ask you tonight to follow in that tradition, to judge me on the basis of fourteen years in the Congress—on my declared stands against an ambassador to the Vatican, against unconstitutional aid to parochial schools, and against any boycott of the public schools (which I attended myself)—and instead of doing this do not judge me on the basis of these pamphlets and publications we have all seen that carefully select quotations out of context from the statements of Catholic Church leaders, usually in other countries, frequently in other centuries, and rarely relevant to any situation here—and always omitting, of course, that statement of

[1] President Kennedy's older brother Joseph Jr. was killed in World War II.
[2] *Alamo:* fort in San Antonio which a band of Texans, including the border heroes James Bowie and Davy Crockett, tried to hold against superior Mexican forces. All 187 defenders were killed March 6, 1836.

the American bishops in 1948 which strongly endorsed church-state separation.

I do not consider these other quotations binding upon my public acts—why should you? But let me say, with respect to other countries, that I am wholly opposed to the state being used by any religious group, Catholic or Protestant, to compel, prohibit or persecute the free exercise of any other religion. And, that goes for any persecution at any time, by anyone, in any country.

And I hope that you and I condemn with equal fervor those nations which deny their Presidency to Protestants and those which deny it to Catholics. And rather than cite the misdeeds of those who differ, I would also cite the record of the Catholic Church in such nations as France and Ireland—and the independence of such statesmen as de Gaulle[1] and Adenauer.[2]

But let me stress again that these are my views—for, contrary to common newspaper usage, I am not the Catholic candidate for President. I am the Democratic party's candidate for President who happens also to be a Catholic.

I do not speak for my church on public matters—and the church does not speak for me.

Whatever issue may come before me as President, if I should be elected—on birth control, divorce, censorship, gambling, or any other subject—I will make my decision in accordance with these views, in accordance with what my conscience tells me to be in the national interest, and without regard to outside religious pressure or dictate. And no power or threat of punishment could cause me to decide otherwise.

But if the time should ever come—and I do not concede any conflict to be remotely possible—when my office would require me to either violate my conscience, or violate the national interest, then I would resign the office, and I hope any other conscientious public servant would do likewise.

[1] *de Gaulle:* Charles de Gaulle, president of France
[2] *Adenauer:* Konrad Adenauer, chancellor of the West German Repub'

But I do not intend to apologize for these views to my critics of either Catholic or Protestant faith, nor do I intend to disavow either my views or my church in order to win this election. If I should lose on the real issues, I shall return to my seat in the Senate satisfied that I tried my best and was fairly judged.

But if this election is decided on the basis that 40,000,000 Americans lost their chance of being President on the day they were baptized, then it is the whole nation that will be the loser in the eyes of Catholics and non-Catholics around the world, in the eyes of history, and in the eyes of our own people.

But if, on the other hand, I should win this election, I shall devote every effort of mind and spirit to fulfilling the oath of the Presidency—practically identical, I might add, with the oath I have taken for fourteen years in the Congress. For, without reservation, I can, and I quote "solemnly swear that I will faithfully execute the office of President of the United States and will to the best of my ability preserve, protect and defend the Constitution, so help me God."

Questions and Comments

1. What, according to Mr. Kennedy, are the issues in the election? Why are they not religious issues?

2. Mr. Kennedy believes in an America where church and state are separated; an America that is officially neither Catholic, Protestant, nor Jewish; an America where religious intolerance someday will end. What supporting statements does he make about each of these beliefs?

   How does Mr. Kennedy relate the kind of America he be-
   ~ in to the kind of Presidency he believes in?

       ou explain the quotation marks in the paragraph
       . Mr. Kennedy mentions his military service?

5. In the next paragraph, why does Mr. Kennedy refer to the Alamo? Why do you think he mentions the names he does?

6. What arguments does Mr. Kennedy put forth to show that he would not permit his church to speak for him as President?

7. Mr. Kennedy states that he would make the decisions of a President in accordance with his conscience. Why do you think he names the issues he does?

8. At the end of the speech Mr. Kennedy, quoting from the oath of the Presidency, includes the phrase "defend the Constitution." What provisions of the Constitution has he mentioned to support the stand taken in his speech?

Word Study

1. Mr. Kennedy said that the Presidency should not arbitrarily be withheld from the members of any religious group. What does *arbitrarily* mean in this context? What is the meaning of the related word *arbitration* as in the arbitration of a dispute?

2. Mr. Kennedy hoped that members of a religious group on both the *lay* and *pastoral* levels would promote the ideal of brotherhood. Tell the meaning of the italicized words in this context.

3. Give the meaning of the italicized words, using clues from the context. Check your guesses in a dictionary.

"I believe in an America . . . where no public official either requests or accepts instructions on public policy from the Pope, the National Council of Churches or any other *ecclesiastical* source. . . ." (page 260)

"It was Virginia's *harassment* of Baptist preachers, for example, that led to Jefferson's statute of religious freedom." (page 261)

"I ask you . . . to judge me . . . on my declared stand against unconstitutional aid to *parochial* scho against any *boycott* of the public schools (which I attended myself). . . ." (page 262)

". . . nor do I intend to *disavow* either my views or my church. . . ." (page 264)

Composition

1. Tell whether you think this is or is not an effective speech. If there are passages designed to appeal to the emotions rather than to reason, point them out. If there are objections to the stand that Mr. Kennedy took, name them.

2. Choose one of the issues Mr. Kennedy called critical and tell whether that issue still exists and what has been done about it.

3. Write an essay on the American ideal of brotherhood, relating the idea to actual practices in the country or in your own community.

At the end of the war with Persia in 479 B.C., victorious Athens was unquestionably the greatest of the Greek city-states. Under the pretense of maintaining political and commercial peace in the Aegean, Athens formed the Confederacy of Delos, further increasing her power and influence. In order to combat Athenian imperialism, Sparta organized the Peloponnesian League. The showdown between these rival powers was inevitable. In 431 B.C. war was declared; twenty-seven years later Sparta emerged victorious.

Pericles made his famous funeral oration at the completion of the first year of the war. In keeping with her custom, Athens was honoring those soldiers who had fallen in battle.

THE FUNERAL ORATION
OF PERICLES

Thucydides

In the same winter the Athenians gave a funeral at the public cost to those who had first fallen in this war. It was a custom of their ancestors, and the manner of it is as follows. Three days before the ceremony, the bones of the dead are laid out in a tent which has been erected; and their friends bring to their relatives such offerings as they please. In the funeral procession cypress coffins are borne in cars, one for each tribe; the bones of the deceased being placed in the coffin of their tribe. Among these is carried one empty bier decked for the missing, that is, for those whose bodies could not be recovered. Any citizen or stranger who pleases, joins in the procession: and the female relatives are there to wail at the burial. The dead are laid in the public sepulchre in the Beautiful suburb of the city, in which those who fall in war are always buried; with the exception of those slain at Marathon, who for their singular and extraordinary valour were interred on the spot where they fell. After the bodies have been laid in the earth, a man chosen by the state, of approved wisdom and eminent reputation, pronounces over them an appropriate panegyric; after which all retire. Such is the manner of the burying; and throughout the whole of the war, whenever the occasion arose, the established custom was observed. Meanwhile these were the first that had fallen, and Pericles, son of Xanthippus, was chosen to pronounce their eulogium. When the proper time arrived, he advanced from the sepulchre to an elevated platform in order to be heard by as many of the crowd as possible, and spoke as follows:

'Most of my predecessors in this place have commended him who made this speech part of the law, telling us that it is well that it should be delivered at the burial of those who fall in battle. For myself, I should have thought that the worth which had displayed itself in deeds, would be sufficiently rewarded by honours also shown by deeds; such as you now see in this funeral prepared at the people's cost. And I could have wished that the reputations of many brave men were not to be imperilled in the mouth of a single individual, to stand or fall according as he spoke well or ill. For it is hard to speak properly upon a subject where it is even difficult to convince your hearers that you are speaking the truth. On the one hand, the friend who is familiar with every fact of the story, may think that some point has not been set forth with that fulness which he wishes and knows it to deserve; on the other, he who is a stranger to the matter may be led by envy to suspect exaggeration if he hears anything above his own nature. For men can endure to hear others praised only so long as they can severally persuade themselves of their own ability to equal the actions recounted: when this point is passed, envy comes in and with it incredulity. However, since our ancestors have stamped this custom with their approval, it becomes my duty to obey the law and to try to satisfy your several wishes and opinions as best I may.

'I shall begin with our ancestors: it is both just and proper that they should have the honour of the first mention on an occasion like the present. They dwelt in the country without break in the succession from generation to generation, and handed it down free to the present time by their valour. And if our more remote ancestors deserve praise, much more do our own fathers, who added to their inheritance the empire which we now possess, and spared no pains to be able to leave their acquisitions to us of the present generation. Lastly, there are few parts of our dominions that have not been augmented by those of us here, who are still more or less in the vigour of life; while the mother country has been furnished by us with everything that can enable her to depend on her own resources whether for war or for peace. That part of our history which tells of the military achievements which gave us our several possessions, or of the ready valour with which either we or our fathers stemmed the tide of Hellenic or foreign aggression, is a theme too familiar to my hearers for me to dilate on, and I shall therefore pass it by. But what was the road by which we reached our position, what the form of government under which our greatness grew, what the national habits out of which it sprang; these are questions which I may try to solve before I proceed to my panegyric upon these men; since I think this to be a subject upon which on the present occasion a speaker may properly dwell, and to which the whole assemblage, whether citizens or foreigners, may listen with advantage.

'Our constitution does not copy the laws of neighbouring states; we are rather a pattern to others than imitators ourselves. Its administration favours the many instead of the few; this is why it is called a democracy. If we look to the laws, they afford equal justice to all in their private differ-ences; if to social standing, advancement in public life falls to reputation for capacity, class considerations not being al-lowed to interfere with merit; nor again does poverty bar the way, if a man is able to serve the state, he is not hindered by the obscurity of his condition. The freedom which we enjoy in our government extends also to our ordinary life. There, far from exercising a jealous surveillance over each other, we do not feel called upon to be angry with our neigh-bour for doing what he likes, or even to indulge in those injurious looks which cannot fail to be offensive, although they inflict no positive penalty. But all this ease in our pri-vate relations does not make us lawless as citizens. Against this fear is our chief safeguard, teaching us to obey the mag-istrates and the laws, particularly such as regard the protec-tion of the injured, whether they are actually on the statute book, or belong to that code which, although unwritten, yet cannot be broken without acknowledged disgrace.

'Further, we provide plenty of means for the mind to re-fresh itself from business. We celebrate games and sacrifices all the year round, and the elegance of our private estab-lishments forms a daily source of pleasure and helps to banish the spleen; while the magnitude of our city draws the produce of the world into our harbour, so that to the Ath-enian the fruits of other countries are as familiar a luxury as those of his own.

'If we turn to our military policy, there also we differ from our antagonists. We throw open our city to the world, and never by alien acts exclude foreigners from any oppor-tunity of learning or observing, although the eyes of an en-emy may occasionally profit by our liberality; trusting less in system and policy than to the native spirit of our citizens; while in education, where our rivals from their very cradles by a painful discipline seek after manliness, at Athens we live exactly as we please, and yet are just as ready to en-counter every legitimate danger. In proof of this it may be noticed that the Lacedæmonians do not invade our country alone, but bring with them all their confederates; while we Athenians advance unsupported into the territory of a neighbour, and fighting upon a foreign soil usually vanquish with ease men who are defending their homes. Our united force was never yet encountered by any enemy, because we have at once to attend to our marine and to despatch our citizens by land upon a hundred different services; so that, wherever they engage with some such fraction of our strength, a success against a detachment is magnified into a victory over the nation, and a defeat into a reverse suffered at the hands of our entire people. And yet if with habits not of labour but of ease, and courage not of art but of nature, we are still willing to encounter danger, we have the double advantage of escaping the experience of hardships in anticipation and of facing them in the hour of need as fearlessly as those who are never free from them.

'Nor are these the only points in which our city is worthy of admiration. We cultivate refinement without extravagance and knowledge without effeminancy; wealth we employ more for use than for show, and place the real disgrace of poverty not in owning to the fact but in declining the struggle against it. Our public men have, besides politics, their private affairs to attend to, and our ordinary citizens, though occupied with the pursuits of industry, are still fair judges of public matters; for, unlike any other nation, regarding him who takes no part in these duties not as unambitious but as useless, we Athenians are able to judge at all events if we cannot originate, and instead of looking on discussion as a stumbling-block in the way of action, we think it an indispensable preliminary to any wise action at all. Again, in our enterprises we present the singular spectacle of daring and deliberation, each carried to its highest point, and both united in the same persons; although usually decision is the fruit of ignorance, hesitation of reflexion. But the palm of courage will surely be adjudged most justly to those, who best know the difference between hardship and pleasure and yet are never tempted to shrink from danger. In generosity we are equally singular, acquiring our friends by conferring not by receiving favours. Yet, of course, the doer of the favour is the firmer friend of the two, in order by continued kindness to keep the recipient in his debt; while the debtor feels less keenly from the very consciousness that the return he makes will be a payment, not a free gift. And it is only the Athenians who, fearless of consequences, confer their benefits not from calculations of expediency, but in the confidence of liberality.

'In short, I say that as a city we are the school of Hellas; while I doubt if the world can produce a man, who where he has only himself to depend upon, is equal to so many emergencies, and graced by so happy a versatility as the Athenian. And that this is no mere boast thrown out for the occasion, but plain matter of fact, the power of the state acquired by these habits proves. For Athens alone of her contemporaries is found when tested to be greater than her reputation, and alone gives no occasion to her assailants to blush at the antagonist by whom they have been worsted, or to her subjects to question her title by merit to rule. Rather, the admiration of the present and succeeding ages will be ours, since we have not left our power without witness, but have shown it by mighty proofs; and far from needing a Homer for our panegyrist, or other of his craft whose verses might charm for the moment only for the impression which they gave to melt at the touch of fact, we have forced every sea and land to be the highway of our daring, and everywhere, whether for evil or for good, have left imperishable monuments behind us. Such is the Athens for which these men, in the assertion of their resolve not to lose her, nobly fought and died; and well may every one of their survivors be ready to suffer in her cause.

'Indeed if I have dwelt at some length upon the character of our country, it has been to show that our stake in the struggle is not the same as theirs who have no such blessings to lose, and also that the panegyric of the men over whom I am now speaking might be by definite proofs established. That panegyric is now in a great measure complete; for the Athens that I have celebrated is only what the heroisms of these and their like have made her, men whose fame, unlike that of most Hellenes, will be found to be only commensurate with their deserts. And if a test of worth be wanted, it is to be found in their closing scene, and this not only in the cases in which it set the final seal upon their merit, but also in those in which it gave the first intimation of their having any. For there is justice in the claim that stedfastness in his country's battles should be as a cloak to cover a man's other imperfections; since the good action has blotted out the bad, and his merit as a citizen more than outweighted his demerits as an individual. But none of these allowed either wealth with its prospect of future enjoyment to unnerve his spirit, or poverty with its hope of a day of freedom and riches to tempt him to shrink from danger. No, holding that vengeance upon their enemies was more to be desired than any personal blessings, and reckoning this to be the most glorious of hazards, they joyfully determined to accept the risk, to make sure of their vengeance and to let their wishes wait; and while committing to hope the uncertainty of final success, in the business before them they thought fit to act boldly and trust in themselves. Thus choosing to die resisting, rather than to live submitting, they fled only from dishonour, but met danger face to face, and after one brief moment, while at the summit of their fortune, escaped, not from their fear, but from their glory.

'So died these men as became Athenians. You, their survivors, must determine to have as unfaltering a resolution in the field, though you may pray that it may have a happier issue. And not contented with ideas derived only from words of the advantages which are bound up with the defence of your country, though these would furnish a valuable text to a speaker even before an audience so alive to them as the present, you must yourselves realise the power of Athens, and feed your eyes upon her from day to day, till love of her fills your hearts; and then when all her greatness shall break upon you, you must reflect that it was by courage, sense of duty, and a keen feeling of honour in action that men were enabled to win all this, and that no personal failure in an enterprise could make them consent to deprive their country of their valour, but they laid it at her feet as the most glorious contribution that they could offer. For this offering of their lives made in common by them all they each of them individually received that renown which never grows old, and for a sepulchre, not so much that in which their bones have been deposited, but that noblest of shrines wherein their glory is laid up to be eternally remembered upon every occasion on which deed or story shall call for its commemoration. For heroes have the whole earth for their tomb; and in lands far from their own, where the column with its epitaph declares it, there is enshrined in every breast a record unwritten with no tablet to preserve it, except that of the heart. These take as your model, and judging happiness to be the fruit of freedom and freedom of valour, never decline the dangers of war. For it is not the miserable that would most justly be unsparing of their lives; these have nothing to hope for: it is rather they to whom continued life may bring reverses as yet unknown, and to whom a fall, if it came, would be most tremendous in its consequences. And surely, to a man of spirit, the degradation of cowardice must be immeasurably more grievous than the unfelt death which strikes him in the midst of his strength and patriotism!

'Comfort, therefore, not condolence, is what I have to offer to the parents of the dead who may be here. Numberless are the chances to which, as they know, the life of man is subject; but fortunate indeed are they who draw for their lot a death so glorious as that which has caused your mourning, and to whom life has been so exactly measured as to terminate in the happiness in which it has been passed. Still I know that this is a hard saying, especially when those are in question of whom you will constantly be reminded by seeing in the homes of others blessings of which once you also boasted: for grief is felt not so much for the want of what we have never known, as for the loss of that to which we have been long accustomed. Yet you who are still of an age to beget children must bear up in the hope of having others in their stead; not only will they help you to forget those whom you have lost, but will be to the state at once a reinforcement and a security; for never can a fair or just policy be expected of the citizen who does not, like his fellows, bring to the decision the interests and apprehensions of a father. While those of you who have passed your prime must congratulate yourselves with the thought that the best part of your life was fortunate, and that the brief span that remains will be cheered by the fame of the departed. For it is only the love of honour that never grows old; and honour it is, not gain, as some would have it, that rejoices the heart of age and helplessness.

'Turning to the sons or brothers of the dead, I see an arduous struggle before you. When a man is gone, all are wont to praise him, and should your merit be ever so transcendent, you will still find it difficult not merely to overtake, but even to approach their renown. The living have envy to contend with, while those who are no longer in our path are honoured with a goodwill into which rivalry does not enter. On the other hand, if I must say anything on the subject of female excellence to those of you who will now be in widowhood, it will be all comprised in this brief exhortation. Great will be your glory in not falling short of your natural character; and greatest will be hers who is least talked of among the men whether for good or for bad.

'My task is now finished. I have performed it to the best of my ability, and in word, at least, the requirements of the law are now satisfied. If deeds be in question, those who are here interred have received part of their honours already, and for the rest, their children will be brought up till manhood at the public expense: the state thus offers a valuable prize, as the garland of victory in this race of valour, for the reward both of those who have fallen and their survivors. And where the rewards for merit are greatest, there are found the best citizens.

'And now that you have brought to a close your lamentations for your relatives, you may depart.'

Questions and Comments

1. What factors, according to Pericles, make it extremely difficult to deliver an acceptable funeral oration?

2. Why does Pericles begin his oration with praise for the ancestors of the Athenians?

3. Pericles calls the Athenian form of government a democracy. What examples does he cite to support this claim?

4. In what way does the Athenian military policy differ from that of Sparta? What proof does Pericles offer to show that the Athenians are more fearless and better disciplined than the Spartans?

5. What, according to Pericles, is the Athenian attitude towards the need for discussion?

6. Pericles says that Athens will have the admiration of "the present and succeeding ages." What reasons does he offer?

7. What is meant by Pericles's statement that "heroes have the whole earth for their tomb"?

8. What quality, according to Pericles, never grows old?

Word Study

1. How do we use the term *marathon* today? Explain its derivation from the battle of Marathon (page 268).

2. What do *panegyric* and *eulogium* mean? What clues in the first paragraph show that the words are synonyms?

3. The spleen is an organ of the body. What does the author mean by the word *spleen* in "the elegance of our private establishments forms a daily source of pleasure and helps to banish the spleen"? Consult a dictionary to explain the relation of the different meanings of the word.

4. Distinguish between the meaning of the italicized words in "*Comfort,* therefore, not *condolence,* is what I have to offer to the parents of the dead who may be here." (page 274)

5. The verb *desert* and the noun *deserts* have different derivations. What does *deserts* mean in "men, whose fame, unlike that of most Hellenes, will be found to be only commensurate with their deserts"? What does *commensurate* mean?

6. Give the meaning of the italicized words, using clues in the context wherever possible and checking your guesses in a dictionary: *surveillance* (page 270), *adjudged* (page 271), *versatility* (page 272), *transcendent* (page 275).

Composition

1. Reread Lincoln's Gettysburg Address and compare it to Pericles's funeral oration. Recall first the historic occasion which prompted each address. Analyze the content of both addresses by comparing what each man said with regard to indebtedness to ancestors, the bravery of the men who had died, what they had died for, and the belief both men had in democratic forms of government.

2. Pericles claimed that in Athens "ordinary citizens, though occupied with the pursuits of industry, are still fair judges of public matters." Discuss this idea and state whether or not the same claim might be made for American citizens.

3. At one point in the oration, Pericles gives a very clear picture of Athenian democracy, enumerating the rights and privileges that citizens of Athens enjoyed. Point out those aspects of American democracy that appear to have had their roots in Athenian democracy. Comment on those features of American democracy not present in Athens.

From the time of the ancient Greeks to the present era the nature of freedom has been a thorny problem for statesmen, philosophers, and theologians. Woodrow Wilson, twenty-eighth President of the United States, in this selection from one of his speeches gives us several penetrating observations on the nature of freedom. *The New Freedom* is the title of a collection of Wilson's speeches.

WHAT IS LIBERTY?

Woodrow Wilson

WHAT is liberty?

I have long had an image in my mind of what constitutes liberty. Suppose that I were building a great piece of powerful machinery, and suppose that I should so awkwardly and unskilfully assemble the parts of it that every time one part tried to move it would be interfered with by the others, and the whole thing would buckle up and be checked. Liberty for the several parts would consist in the best possible assembling and adjustment of them all, would it not? If you want the great piston of the engine to run with absolute freedom, give it absolutely perfect alignment and adjustment with the other parts of the machine, so that it is free, not because it is let alone or isolated, but because it has been associated most skilfully and carefully with the other parts of the great structure.

What is liberty? You say of the locomotive that it runs free. What do you mean? You mean that its parts are so assembled and adjusted that friction is reduced to a minimum, and that it has perfect adjustment. We say of a boat skimming the water with light foot, "How free she runs," when we mean, how perfectly she is adjusted to the force of the wind, how perfectly she obeys the great breath out of the heavens that fills her sails. Throw her head up into the wind and see how she will halt and stagger, how every sheet will shiver and her whole frame be shaken, how instantly she is "in irons," in the expressive phrase of the sea. She is free only when you have let her fall off again and have recovered once more her nice adjustment to the forces she must obey and cannot defy.

Human freedom consists in perfect adjustments of human interests and human activities and human energies.

Now, the adjustments necessary between individuals, between individuals and the complex institutions amidst which they live, and between those institutions and the government, are infinitely more intricate today than ever before. No doubt this is a tiresome and roundabout way of saying the thing, yet perhaps it is worth while to get somewhat clearly in our minds what makes all the trouble today. Life has become complex; there are many more elements, more parts, to it than ever before. And, therefore, it is harder to keep everything adjusted,—and harder to find out where the trouble lies when the machine gets out of order.

You know that one of the interesting things that Mr. Jefferson said in those early days of simplicity which marked the beginnings of our government was that the best government consisted in as little governing as possible. And there is still a sense in which that it true. It is still intolerable for the government to interfere with our individual activities except where it is necessary to interfere with them in order to free them. But I feel confident that if Jefferson were living in our day he would see what we see: that the individual is caught in a great confused nexus of all sorts of complicated circumstances, and that to let him alone is to leave him helpless as against the obstacles with which he has to contend; and that, therefore, law in our day must come to the assistance of the individual. It must come to his assistance to see that he gets fair play; that is all, but that is much. Without the watchful interference, the resolute interference, of the government, there can be no fair play between individuals and such powerful institutions as the trusts. Freedom today is something more than being let alone. The program of a government of freedom must in these days be positive, not negative merely.

Well, then, in this new sense and meaning of it, are we preserving freedom in this land of ours, the hope of all the earth?

Have we, inheritors of this continent and of the ideals to which the fathers consecrated it,—have we maintained them, realizing them, as each generation must, anew? Are we, in the consciousness that the life of man is pledged to higher levels here than elsewhere, striving still to bear aloft the standards of liberty and hope, or, disillusioned and defeated, are we feeling the disgrace of having had a free field in which to do new things and of not having done them?

Questions and Comments

1. What two analogies does Woodrow Wilson give to develop his definition of human freedom?

2. What other analogy can you think of as an illustration of his definition?

3. How would you apply Wilson's definition of freedom to the home? To the school?

4. Wilson says, "Life has become complex; there are many more elements, more parts, to it than ever before." To what new elements and new parts do you think Wilson refers?

5. "We hold these truths to be self-evident, that all men are created equal, that they are endowed by their Creator with

certain unalienable Rights, that among these are Life, Liberty and the pursuit of Happiness." These words, as you know, are from the Declaration of Independence by Thomas Jefferson. You also know that Jefferson said that the best government consisted in as little governing as possible. How does Wilson reconcile Jefferson's ideas with his own definition of liberty?

Word Study

1. Wilson says "the individual is caught in a great confused nexus of all sorts of complicated circumstances." What does *nexus* mean as revealed by this context?

2. By *trusts* Wilson means corporations of possibly monopolistic nature. When we speak of *trust companies* today, what do we mean?

Composition

1. Give your answer to the questions Wilson asks in the last paragraph. Give examples to support your answer.

2. Give your own opinion of Wilson's statement "The program of a government of freedom must in these days be positive, not negative merely." Relate your opinion to present-day problems of government.

3. Give your own definition of freedom, using analogies or illustrations to develop your definition.

McCORMICK-MATHERS

NEW DIMENSIONS IN LITERATURE

SERIES

Introduction to the Short Story
Introduction to Drama
Introduction to Poetry
Introduction to Nonfiction

A Study of the Short Story
A Study of Drama
A Study of Poetry
A Study of Nonfiction